GMAT
SENTENCE
CORRECTION
BIBLE

POWERSCORE
TEST PREPARATION

First Edition published November 2006

Published by
PowerScore Publishing, a division of PowerScore Incorporated
37V New Orleans Road
Hilton Head Island, SC 29928

Author: Victoria Wood   ISBN: 0-9721296-5-0
                               ISBN: 978-0-9721296-5-7

Printed in Canada, March 2008

CONTENTS

CHAPTER ONE: INTRODUCTION

CHAPTER TWO: THE BASICS OF SENTENCE CORRECTION

CHAPTER THREE: THE BASICS OF GRAMMAR

CHAPTER FOUR: ERRORS INVOLVING VERBS

CHAPTER FIVE: ERRORS WITH NOUNS AND PRONOUNS

CHAPTER SIX: ERRORS INVOLVING MODIFIERS

CHAPTER SEVEN: ERRORS INVOLVING CONJUNCTIONS

CHAPTER EIGHT: ERRORS IN CONSTRUCTION

CHAPTER NINE: ERRORS INVOLVING STYLE

CHAPTER TEN: MULTIPLE ERRORS

CHAPTER ELEVEN: SENTENCE CORRECTION STRATEGIES

CHAPTER TWELVE: TEST READINESS

APPENDIX

CHAPTER ANSWER KEY

GLOSSARY

About PowerScore

PowerScore is one of the world's fastest growing test preparation companies. Headquarted on Hilton Head Island in South Carolina, PowerScore offers GMAT, GRE, LSAT, and SAT preparation courses in over 75 locations in the U.S. and abroad. For more information, please visit our website at www.powerscore.com.

Chapter One: Introduction

Introduction

Welcome to the PowerScore GMAT Sentence Correction Bible. The purpose of this book is to provide you with a thorough review of grammar, usage, and word choice for use in attacking the Sentence Correction questions on the Graduate Management Admission Tests (GMAT). By carefully studying and correctly applying the techniques we employ, we are certain that you will increase your Sentence Correction score.

This book has been carefully designed to reinforce your understanding of the concepts behind the Sentence Correction questions. The concepts and techniques discussed herein are drawn from our live GMAT courses, which we feel are the most effective in the world.

In order to apply our methods effectively and efficiently, we strongly recommend that you carefully read and re-read each of the discussions regarding basic grammar and error types. We also suggest that as you finish each question you look at both the explanation for the correct answer choice and the explanations for the incorrect answer choices. Closely examine each problem and determine which elements led to the correct answer, and then study the analyses provided in the book and check them against your own work. By doing so you will greatly increase your chances of recognizing the patterns present in all Sentence Correction questions.

This book also contains a variety of drills and exercises that supplement the discussion of techniques and question analysis. The drills help strengthen specific skills that are critical for GMAT excellence, and for this reason they are as important as the questions. In the answer keys to these drills we will often introduce and discuss important GMAT points, so we strongly advise you to read through all explanations.

On page 263 there is a complete quick-reference answer key to all problems in this book. The answer key contains a legend of question identifiers, as well as chapter-by-chapter answer keys.

Because access to accurate and up-to-date information is critical, we have devoted a section of our website to Sentence Correction Bible students. This free online resource area offers supplements to the book material, answers questions posed by students, offers study plans, and provides updates as needed. There is also an official book evaluation form that we strongly encourage you to use.

The exclusive GMAT Sentence Correction Bible online area can be accessed at:

www.powerscore.com/scbible

If we can assist you in your GMAT preparation in any way, or if you have any questions or comments, please do not hesitate to contact us via e-mail at scbible@powerscore.com. Additional contact information is provided at the end of this book. We look forward to hearing from you!

A Brief Overview of the GMAT

The Graduate Management Admission Test is required for admission at over 1000 business schools worldwide. According to the Graduate Management Admission Council (GMAC), the makers of the test, "The GMAT is specifically designed to measure the verbal, quantitative, and writing skills of applicants for graduate study in business. It does not, however, presuppose any specific knowledge of business or other specific content areas, nor does it measure achievement in any particular subject areas." The GMAT is given in English, and consists of the following four separately timed sections:

- **Analytical Writing Assessment.** 2 essays, 30 minutes each; one essay asks for an analysis of an issue, the other asks for an analysis of an argument.

- **Quantitative Section.** 37 multiple-choice questions, 75 minutes; two question types: Problem Solving and Data Sufficiency.

- **Verbal Section.** 41 multiple-choice questions, 75 minutes; three question types: Reading Comprehension, Critical Reasoning, and Sentence Correction.

An optional break of 5 minutes is allowed between each section, and so the order of the test sections is always identical:

Analytical Writing Assessment

Analysis of an Issue	30 minutes	1 question
Analysis of an Argument	30 minutes	1 question
Break	5 minutes	

Quantitative Section

Data Sufficiency Problem Solving	75 minutes	37 questions
Break	5 minutes	

Verbal Section

Critical Reasoning Reading Comprehension Sentence Correction	75 minutes	41 questions

When you take an actual GMAT, you must present an ID. This is done in case of test security problems..

Although the 5-minute breaks are optional, you should always take the entire break time in order to avoid fatigue.

The Analytical Writing Assessment

The Analytical Writing Assessment (AWA) appears at the beginning of the GMAT, immediately after the computer tutorial. The AWA consists of two essays, and you have thirty minutes to complete each essay. There is no break between the two sections. The two essay topics are Analysis of an Argument and Analysis of an Issue.

The AWA was developed in 1994 in response to requests from business schools to add a writing component to the GMAT. Studies had shown that strong writing and communication abilities are critical for strong business performance, and business schools wanted to have a means of assessing candidates' communication abilities. According to GMAC, "The AWA is designed as a direct measure of your ability to think critically and to communicate your ideas. More specifically, the Analysis of an Issue task tests your ability to explore the complexities of an issue or opinion and, if appropriate, to take a position informed by your understanding of those complexities. The Analysis of an Argument task tests your ability to formulate an appropriate and constructive critique of a specific conclusion based upon a specific line of thinking."

At the conclusion of the GMAT you have the option to cancel your score. Unfortunately, there is no way to determine exactly what your score would be before cancelling.

If you choose to accept your score, the results of your test (excluding the Writing scores) are available immediately.

Each Analytical Writing Assessment essay is initially scored on a 0 to 6 scale in half-point increments by two readers—one human reader, and one machine reader, the "e-rater." The two scores are averaged to produce a final score for each essay. The final score of each essay are then averaged together to create an overall score on a scale from 0 to 6, in half-point increments.

The Quantitative Section

The Quantitative section of the GMAT is comprised of questions that cover mathematical subjects such as arithmetic, algebra, and geometry. There are two question types—Problem Solving and Data Sufficiency.

Problem Solving questions contain five separate answer choices, each of which offers a different solution to the problem. Approximately 22 of the 37 Quantitative section questions will be in the Problem Solving format.

Data Sufficiency questions consist of a question followed by two numbered statements. You must determine if the numbered statements contain sufficient information to solve the problem—individually, together, or not at all. Each Quantitative section contains approximately 15 Data Sufficiency questions, and this type of problem is unique to the GMAT and can be exceptionally challenging.

The Verbal Section

The GMAT Verbal section is a test of your ability to read for content, analyze argumentation, and to recognize and correct written errors. Accordingly, there are three types of problems—Reading Comprehension, Critical Reasoning, and Sentence Correction.

Reading Comprehension questions examine your ability to analyze large amounts of material for content and understanding. Passages range up to 350 words in length, and each passage is accompanied by 3 to 8 questions. Passage topics are drawn from a variety of areas, including business, science, politics, law, and history.

Critical Reasoning questions present a short argument followed by a question such as: "Which of the following weakens the argument?" "Which of the following parallels the argument?" or "Which of the following must be true according to the argument?" The key to these questions is understanding the reasoning types and question types that frequently appear. Within the Verbal Section you will encounter approximately 10 to 14 Critical Reasoning questions.

For more help with Critical Reasoning questions, consult the PowerScore GMAT Critical Reasoning Bible.

Each Sentence Correction problem presents a sentence containing an underlined section. Five answer choices follow the problem, and each suggests a possible phrasing of the underlined section. The first answer choice is a repeat of the underlined section, and the remaining four answers are different than the original. Your task is to analyze the underlined section and determine which of the answers offers the best phrasing.

Experimental Questions

During the GMAT you will encounter questions that will not contribute to your score. These questions, known as "experimental" questions, are used on future version of the GMAT. Unfortunately, you will not be informed during the test as to which questions do not count, so you must give your best performance on each question.

About 1/4 of the questions on the GMAT are experimental, with the questions roughly split between the Quantitative and Verbal sections.

As opposed to the traditional paper-and-pencil format used by many other tests, the GMAT is administered on a computer. Consequently, only one question at a time is presented, the order of questions is not predetermined, and the test actually responds to your answers and shapes the exam in order to most efficiently arrive at your proper score. This format is known as a Computer Adaptive Test, or CAT.

For example, the first question in the Verbal or Quantitative section will be a medium difficulty question. If answered correctly, the computer will supply a somewhat harder question on the assumption that your score is somewhere above that level. If this next question is answered correctly, the following question will again be more difficult. This process continues until a question is missed. At that point, the test will supply a somewhat easier question as it tries to determine if you have reached your score "ceiling." By increasing or decreasing the difficulty of the questions based on prior response, the test attempts to quickly pinpoint your appropriate score level and then confirm that level. Consequently, the first several questions are used to broadly establish your general scoring range:

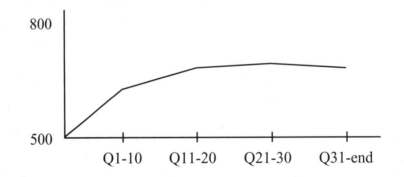

In the diagram above, correct responses to the first several questions lead to significant jumps in score, whereas later questions make smaller adjustments. A strong beginning followed by a weak finish will produce a higher score than a weak beginning followed by a strong finish. For this reason it is essential that your performance early in the section be as strong as possible, even if this requires using more than the average time allotted per question.

The CAT format has certain features that appreciably alter the testing experience:

- The CAT format does not allow you to "skip" a question; that is, you cannot leave a question blank nor can you come back to a question. In order to move forward in the test you *must* answer the question on the screen. If you do not know the answer, you must make an educated guess. And since the test adapts to your previous responses, once you complete a question, you cannot return to that question.

- You cannot write on the computer screen, but scratch paper is available and should be used (more on this in a moment).

- Facility with a computer is clearly an advantage; fast typing is also an advantage in the Analytical Writing Sections where your response must be typed into the computer.

- The test penalizes examinees who do not finish all the questions in the section. Thus, since the number of questions answered is incorporated into the calculation of scores, it is essential that you complete every question in each section. There is a strong penalty for leaving questions unanswered, and so it is better to miss a question than to leave it unanswered.

- The results of your test (excluding the Writing scores) are available at the conclusion of the exam.

Question Difficulty Matters

Complicating the GMAT CAT scoring system is that question difficulty affects your overall score. Each question is assigned a predetermined "weight," and more difficult question have a greater weight. Consequently, it is important that you answer difficult questions and not just "skip" any question that appears difficult. Answering fifteen easy questions will produce a lower score than answering fifteen difficult questions.

General Pacing

Since completing every question in a section is critical, pacing is equally important. Based purely on the number of questions and the total time per section, the following lists the the average amount of time you can spend per question:

> Quantitative Section: 37 questions, 75 minutes
> Average time per question: *2 minutes, 1 second*

> Verbal Section: 41 questions, 75 minutes
> Average time per question: *1 minute, 49 seconds*

Score-Specific Pacing

The following references provide alternate pacing strategies depending on desired score.

Basic Quantitative Strategy for various scoring ranges:

> 700-800: Complete every question, average of just under 2 minutes per question

> 600-690: Attempt to complete every question, average of 2 minutes, 15 seconds per question, keep enough time to guess on uncompleted questions

> 500-590: Attempt to complete at least 75% of questions, average of 2 minutes, 35 seconds per question, keep enough time to guess on uncompleted questions

Basic Verbal Strategy for various scoring ranges:

> 700-800: Complete every question, average of 1 minute, 45 seconds per question

> 600-690: Attempt to complete every question, average of 2 minutes per question, keep enough time to guess on uncompleted questions

> 500-590: Attempt to complete at least 75% of questions, average of 2 minutes, 20 seconds per question, keep enough time to guess on uncompleted questions

However, since the questions at the start of each section are more critical than later questions, a greater amount of time than the average can be allotted to the early questions, and then the pace can be accelerated as the sections proceeds.

Timing Your Practice Sessions

One of the most important tools for test success is a timer. When working with paper tests or the *Official Guide for GMAT Review,* your timer should be a constant companion during your GMAT preparation.

Although not all of your practice needs to be timed, you should attempt to do as many questions as possible under timed conditions. Time pressure is the top concern cited by test takers, and practicing with a timer will help acquaint you with the challenges of the test. After all, if the GMAT was a take-home test, no one would be too worried about it.

When practicing with a timer, keep notes about how many questions you complete in a given amount of time. You should vary your approach so that practice does not become boring. For example, you could track how long it takes to complete 3, 5, or 8 questions. Or you could see how many questions you can complete in 6 or 10 minutes. Trying different approaches will help you get the best sense of how fast you can go while still maintaining a high degree of accuracy.

A timer is invaluable because it is both an odometer and speedometer for your practice. With sufficient practice you will begin to establish a comfortable Sentence Correction speed, and the timer allows you to make sure you are maintaining this pace. Whether you use a watch, stopwatch, or kitchen timer is irrelevant; just make sure you time yourself rigorously.

Silent countdown timers can be purchased through our website at www.powerscore.com

Taking a standardized test on a computer is an unusual experience. The natural tendency to mark up the page is thwarted since you cannot write on the computer screen. Consequently, using noteboards, laminated pages provided in place of scratch paper by the test administrator, is an important aid to smooth test performance. A special marker and a spiral-bound booklet of five noteboards will be supplied by the test administrator, and more noteboards can be requested during the exam.

During the pre-test tutorial, use part of one noteboard to quickly draw out the following chart:

A									
B									
C									
D									
E									

As you progress though each question, you can use the chart to keep track of eliminated answer choices as is necessary. For example, if you are certain answer choices (A) and (C) are incorrect in problem #2, simply "X" them out on the chart:

	2								
A	X								
B									
C	X								
D									
E									

In this fashion you can overcome the inability to physically mark out answer choices on the computer screen.

You should also familiarize yourself with GMAT CAT computer controls since computer aptitude is clearly an advantage. Although the test is given on standard computers, the GMAT CAT program does not allow the use of certain keys, such as the "tab" key. *The Official Guide for GMAT Review* contains a detailed explanation of the GMAT CAT computer controls, and the free GMATPrep Software contains test tutorials to help you gain experience with the computer controls. Additionally, in the Analytical Writing Sections, your typing ability affects overall performance, and thus you must have at least basic typing skills.

The GMAT Scoring Scale

Every GMAT score report contains four sections:

- A Quantitative Score—on a scale of 0 to 60
- A Verbal Score—on a scale of 0 to 60
- A Total Score—on a scale of 200 to 800
- An Analytical Writing Assessment Score—on a scale of 0 to 6

The Quantitative and Verbal scores are section scores, and these two section scores are combined to create the Total Score. The Total Score is the one most familiar to GMAT test takers and is given on the famous 200 to 800 scale, with 200 being the lowest score and 800 the highest score.

Each Analytical Writing Assessment essay is initially scored on a 0 to 6 scale by two readers—one human reader and one machine reader, the "E-rater." The two scores are averaged to produce a final score for each essay. The final scores of each essay are then averaged together to create an overall score. Approximately 90% of all test takers receive a score of 3 or higher. Your AWA score has no effect on your Total Score.

The GMAT Percentile Table

It is important not to lose sight of what the GMAT Total Score actually represents. The 200 to 800 test scale contains 61 different possible scores. Each score places a student in a certain relative position compared to other test takers. These relative positions are represented through a percentile that correlates to each score. The percentile indicates where the test taker ranks in the overall pool of test takers. For example, a score of 680 represents the 90th percentile, meaning a student with a score of 680 scored better than 90 percent of the people who have taken the test in the last two years. The percentile is critical since it is a true indicator of your positioning relative to other test takers, and thus business school applicants.

Charting out the entire percentage table yields a rough "bell curve." The number of test takers in the 200s and 700s is very low (only 7% of all test takers receive a score in the 700s; only 2% in the 200s), and most test takers are bunched in the middle, comprising the "top" of the bell. In fact, approximately 30% of all test takers score between 450 and 550 inclusive, and about 60% of all test takers score between 400 and 600 inclusive.

The median score on the GMAT scale is 540. The median, or middle, score is the score at which approximately 50% of test takers have a lower score and 50% of test takers have a higher score.

It is important to remember that you do not have to answer every question correctly in order to receive an excellent GMAT score. There is room for error, and accordingly you should never let any single question occupy an inordinate amount of your time.

The use of the GMAT in business school admissions is not without controversy. Experts agree that your GMAT score is one of the most important determinants of the type of school you can attend. At many business schools an "admissions index" consisting of your GMAT score and your undergraduate grade point average is used to help determine the relative standing of applicants, and at some schools a sufficiently high admissions index virtually guarantees your admission.

For all the importance of the GMAT, the exam is not without flaws. As a standardized test currently given in the computer adaptive format there are a number of skills that the GMAT cannot measure, including listening skills, note-taking ability, perseverance, etc. GMAC is aware of these limitations and on a regular basis they warn all business school admission offices about using the GMAT scores as the sole admission criterion. Still, because the test ultimately returns a number for each student, the tendency to rank applicants is strong. Fortunately, once you get to business school the GMAT is forgotten. For the time being consider the test a temporary hurdle you must leap in order to reach the ultimate goal.

For more information on the GMAT, or to register for the test, contact the Graduate Management Admission Council at (800) 462-8669 or at their website at www.mba.com.

CHAPTER TWO: THE BASICS OF SENTENCE CORRECTION

GMAT Sentence Correction

The Verbal section of the GMAT contains 41 multiple choice questions in three question types—Reading Comprehension, Critical Reading, and Sentence Correction. This book focuses strictly on Sentence Correction, which consists of 10 to 15 questions per test. You have 75 minutes to complete all 41 questions, with an average of one minute and forty-five seconds per question. Because nearly all students report that the time constraints of the Verbal portion are a major obstacle, you should dedicate less than sixty seconds to each Sentence Correction question. This will help compensate for the time spent reading long passages and tackling more difficult Critical Reasoning questions. By studying the GMAT's pattern of errors outlined in this book, you'll learn to quickly recognize improper sentence construction, saving valuable time for other portions of the Verbal test.

Sentence Correction Question Directions

The directions for Sentence Correction questions are only given once on the test, just before the first Sentence Correction question. Test questions tend to arrive in bunches; you may have three Sentence Correction questions, followed by three Critical Reasoning questions and two Reading Comprehension questions, and finally another Sentence Correction question. The directions will not be repeated after the first Sentence Correction question. For this reason, as well as for saving time on the GMAT, you should familiarize yourself with the directions now:

> A sentence correction question will introduce a sentence. All or part of the sentence may be underlined. Five ways to phrase the underlined portion will be listed under the sentence. The first answer choice is identical to the underlined portion; the remaining four answer choices are different. If the original underlined portion is best, select the first answer. Otherwise, choose another phrase.
>
> These questions assess your skill in recognizing the proper use and effectiveness of sentences in standard written English. Your answer must follow the rules of standard written English by using correct grammar, word choice, and sentence construction. Choose the best phrasing that creates the most effective sentence. Your choice should not be awkward, ambiguous, redundant, or grammatically incorrect; rather, the sentence should be clear and concise.

Examine the directions closely, as they contain clues about attacking Sentence Correction questions. First, notice the line "The first answer choice is identical to the underlined portion." Because you have already read the underlined portion of the sentence, you should never read the first answer choice. There is

Unlike the ACT or SAT, the GMAT mixes Sentence Correction questions with Reading Comprehension and Critical Reading questions. They are not separated by format or content.

no point in reading the same phrase twice, as it wastes valuable time.

Next examine the line "choose the best phrasing." By stating up front that the answers have comparative value and some are better than others, the makers of the test compel you to read every other answer choice before making a selection. If you read only one or two answer choices and then decide that you have the correct one, you could end up choosing an answer that has some merit but is not as good as a later answer. One of the test makers' favorite tricks is to place a highly attractive wrong answer choice immediately before the correct answer choice in the hopes that you will pick the wrong answer choice and then move on to the next question without reading any of the other answers.

You must read Answer Choices (B), (C), (D), and (E) before making a selection.

This phrase is also important because it implies that you are looking for the *best* answer, and not necessarily the *perfect* answer. You may feel that there is a better way to express the meaning of the sentence, but your ideal sentence is not listed. You must pick the answer that is superior to the remaining answer choices, whether or not you agree with its format or diction.

The best answer is not always a perfect answer.

Now analyze the passage "Your answer must follow the rules of standard written English." Standard English is the variety of English used as the model for proper communication, reflecting correct grammar and usage as dictated by textbooks and style manuals. The GMAT tests the standards of *written* English, which tend to be more formal than the rules of *spoken* English. For example, did you know that contractions (*he's, we'll, shouldn't*) are considered standard spoken English but are not deemed standard written English? Try to find the use of a contraction in a newspaper; unless a speaker is being quoted, contractions are not used. You should also be aware that the GMAT tests standard written American English, although this is not stated in the directions. Because the GMAT is largely used for admission to American universities, these directions are implied. It bears mentioning to students of standard written British English who many need to brush up on a few differences between the written languages (such as idiom and spelling).

Finally, study the last sentence of the directions, which says, "Your choice should not be awkward, ambiguous, redundant, or grammatically incorrect." The rules of standard written English will ensure that your answer is not grammatically incorrect, but they do not always cover awkwardness, ambiguity, or redundancy. You might be presented with two answer choices that are grammatically sound but forced to choose the one that is more smooth and concise. We cannot adequately stress the importance of reading Answer Choices (B), (C), (D), and (E) before selecting the correct answer.

The Parts of a Sentence Correction Question

Each Sentence Correction question contains two parts: the sentence and the five answer choices. All or part of the sentence will be underlined, and the first answer choice is identical to the underlined portion of the sentence:

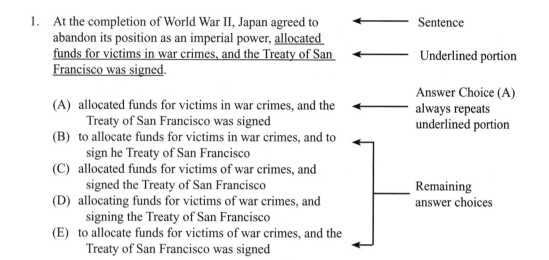

1. At the completion of World War II, Japan agreed to abandon its position as an imperial power, <u>allocated funds for victims in war crimes, and the Treaty of San Francisco was signed</u>.

    (A) allocated funds for victims in war crimes, and the Treaty of San Francisco was signed
    (B) to allocate funds for victims in war crimes, and to sign he Treaty of San Francisco
    (C) allocated funds for victims of war crimes, and signed the Treaty of San Francisco
    (D) allocating funds for victims of war crimes, and signing the Treaty of San Francisco
    (E) to allocate funds for victims of war crimes, and the Treaty of San Francisco was signed

As a technical note, an empty answer bubble appears next to each answer choice (rather than the letters A through E) on the real GMAT CAT. However, for the convenience of discussion, we will present problems with the answer choices lettered (A) through (E).

Just as the Verbal portion of the test assesses several different verbal abilities, the Sentence Correction questions test three different areas of language proficiency.

1. <u>Grammar</u>

   At the root of every Sentence Correction problem is a grammatical error. Using the rules of standard written English, the correct answer choice must create a final sentence that is free of errors such as subject-verb disagreement, incorrect pronoun choice, and misplaced modifiers.

2. <u>Concise expression</u>

   The GMAT will also assess a test taker's ability to create sentences that express a complete idea in as few words as possible. This does not always mean the shortest sentence is the best answer; it may take a long sentence to fully express the intended meaning. However, the correct sentence should be free of extraneous words and redundant phrases.

3. <u>Correct diction</u>

   Some Sentence Correction questions will assess diction, which means the choice of appropriate words. The correct answer must use words that are meaningful to the context of the sentence while following the rules of idiom and standard written English.

Grammatical offenses are at the root of all GMAT Sentence Correction errors. Problems with wordy phrases or incorrect word choice are usually secondary errors.

Although the makers of the GMAT purposefully create sentences intended to trick the novice test-taker, they also tend to repeat the same types of errors and test questions. This book reviews all of the grammatical and stylistic errors that occur in official ETS publications; your key to acing the Sentence Correction portion of the GMAT is to study and understand these prevailing errors. By recognizing a repeated pattern, you can dissect a Sentence Correct question quickly and correctly.

Sentence Correction Strategies ▐████████████████████

The foundation of a great GMAT Sentence Correction score is a firm under-standing of the grammatical concepts tested. Therefore, Chapters Three through Eleven present an in-depth look at grammar and its potential weak-nesses on the GMAT. Chapter Twelve explains how to use this knowledge to tackle test questions.

CHAPTER THREE: THE BASICS OF GRAMMAR

Grammar Education

When most prospective test takers learn that the GMAT will evaluate their grammar and usage, a slight panic ensues. "Grammar? Like adjectives and adverbs? Pronoun and antecedent agreement? I can't remember that stuff!"

These anxious grammar-phobes are not alone; few students who graduated high school in the last forty years ever had a formal grammar course. Basic grammar might have been taught briefly, possibly as a week-long introduction to a composition course, but this foundation of all reading and writing has been fighting its expulsion from the "grammar" school curriculum since the late 1950s. At that time, MIT professor Noam Chomsky and several other leading linguists declared that grammar was learned naturally. They believed that grammar was easily absorbed in the context of speech, reading, and writing, rather than in isolation as a course by itself. Their question—"Why should children be formally taught their own language?"—led to the abandonment of grammar education by both teachers and textbook companies alike. With the inclusion of science, technology, and other new disciplines in the curriculum, overworked school teachers were happy to remove an extra subject from the school day, and underfunded school districts were happy to remove pointless textbook costs from the budget. This naturalist theory filtered all the way to the members of the National Council of Teachers of English, the guardians and gurus of reading and writing instruction, who published articles as late as the 1990s which declared grammar instruction had little or no effect on students.

Two influential groups disagree, and their dissent may change the face of grammar instruction once again. The first group, college instructors, recently ranked grammar and usage in a survey by ACT as the most important skill out of six language arts aspects for college freshman (ironically, high school teachers ranked grammar and usage as the least important skill of the six). In this technological age of online message board emoticons and cellular text messaging shorthand, college professors are reporting decreasing grammar skills among incoming freshman; it is little surprise, then, that universities are demanding increased grammar instruction from elementary and secondary schools. With so many choices and so much competition among public and private high schools, teachers may feel pressure to meet the demands of college educators in order to ensure more of their graduating seniors are accepted to post-secondary schools, thus attracting more prospective students to their district.

Even more influential in dictating high school curriculum is the second group—standardized test makers. Although the GMAT has long tested grammatical skills, high school administrators have not concerned themselves with meeting standards for post-graduate examinations. However, a new SAT test was revealed in 2005 that included an essay question and two sections of multiple choice grammar questions. This new section was likely created in order to gain acceptance with the increasing number of colleges who were leaning toward the grammar-heavy ACT. Many school districts across the country are now scrambling to include grammar in their elementary and secondary curriculums—as well as to teach grammar to their teachers—in order to prepare their students for this final test of their academic career.

Unless you have school-aged children, the debate concerning grammar education in our elementary and secondary schools is probably irrelevant to you now. But grammar is necessary for acing the GMAT. If you have purchased this book, you are likely one of the millions of students who attended school when grammar was trivialized or forgotten. It's not your fault. Whether you have never studied an antecedent or just can't remember what an antecedent is, the Sentence Correction Bible will categorize and explain common GMAT errors and question types.

Standard Written English

Standard written English is the group of accepted symbols used to convey speech and thought. The choice and arrangement of these symbols constitutes grammar and usage. To help you understand, consider math for a moment:

$$2 + 2 = 3$$

This equation violates the accepted symbols used in math. A student who uses these representations will most likely be perceived as uneducated or unintelligent. Similarly, a student who uses incorrect writing symbols might be also perceived as an inferior student:

The girl ran wild through the forest.

Like the math problem, this sentence violates the accepted symbols used in writing. Correct both the equation and the sentence by using the correct representations:

$$2 + 2 = 4$$
The girl ran wild*ly* through the forest.

Written language and the symbols used to convey speech and thought constantly evolve. What's more, there is not a specific reason why one representation is favored over another. Instead, standard written English is determined by observing how educated writers form sentences and paragraphs. Without

The French and Spanish languages are governed by official academies responsible for approving all changes to the languages. The English language has no such institution to monitor rules, so standard written English is derived from the speech and writing of the educated population.

an official governing body to regulate the symbols and representations, our written language is bound to experience frequent changes. The GMAT tests long-standing constants that are accepted by authors, publishers, universities, and other scholars. Your task is to learn, recognize, and mimic these nationwide standards.

> **Important Note:** There is no way around it—grammar is boring, dry, and often tedious. The remainder of this chapter examines the fundamentals of grammar and uses short exercises to reinforce the basic concepts needed for understanding the GMAT Sentence Correction section. There are dozens of examples of GMAT questions and over 140 practice problems, but these examples do not begin until the next chapter. If you feel that you have a firm understanding of grammar, including the parts of speech and parts of a sentence, please skip to Chapter Four to begin learning how to apply these concepts to the GMAT. However, if you are not completely comfortable with grammar and usage, it is important to plod through the rest of this chapter—however boring—in order to understand concepts discussed later in the book.

Parts of Speech

Each word in a sentence serves a specific purpose and is categorized as a part of speech based on its function. There are eight parts of speech used to create sentences, and a basic knowledge of each is required to understand the errors on the test.

We have provided definitions for each part of speech, as well as a brief summary or explanation of their possible roles in a sentence. New vocabulary terms and definitions within the summary are highlighted in bold. You do not need to know these definitions to take the GMAT. We simply use them for the convenience of discussion and for students who had formal grammar instruction. These summaries are also in no way a comprehensive study of grammar. We provide only the resources you need to excel on the GMAT.

Most of the sentences used as examples will identify the part of speech in question using the listed abbreviation immediately above the word.

The problem sets in this chapter are not indicative of GMAT test questions. They do not follow the Sentence Correction form described in Chapter Two. Rather, they are simple exercises to help you learn to identify the parts of speech. If you feel that you have a firm understanding of basic grammar, you may want to skip this chapter and move on to Chapter Four.

If you have trouble remembering the functions of the eight parts of speech, use the similes in these corresponding sidebars as mnemonic devices.

Sentences are like motion pictures. It takes a carefully planned cast and crew to produce a quality film, just as it takes the carefully planned parts of speech to produce a quality sentence.

1. Nouns

Nouns are like actors and actresses. They are the celebrities of the sentence, and the other, less-important words work to make the stars shine. Nouns are very demanding and quite spoiled, and they are used to being the VIP—the Very Important Part of speech—in every sentence.

> **noun** (n.) – a part of speech that names a person, place, or thing

Common nouns name common things: *cat, governor, high school, weather*. **Proper nouns** are almost always capitalized and name specific people, places, or things: *Fido, Governor Adams, Adrian High School, The Weather Channel*. Nouns can occur anywhere in a sentence:

The *bus* arrived. [n.]

After receiving her test *score*, *Ling* was accepted to six *colleges*. [n.] [n.] [n.]

A sentence can have unlimited common and proper nouns, as long as the sentence continues to make sense.

A **singular noun** names one person, place, or thing (*cat, house*), while a **plural noun** names more than one person, place, or thing (*cats, houses*).

Beware of words that look like nouns, but function as adjectives. For example, in "birthday present," *birthday* is not a noun; it is modifying the real noun, *present*.

Nouns can be further categorized as count nouns, non-count nouns, and collective nouns. **Count nouns** can be counted (one *pen*, seven *blocks*, two thousand *ducks*) while **non-count nouns** (sometimes called mass nouns) cannot be counted (*gravity, grass, wood*). **Collective nouns** are singular count nouns that identify a group (*committee, choir, faculty*).

Noun Mini-Drill

Read the following passages. Place each of the nouns from the passage into the corresponding boxes below the passage. The first one has been done for you. *Answers are provided on page 51.*

1. General Washington led the Continental Army across the Delaware River by the cover of darkness. Over one thousand unsuspecting Hessian soldiers were camped out in the homes and businesses of Trenton, where they had just celebrated Christmas far from their German homeland.

Common Nouns	Proper Nouns
	General Washington

Nouns occur in every sentence on the GMAT. You must be able to isolate them in order to verify subject-verb agreement, noun agreement, parallel structure, and many other grammatical concepts covered in the next five chapters.

2. A jazz band is a musical ensemble that consists of two sections. The rhythm section includes a set of drums, the bass, and an instrument capable of playing chords, such as a piano. The horns group contains several trumpets, saxophones, and trombones.

Singular Nouns	Plural Nouns

3. The moving company bases its prices on the number of pieces of furniture, the weight of the load, and the time spent packing your home. A contract is required, and all money must be paid up front.

Count Nouns	Non-Count Nouns

2. Pronouns

pronoun (pr.) – a person, place, or thing which replaces a noun

Pronouns are like body doubles.

Just as movie stars have body doubles to take their place during rehearsals or less important scenes, the noun has a pronoun to take its place when its overworked. The Pronoun is selected for his similarity to the Noun, both in style and in function.

Pronouns, such as *he*, *we*, and *them*, are words that are used to replace a noun. Imagine a sentence with pronouns:

> When Mrs. Hanson told Jacob that *he* could take home *their* classroom guinea pig for the summer, *he* called *his* mother and told *her* that *she* would need to pick *it* up after school.

And then imagine it without:

> When Mrs. Hanson told Jacob that Jacob could take home Mrs. Hanson's students' guinea pig for the summer, Jacob called Jacob's mother and told Jacob's mother that Jacob's mother would need to pick up Mrs. Hanson's classroom guinea pig after school.

Yikes.

The word that a pronoun replaces is called an **antecedent**. In the previous sentences, *Mrs. Hanson's classroom guinea pig* was an antecedent for *it. Jacob* was an antecedent for *he* and *his*. While most pronouns will have an antecedent, beware of the occasional sentence without an antecedent. Take the following sentence for example:

> *Everyone* must take a seat before the orchestra begins.

Everyone does not have an antecedent because it is understood that *everyone* refers to all of the people in the room at the time the orchestra begins.

Several pronoun concepts are tested in Sentence Correction, including pronoun-antecedent agreement and implied and ambiguous pronouns. These potential errors are covered in detail in Chapter Five. Your ability to quickly spot a pronoun and its antecedent can save you valuable time.

Types of Pronouns

There are seven different types of pronouns, and a basic understanding of each is important for succeeding on the GMAT. Some pronouns may fall into more than one categories, depending on their function in a sentence.

1. Personal pronouns

As the name implies, these pronouns get personal; they refer to a specific person or thing, and include pronouns like *I*, *he*, *hers*, and *us*.

> Although *she*^{pr.} was best known for her art, Rosa also published cook books.

> After the kids watched the movie, the baby-sitter served *them*^{pr.} dinner.

2. **Demonstrative pronouns**

Demonstrative pronouns demonstrate. They point to nouns that are nearby in time or in space. There are four demonstrative pronouns: *this*, *that*, *these*, and *those*.

These^{pr.} shirts should be marked half price.

These shirts should be marked half price.

That cannot happen again.

3. **Interrogative pronouns**

This type of pronoun interrogates, or asks questions. The four main interrogative pronouns are *who*, *whom*, *which*, and *what*.

Who took the last slice of pizza?

Which band member is your favorite?

4. **Relative pronouns**

Relative pronouns relate. They connect a phrase to the antecedent. There are four specific relative pronouns: *who*, *whom*, *that*, and *which*.

The nurse *who* gave you the injection has the day off.

The only thing *that* matters is your safety.

Remember, you do not have to memorize the names of the seven types of pronouns. You simply must understand that pronouns take many different roles in a sentence. You can refer back to this page as needed as we discuss pronouns throughout the book.

5. **Indefinite pronouns**

These pronouns aren't definite; they refer to a person or thing that is identified, but isn't specific. There are dozens of indefinite pronouns, and some examples include *everybody*, *few*, *each*, and *somebody*.

Many of the balloons popped before they were released.

You can put *anything* on the pizza you want.

6. **Reflexive pronouns**

Reflex pronouns reflect back onto the noun. They are *myself*, *yourself*, *herself*, *himself*, *itself*, *ourselves*, *yourselves*, and *themselves*.

The CEO does the hiring *himself*.

I gave *myself* a haircut.

7. Intensive pronouns

These pronouns intensify or emphasize the antecedent. They take the exact same form as reflexive pronouns, but they follow the noun more closely.

I *myself* [pr.] would prefer to eat in the non-smoking section.

The office manager *herself* [pr.] said that we're all getting bonuses.

Pronoun Mini-Drill

In each of the following sentences, underline the pronoun(s). If an antecedent is present, draw an arrow from the pronoun to the antecedent. The first one has been done for you. *Answers are provided on page 52.*

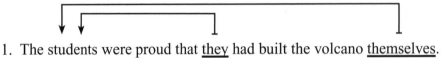

1. The students were proud that <u>they</u> had built the volcano <u>themselves</u>.

2. The new law, which went into effect last month, requires more paperwork.

3. Everyone at the meeting agreed that the resolution would pass.

4. Doug himself should make the phone call if he wants to have an impact.

5. Daily use of vitamins and moisturizer helps your skin replenish itself.

6. What is the difference in gas mileage between the SUV and the sedan?

7. After she retired, Tanya worked part-time for Virginia as her bookkeeper.

3. Verbs

verb (vb.) – a word showing action or state of being

Every sentence must contain a verb. The most simple sentence in the English language is only three letters long, containing a pronoun and a verb:

I am.

Most sentences are more descriptive, but they all contain at least one verb:

vb.
I <u>went</u> to the amusement park.

vb.
The roller coaster <u>sped</u> down the hill.

Some verbs are made up of more than one word. **Helping verbs** (hv.) such as *be*, *shall*, *can*, *must*, and *would* are added to action verbs to help express time and mood. Look at the following sentence:

hv. vb.
The band <u>is playing</u> at Main Street Café.

In this sentence, *is* joins *playing* to show that the band is currently at Main Street Café. If *was* were substituted for *is*, the sentence would take on a new meaning because then the band had played at Main Street Café in the past. Other helping verbs include *can*, *could*, *may*, *might*, *must*, *need*, *ought to*, *shall*, *should*, *will*, *would*, and *used to*. The verb phrase may contain several helping verbs:

hv. hv. hv. vb.
In January, Jenica <u>will have been working</u> here for four years.

The helping verbs in this sentence indicate that Jenica began working in the past and will continue working into the future. Helping verbs are necessary to convey timing.

One verb is used more than any other verb in our vocabulary: *be*. Look at the conjugation of *to be*:

	Present Tense	Past Tense
I	am	was
you (singular)	are	were
he/she/it	is	was
we	are	were
you (plural)	are	were
they	are	were

Verbs are like the directors of a film. They yell "Lights, Camera, Action!" and direct the Nouns through the scene. They dictate whether the Noun must glare, cry, walk, talk, run, dance, or drive.

Because "to be" is used so often, you will encounter many test questions in your studies that include errors with the verb.

Be can be a helping verb, as in the previous example:

         hv. vb.
The band is playing at Main Street Café.

And *be* can also be a **linking verb** (lv.), which, rather than showing action, links a noun or pronoun to additional information about that noun or pronoun:

                  lv.
The smoked herring is delicious.

In this sentence, the noun, *herring*, is not performing any action (such as swimming or fleeing). Instead, a linking verb provides information about the herring: it is delicious. Look at another:

   lv.
I am a sales representative for a paper company.

Other linking verbs include sensory verbs (*see, hear, taste, smell, feel*) and verbs that reflect a state of being (such as *appear, become, prove, remain, seem*).

             lv.
Cassandra seems moody.

           lv.
The dirty sock smells repulsive.

Note that many linking verbs can also be regular verbs which show action:

         vb.
The boy smells the dirty sock.

In this sentence, *smells* is an action verb because it shows what the boy is doing. To test a sensory verb or a state of being verb for its classification as a linking verb or an action verb, substitute the verb *to be* in the sentence. If the sentence still makes sense, the original verb is a linking verb. If the sentence no longer makes sense, the original verb is an action verb:

    The dirty sock smells repulsive.
    The dirty sock is repulsive.
    Smells = linking verb

This sentence makes sense, so *smells* is functioning as a linking verb in the original sentence.

    The boy smells the dirty sock.
    The boy is the dirty sock.
    Smells = action verb

The second sentence does not make sense in this example, thus *smells* occurs as an action verb in the first sentence.

Verbals are words that are based on verbs, but function as other parts of speech in the sentence. One type of verbal is the **infinitive**, which is the root of the verb combined with the word *to*:

> to draw
> to eat
> to remember
> to waste

Infinitives can act as adjectives and adverbs but are most often nouns:

<pre>
        vb.   n.
I <u>learned</u> <i>to cook</i> when I was in college.
</pre>

Some students may struggle with this concept, wanting to group *to cook* with the verb, *learned*. But replace *to cook* with a true noun:

<pre>
        vb.   n.
I <u>learned</u> <i>biology</i> when I was in college.
</pre>

This should help you clearly see that *to cook* is a noun which follows the verb.

Another verbal is the **gerund**. Gerunds are often mistaken with verbs because they end in *–ing*, but gerunds function as a noun. Look at how *running* can be used as an action verb or a gerund:

<pre>
    hv.   vb.
I <u>was running</u> for my life!
</pre>

<pre>
   n.   lv.
Running <u>is</u> my favorite form of exercise.
</pre>

Again, if you have trouble visualizing *running* as a noun in the second sentence, replace it with an unquestionable noun:

<pre>
   n.   lv.
Running <u>is</u> my favorite form of exercise.
</pre>

<pre>
    n.   lv.
Aerobics <u>is</u> my favorite form of exercise.
</pre>

Few students will question that *aerobics* is a noun, and it should help you see that *running* functions as a noun in the same sentence.

Substituting is a common method used by great test takers on all sections of the test. By replacing the unfamiliar with the familiar, you are able to solve problems that might have originally appeared too difficult.

The final verbal is the participle. **Participles** are verb forms that function as adjectives and most often end in *–ing* (present participles) or *–ed* (past participles). Look at how the word *frighten* can be used as verb and as a verbal adjective:

      hv.   vb.

The dog <u>is frightening</u> the mailman.

adj.

The *frightening* dog lunged at the mailman.

adj.

The *frightened* dog hid from the mailman.

As with the two previous verbals, substitute a true adjective into the sentence in order to confirm that the verbal is a participle:

adj.
The *frightening* dog lunged at the mailman.

adj.
The *scary* dog lunged at the mailman.

And:

adj.
The *frightened* dog hid from the mailman.

adj.
The *timid* dog hid from the mailman.

Because every sentence contains a verb, errors with verbs are extremely popular test questions, and we will discuss verb tense and verb form in more detail later.

> Every sentence must contain a verb, so it should be no surprise that verb errors are prevalent on the GMAT. If you can discern verbs from infinitives, gerunds, and participles, you can quickly catch errors in agreement, tense, and form. Verbs are thoroughly covered in Chapter Four.

Verb Mini-Drill

Underline all of the verbs in the following sentences. Above each verb, indicate (v.) for an action verb, (hv.) for a helping verb, or (lv.) for a linking verb. The first one has been done for you. *Answers are provided on page 53.*

1. The cast of the movie hv. v. <u>is rumored</u> to include several leading celebrities.

Beware of verbals! These verb forms function as nouns, adjectives, and adverbs—not verbs.

2. Cheetahs can accelerate faster than a Lamborghini and reach speeds of seventy miles and hour.

3. Learning to ride a bike is one of the many milestones of childhood.

4. The town council has been planning to increase taxes and decrease parking fines.

5. In the writing class, students work in study groups, read at home, and present projects in class.

6. Running from the dog, the daring squirrel sprinted into the house.

7. At the time of the incident, the doctor looked guilty of malpractice.

8. Dancing has been voted the campers' favorite activity while sailing has been elected their least favorite activity.

4. Prepositions

Prepositions are like the set decorators on a movie stage. They create a scene to show where the Noun is in time and space. When the director yells "Action!" the preposition has already "pre-positioned" the noun or pronoun.

Preposition (prep.) – word used to link a noun or pronoun to other words

Prepositions describe a relationship or situation between words in the sentence. Try to define one, like *above* or *around* or *on*. Chances are you'll use your hands to try to show the relationship of two things or the way two things are situated. The most common prepositions include:

about, across, after, against, among, around, as, at, before, behind, between, by, during, for, from, in, including, into, like, off, on, over, through, to, towards, under, upon, with, within, and without

Prepositions never occur alone; they are always in a prepositional phrase. **Prepositional phrases** begin with a preposition and end with a noun or pronoun, which is called the **object of the preposition**. Look at several prepositional phrases with the preposition and its object identified:

prep.   n.
to the store

prep.   n.
by the bubbling brook

prep.   n.
from a distant land

Prepositions most often describe time (*at*, *by*, *during*), place (*above*, *on*, *within*), or movement (*to*, *towards*).

Because many prepositions are only two or three letters long, they are popular errors on the GMAT. The test makers hope that you will not notice an error in such a small word.

Preposition Mini-Drill

Little prepositions tend to cause big problems in idiom and parallel structure, as discussed in many of the upcoming chapters. A close reading and quick identification of prepositions can lead to speedy solutions.

Underline all of the prepositional phrases in the following sentences. Write (prep.) above each preposition and (n.) or (pr.) above each object of the preposition, depending on whether it is a noun or a pronoun. The first one has been done for you. *Answers are provided on page 54.*

prep.   n.
1. I am supposed to meet James <u>at the pool hall</u>.

2. On the Oregon Trail, women and children rode in the wagon, while men

    walked alongside the caravan with the livestock.

3. Before Milo left for vacation, he took his dog to to the vet for boarding.

5. Adjectives

Adjective (adj.) – word which describes or modifies a noun or a pronoun

Adjectives are called modifiers because they modify a noun or pronoun in a sentence. They make an apple *shiny* and *red* or an orange *juicy* and *sweet*. They help make our language more colorful and descriptive, and most authors are armed with an arsenal of adjectives. Take this passage from *The Great Gatsby*, by F. Scott Fitzgerald:

> A stout, middle-aged man, with enormous owl-eyed spectacles, was sitting somewhat drunk on the edge of a great table, staring with unsteady concentration at the shelves of books.

Adjectives are the hair and make-up artists to the stars. Their only job is to make the Noun or Pronoun look glamorous.

Remove the adjectives and adjective phrases and the sentence loses its brilliance:

> A man was sitting somewhat drunk on the edge of a table, staring with concentration at the shelves.

We no longer know the man's appearance, his age, or the degree of his concentration. Plus, we have lost details about the table and the shelves. Adjectives help make the literary world more vivid and interesting.

Adjectives most often come before the noun or pronoun they are modifying:

> adj.   n.   adj.   n.
> The choppy water caused the small boat to roll.

>   adj.   n.   adj.   adj.   n.
> I bought an inexpensive purse in a charming French village.

Adjectives can also come after a linking verb to modify the noun or pronoun before the linking verb:

>   n.   lv.   adj.
> The water is choppy.

>   pr.   lv.   adj.
> They are inexpensive.

The determiners a, an, and the are a special group of adjectives called articles.

Errors with adjectives will be discussed later, but it is important to know that adjectives are often confused with the next part of speech, adverbs.

6. Adverbs

> **Adverb** (adv.) – word which describes or modifies a verb, an adjective, or another adverb

Adverbs are like camera-men. Their main responsibility is to accurately capture the action dictated by the director, the verb.

Adverbs are also modifiers. However, unlike an adjective which modifies a noun or pronoun, adverbs modify a verb, an adjective, or another adverb. Three examples follow.

Adverb modifying a verb:

adv.   vb.
Jamie quickly ran the ball down the field

Adverb modifying an adjective:

adv. adj. n.
Jamie ran the ball down the very long field.

Adverb modifying another adverb:

v.   adv. adv.
Jamie ran quite slowly up the field.

It is true that most words that end in –*ly* are adverbs: *quickly*, *sadly*, *loudly*, *carefully*. But adverbs do not have to end in –*ly*, such as *quite* and *very*, and not all words that end in –*ly* are adverbs. Words such as *friendly*, *lonely*, and *sparkly* are adjectives.

Adjective and Adverb Phrases

Modifiers and modifying phrases are carefully studied in Chapter Six.

One final note about adjectives and adverbs before their specific errors are discussed later: phrases—especially prepositional phrases—can also take on the modifying role of an adjective or an adverb:

vb.   adv.
Jamie runs <u>like the wind</u>.

Like the wind, typically a prepositional phrase, takes the role of an adverb. It tells the reader how Jamie runs, thus modifying a verb. *Like the wind* is an adverb phrase. Look at another:

adj.
Jamie, <u>the star athlete at my high school</u>, runs every day.

The noun phrase, *the star athlete at my school*, has become an adjective. It modifies *Jamie*, the main noun, making it an adjective phrase.

Read again the sentence from *The Great Gatsby*:

> A stout, middle-aged man, with enormous owl-eyed spectacles, was sitting somewhat drunk on the edge of a great table, staring with unsteady concentration at the shelves of books.

Now study it with the adjectives and adverbs underlined:

adj. adj.   adj.   adj. phrase
A <u>stout</u>, <u>middle-aged</u> man, <u>with enormous owl-eyed spectacles</u>,

     adv. adv.   adv. phrase
was sitting <u>somewhat</u> <u>drunk</u> <u>on the edge of a great table</u>,

    adv. phrase   adv. phrase
staring <u>with unsteady concentration</u> <u>at the shelves of books</u>.

Look at the sentence with all of the adjectives and adverbs removed:

 n. hv. vb.   vb.
Man was sitting, staring.

This exercise makes it easy to see why adjectives and adverbs are so important to the English language.

Adjective and Adverb Mini-Drill
Underline the adjectives and adverbs in the sentences below. Mark individual adjectives and adverbs with (adj.) and (adv.), and phrases with (adj. phrase) and (adv. phrase). Use the passage above as an example. *Answers on page 54.*

1. The angry motorist carelessly wove through four lanes of traffic.

2. The first USS *Allegheny*, named for the Allegheny river, was an

    iron-hulled gunboat that ran on steam.

3. The nervous applicant did not effectively communicate his career goals.

4. Frustrated with the new dress code, Kacey openly and defiantly disobeyed

    her supervisor by wearing jeans to work.

7. Conjunctions

Conjunction (conj.) – word which links words or phrases

There are three types of conjunctions: coordinating conjunctions, subordinating conjunctions, and correlative conjunctions. **Coordinating conjunctions** are the most common, of which there are seven:

and	*but*	*or*	*yet*	*for*	*nor*	*so*

Coordinating conjunctions are used to join nouns, pronouns, verbs, prepositional phrases, adjectives, and even adverbs:

Nouns:	Coke or Pepsi
Pronouns:	he nor she
Verbs:	rocking and rolling
Prepositions:	of the people, for the people, and by the people
Adjectives:	red, white, and blue
Adverbs:	quickly but quietly

Coordinating conjunctions are also used to join two complete sentences:

Toni wrecked the car. She was not injured.
Toni wrecked the car, *but* she was not injured.

You can choose to be quiet. You can choose to leave.
You can choose to be quiet, *or* you can choose to leave.

Taking two complete sentences and joining them with a coordinating conjunction is appropriately called **coordination**. It takes two equally important sentences and fuses them together with a comma and a conjunction.

Subordinating conjunctions include words like *although*, *once*, *rather than*, and *until*. They are also used to join two sentences, but one of the sentences is rearranged to become a phrase:

The car was low on gas. Gretchen turned off the air conditioner.
<u>Because the car was low on gas</u>, Gretchen turned off the air conditioner.

The cat had her rabies vaccination. I decided to let her outside.
I decided to let the cat outside <u>now that she had her rabies vaccination</u>.

I decided not to invest in the internet. I put my savings into a restaurant.
<u>Rather than investing in the internet</u>, I put my savings into a restaurant.

Subordination will be discussed in further detail later in this book.

Conjunctions are like agents. Agents set up meetings between all of the key players and then negotiate salaries, effectively determining which player is most important. Conjunctions joins parts of speech and parts of sentences, often indicating the significance of each part.

Conjunctions are a main error indicator. They can signal problems with parallel structure, subordination, logical comparisons, and faulty word choice. Consequently, they are reviewed in many of the following chapters.

Correlative conjunctions are a type of coordinating conjunction, but like twins, they travel in pairs. Correlative conjunctions include:

either..or   neither..nor   both..and   not only..but also
not..but   whether..or   as..as

Look at a few examples:

I can *either* take the bus *or* participate in a carpool.

The amazing piano player is *both* blind *and* deaf.

Swimming is *not only* great exercise *but also* an enjoyable pastime.

Conjunctions are common parts of speech, and therefore they are common errors on the test.

Correlative conjunctions MUST occur in these specific pairs. If they are paired with different words on the GMAT, the sentence must be corrected.

Conjunction Mini-Drill

Underline the conjunctions in the following sentences. Identify each one as a coordination conjunction (cc.), a subordination conjunction (sc.), or a correlative conjunction (twin). The first one has been done for you. *Answers are provided on page 54.*

1. Do you want heads <u>or</u> tails?
   > cc.

2. Jeff wants to go to Harvard or Yale, but he is worried about his test scores.

3. Once the immigrants reached Ellis Island, they were subject to medical examinations and interviews.

4. The sociology experiment tests whether people return money they have found or keep it for themselves.

8. Interjections

Interjection (int.) – word used to convey emotion

Interjections are added to a sentence to show emotion, so they do not affect any other part of the sentence. Words like *Wow!*, *Oh*, and *Eh?* are interjections. Because they are not common in formal writing, interjections are not tested on the GMAT. Hurray!

Interjections are like publicists. They are emotional, excitable, and animated, screaming "PARTY!," "WOW!," and "POW!"

Sentences are created by combining parts of speech. A sentence can contain only a noun and a verb:

> n.   vb.
> Bob yelled.

Or a sentence can contain several or all of the parts of speech:

> int.   n. conj.   adv.   vb. prep.   adj.
> "Touchdown!" Dan and Keith excitedly yelled at the television screen.

As we have seen, some words can function as several different parts of speech. Take, for example, the word *dog*. *Dog* can be a noun, an adverb, or a verb, depending on how it is used in the sentence:

As a noun:	Ricardo wanted a *dog* for his birthday.
As an adjective:	I am *dog*-tired.
As a verb:	The FBI will *dog* him until he is caught.

It is imperative to understand the seven parts of speech. Not only are they the foundation of grammar and usage, but they are also the key to understanding specific errors on the test. You can review each part of speech now, or refer back to these pages as you encounter specific errors in the following chapters.

The Subject and the Predicate

A sentence can be divided into two parts: a subject and a predicate.

Subject (subj.) – the part of the sentence that contains the word or phrase that performs the action of the verb in the sentence. The subject is a noun, pronoun, or noun phrase and names whom or what the sentence is about.

Predicate (pred.) – the part of the sentence that contains the verb as well as the objects and phrases controlled by the verb.

All sentences must have both a subject and a predicate. The subject can be simple, containing only a noun or pronoun:

> subj.   pred.
> Elaina || won the race.

Movies can be short, five minute clips, or enduring, three-hour epics. Similarly, sentences can be short and simple, or long and complex.

A movie has two essential elements: character and plot.

Similarly, a sentence has two essential elements: a subject and a predicate. A subject, much like a character in a movie, must show who or what the sentence is about. A predicate dictates the action for the subject, just as a plot dictates the action for a character.

Or the subject can be more complex:

subj.   pred.

<u>Elaina, the girl who had spent a year on crutches,</u> || <u>won the race</u>.

The complete subject of this sentence is Elaina, the girl who had spent a year on crutches. On the GMAT, you'll usually only need to locate the **simple subject**, which is the main noun or pronoun with its modifiers removed. The simple subject of the sentence in the example is simply *Elaina*.

A **compound subject** has two nouns or pronouns that perform the same action in the sentence:

subj.   subj.   pred.

<u>Elaina</u> and <u>TJ</u> || <u>ran in the race</u>.

In this sentence, *Elaina and TJ* is a compound subject.

To find a subject, find the verb and ask yourself "Who or what [*insert verb*]?"

The little girl waved to the crowd.
Who waved? The little girl.
Simple subject? Girl.

subj.   pred.

<u>The little *girl*</u> || <u>waved to the crowd</u>.

Predicates can also be simple:

subj.   pred.

<u>The little boy</u> || <u>pouted</u>.

Or more complex:

subj.   pred.

<u>The little boy</u> || <u>pouted about the spilt milk</u>.

A **simple predicate** contains just the verb, verb phrase, or compound verb. In the previous sentence, the simple predicate is *pouted*.

A **compound predicate** occurs when two or more verbs are performed by the same subject:

subj.   pred.   pred.

<u>The little boy</u> || <u>pouted about the spilt milk</u> and <u>cried in the corner</u>.

In this sentence, the little boy completed two actions: *pouted about the spilt milk* and *cried in the corner*. The sentence also has a simple compound predicate: *pouted and cried*.

Inverted sentences occur when a predicate occurs before its subject:

At the end of the movie are the credits.

Inversion can be dangerous to the novice test taker who is searching for the subject. Many students are tempted to choose *end* or *movie* as the subject. However, if this sentence were rearranged, the subject is more obvious:

subj.   pred.
The credits ‖ are at the end of the move.

Inverted sentences that begin with "there" are called expletives. They are explained in more detail in the next chapter.

Inverted sentences often begin with the words *here* or *there*:

There were eight people in the office.

Rearranged:

subj.   pred.
Eight people ‖ were there in the office.

Inversion also occurs with a **split predicate**, in which part of the predicate occurs after the subject and part occurs before the subject. Authors might split a predicate to add variety to their writing:

At the height of its popularity, the TV show went off the air.

The beginning clause *at the height of its popularity* is actually a part of the predicate:

subj.   pred.
The TV show ‖ went off the air at the height of its popularity.

Look at one more example of a split predicate:

In 2005, despite my recent knee surgery, I ran a marathon.

The previous sentence creates more drama than its rearranged counterpart:

subj.   pred.
I ‖ ran a marathon in 2005 despite my recent knee surgery.

Locating the subject of a sentence and its predicate verb is an important skill on the GMAT which we will discuss in more detail at the end of the chapter.

Subject and Predicate Mini-Drill

In the following sentences, underline the subject once and the predicate twice. Mark the simple subject with (ss.) and the simple predicate with (sp.). The first one has been done for you. *Answers are provided on page 55.*

Locating the subject and predicate is crucial to finding agreement errors.

1. The new office *manager* *was forced* to discipline several employees during his first week of work.

2. The playful puppy, a terrier and shepherd mix, pounced on the flowers and chased the birds.

3. There seems to be a problem with the copier.

4. The injured plaintiff and the insurance company reached a settlement which will remain undisclosed.

5. After nearly fifty years of marriage, my grandparents decided to divorce.

6. Even more important is the proper use of power in the department.

7. The most important point of the story is that a true friend never intentionally hurts you.

Direct and Indirect Objects

Many predicates contain a direct object or indirect object.

Direct Object (do.) – the noun or pronoun in the predicate that receives the action of the verb

Indirect Object (io.) – the noun or pronoun in the predicate that is indirectly affected by the verb

While the subject is the noun or pronoun that performs the action, the direct object is the noun or pronoun that receives the action.

vb.   do.
Grant ‖ hit the *ball* out of the park.

Who hit? *Grant*. *Grant* is the subject. But what received the action? What was hit? The *ball*. *Ball* is the direct object.

To locate the direct object, ask "Who or what was [insert *verb*]?" Look at the another example and ask yourself, "What was found?"

do.
Shayna found the *keys* in the backyard.

Sentences may also have an indirect object:

vb. io.   do.
Mom ‖ gave *me* my *allowance*.

Who gave? *Mom*. *Mom* is the subject. What was given? The *allowance*. *Allowance* is the direct object. But what about the word *me*? *Me* cannot be the direct object because Mom did not give *me* away—she gave away the allowance. The word *me* is an indirect object. It is indirectly affected by the verb.

To find an indirect object, ask "Who or what received the [insert *direct object*]?" Study another sentence with an indirect object:

After finding their bridal registry, I bought *Jack and Jill* a *coffee maker*.

What was bought? Not Jack and Jill! A coffee maker was bought, so *coffee maker* is the direct object. Who received the coffee maker? Jack and Jill, making them the indirect objects.

The supporting characters in a movie are different from the main character. Because the movie is about the main character, the main character experiences all of the action and the plot. The supporting characters are often affected by the action, but they are static characters and unchanged. Similarly, direct and indirect objects receive the action of the verb, but they are in the predicate and not directly affected by the action.

Not all sentences will have a direct object, and even fewer have an indirect object.

Direct and Indirect Object Mini-Drill

In the following sentences, underline any direct and indirect objects. Mark the direct object with (do.) and the indirect object with (io.). Not all sentences will have a direct or indirect object. The first one has been done for you. *Answers are provided on page 56.*

1. The agent sold <u>Mrs. Petty</u> the <u>house</u> by the lake.
   <small>io.</small>   <small>do.</small>

2. The city raised the speed limit by 15 miles per hour after conducting a
   traffic study.

3. Gary sent his mother flowers on her birthday.

4. The new intern slept through the staff meeting.

5. Upon her death, the lonely old woman left her gardener her entire estate,
   causing the neighbors to speculate on their relationship.

6. While the catcher chased the overthrown ball, one runner easily stole
   third base and another scored.

7. As a homework assignment, each student in the school wrote the governor
   a letter about the loss of the the statewide music program.

Phrases

Phrase – a group of related words that do not contain a subject and a verb. A phrase can have a subject, or a verb, but not both.

Phrases, if separated from the rest of the sentence, cannot stand on their own as a complete sentence. Sentences may contain phrases in the subject, in the predicate, or in both. We have already examined some phrases in our discussion of verbs, adjectives, and adverbs, but a review is below along with an introduction to some other phrases:

Noun Phrase – a phrase that contains a noun and any words that modify the noun

Examine a noun phrase in italics in the following sentence:

The <u>first gold *medal* from high school</u> hangs in my office now.

Medal is the subject of the sentence. It is modified by *first*, *gold*, and *from high school*. All of these elements combined create the phrase *first gold medal from high school*. Notice that the phrase cannot stand alone as a sentence.

Prepositional Phrase – a phrase including a preposition and a noun or pronoun. They also may include one or more adjectives.

Prepositional phrases are the most common phrases in the English language:

The ship sailed <u>*through* the fierce storm</u>, finding port <u>*in* the Florida Keys</u>.

Prepositions are always accompanied by a prepositional phrase.

Adjective Phrase – a phrase that modifies a noun or a pronoun.

Adjective phrases may contain actual adjectives, or just be a phrase that acts as an adjective:

Jamie, <u>the star athlete at my high school</u>, runs every day.

As we learned earlier, adverb phrases are similar.

Adverb Phrase – a phrase that modifies a verb, adjective, or adverb.

Jamie runs <u>like the wind</u>.

Movies are made up of multiple scenes. A scene is a continuous block of storyline that is set in a single environment. When scenes are put together, the movie unfolds. In the same way, sentences contain phrases and clauses. These phrases and clauses are continuous blocks of words, which, when put together with other phrases and clauses, create a sentence.

Sentences can contain several different types of phrases:

In the early evening, I often find myself thinking back on the purple sunsets of my childhood.

This sentence contains a noun phrase, verb phrase, and prepositional phrase:

Noun phrase: *purple sunsets of my childhood*
Verb phrase: *thinking back on*
Prepositional phrases: *in the early evening, of my childhood*

Clauses

Clauses are similar to phrases, but clauses must contain both a subject and a verb.

Clause – a group of related words that contain both a subject and a verb but is not a sentence

There are two types of clauses:

Independent Clause – a clause that could act as a sentence if a period were added to the end. Independent clauses carry the most weight or importance in a sentence.

Dependent Clause – a clause that depends on an independent clause to make sense. Dependent clauses could not stand alone as a sentence, even if a period were added. Dependent clauses carry less weight and importance than an independent clause.

If a dependent clause appears in a sentence, it will always have an independent clause on which to lean. Look at an example:

Although he was acquitted of embezzlement charges, Mike lost his job and his home.

Independent clause: *Mike lost his job and his home*
If we put a period after *home*, this would be a complete sentence.

Dependent clause: *Although he was acquitted of embezzlement charges*
If we put a period after *charges*, we create a fragment, not a sentence. This clause depends on the remainder of the sentence in order to make sense.

Dependent clauses
function as a noun,
adjective, or adverb.

Dependent clauses often begin with subordinating conjunctions, such as *although, as, because, before, even though, despite, even though, regardless of, since, so that, unless, which,* and *while.* The most important piece of information in the previous sentence, that Mike lost his job and his home, is carried by the independent clause. The fact that he was acquitted of the embezzlement charges is in the dependent clause, and is not the main reason for the sentence. This fact is less important.

Dependent clauses do not have to contain a subordinating conjunction; they simply must have a subject and a verb:

Rodney, *who is a paramedic*, helped the woman who had fallen.

This relative clause, *who is a paramedic*, contains the relative pronoun *who* and the verb *is*. Although the clause cannot make sense without the rest of the sentence, it contains a subject and a verb, thus making it a dependent clause.

An independent clause can be accompanied by a dependent clause, as just demonstrated, or by another independent clause. Two independent clauses separated by a coordinating conjunction is called **coordination**:

The man had a confirmed seat on the flight, but the airline would not let him board the plane.

Conjunction: *but*
Independent clause: *The man had a confirmed seat on the flight*
Independent clause: *The airline would not let him board the plane*

GMAC uses phrases
and clauses to create
complex sentences,
making errors much
more difficult to locate.
You must be able to
search each phrase or
clause for errors, as well
as remove the phrases
or clauses to simplify
the sentence. Errors
involving phrases and
clauses are covered in
nearly all of the remain-
ing chapters.

In a coordinating sentence, the two independent clauses carry the same weight. It is of equal importance to know that the man had a confirmed seat and that he was denied access to the plane.

We can turn the first independent clause (*the man had a confirmed seat on the flight*) into a dependent clause and still convey the same meaning, but diminish the importance of the confirmed seat:

Even though the man had a confirmed seat on the flight, the airline would not let him board the plane.

This is called **subordinating** a clause. It takes one of the clauses and reduces its importance (*even though the man had a confirmed seat on the flight*), thus increasing the importance of the remaining independent clause (*the airline would not let him board the plane*). You may encounter a GMAT question which requires you to select the correct subordinating clause.

Clauses Mini-Drill

In the following sentences, underline any independent clauses. Place any dependent clauses in parenthesis. The first one has been done for you. *Answers are provided on page 57.*

1. (Unless you ace the exam,) <u>your biology grade looks dismal</u>.

2. Trey purchased a new computer, but it didn't come with a monitor.

3. Leticia wanted to become an oncologist because she had experienced cancer firsthand.

4. If the new dress code is enacted, I won't be able to wear shorts to school.

5. Jose threw his first strike following a six game slump.

6. Anna Maria is going to attend culinary school in France, and her brother hopes to visit her often.

7. My daughter doesn't know about the purse that I bought yesterday.

8. Despite the published dangers of smoking, millions of teenagers become addicted to cigarettes every year.

Finding the Main Subject and Verb

Every sentence must have a subject and a verb. Your first step to acing the Sentence Correction section is to be able to identify these two parts of the sentence, because nearly one-fourth of the questions are going to test your knowledge of subjects or verbs. If another type of error does not immediately present itself to you, you must search out the subject and the verb.

As we discussed earlier, the subject of a sentence is the noun or pronoun that performs the action in the sentence. To identify the subject, it is easiest to first locate the verb:

> JaLisa's skateboard flew through the air.

> Verb: *flew*
> What flew? *Skateboard.*

Many might be tempted to select *JaLisa* as the subject. Thankfully, though, JaLisa was not flying through the air – the skateboard flew through the air. *Skateboard* is the subject of the sentence. *JaLisa*, normally a noun, takes on the function of an adjective when the possessive is used. *JaLisa's* modifies skateboard.

Errors frequently occur when the subject becomes lost in the sentence, and the writers of the test will attempt to trick you into incorrectly identifying the subject. They may do this by using a complex sentence with multiple nouns or verbs:

> Although her grade point average was falling, Cheyenne's SAT score rose after taking a preparation course.

> Verb: *rose*
> What rose? *Score.*

The novice GMAT enthusiast might select *was falling* as the main verb. However, *was falling* is located in a dependent clause. The main verb must be in an independent clause.

The sentence might also confuse you because there are so many noun-like words to pick from in finding the subject. Remember, *Cheyenne's* is a possessive and thus an adjective, just as *SAT* is an adjective. The only true nouns in the sentence are *average*, *score*, and *course*. *Score* is in the independent clause and it performs the verb, *rose*, so *score* is the subject.

Your ability to locate the main subject and verb is tested in sentences with agreement errors, one of the most common question types on the test.

Verbs appear in both dependent and independent clauses. However, the main verb is always in an independent clause.

To help identify the subject of a sentence, there is an important rule to remember:

The main subject of the sentence is never in prepositional phrases, in phrases or clauses separated by commas, or in dependent clauses.

Look at the another example:

Even though they faced the obvious obstacles, veterinarians and oncologists administered chemotherapy to Bubba, a 154-pound Queensland grouper, at the Shedd Aquarium in Chicago.

The first part of the sentence, *even though they faced obvious obstacles*, is a dependent clause. It has a subject (*they*) and a verb (*faced*), but based on the rule that a sentence's main subject cannot be in a dependent clause, we know that these are not the main subject and verb for the entire sentence. Also, there are three prepositional phrases in the sentence (*to Bubba*, *at the Shedd Aquarium* and *in Chicago*), and we know that the subject cannot be in there, either. Finally, we can cross out the phrase in the center of the sentence because it is separated by commas (*a 154-pound Queensland grouper*). Using the rule for finding the main subject, you can begin to find the subject of more complex sentences by mentally crossing out the phrases and dependent clauses.

~~Even though they faced the obvious obstacles~~, veterinarians and oncologists administered chemotherapy ~~to Bubba, a 154-pound Queensland grouper, at the Shedd Aquarium in Chicago~~.

By crossing out the dependent clause and the prepositional phrase, the subject and verb become clear:

Verb: *administered*
Who administered? *Veterinarians and oncologists*

Veterinarians and oncologists is the compound subject. The remaining word, *chemotherapy*, is the direct object.

While most sentences will have an easily-identifiable subject, complex questions may require you to cross out the phrases and clauses in order to locate the subject. Look at the sentence below:

Because the school board concentrated on English and mathematics as the fundamental cores of education, rather than supplementing the curriculum with a music program, many students from East Lake High were robbed of an opportunity to apply for the Lake County Scholarship, as it was awarded to those who excelled in orchestra.

Some test takers might be able to pinpoint the subject immediately, but others will need to start slashing the phrases and dependent clauses. Start with the dependent clauses, as they are often the longest, and might include prepositional phrases:

~~Because the school board concentrated on English and mathematics as the fundamental cores of education~~, rather than supplementing the curriculum with a music program, many students from East Lake High were robbed of an opportunity to apply for the Lake County Scholarship, ~~as it was awarded to those who excelled in orchestra~~.

Then kill the prepositional phrases:

~~Because the school board concentrated on English and mathematics as the fundamental cores of education~~, rather than supplementing the curriculum with a music program, many students ~~from East Lake High~~ were robbed ~~of an opportunity to apply for the Lake County Scholarship~~, ~~as it was awarded to those who excelled in orchestra~~.

Finally, remove any phrases separated by commas that may interrupt the flow of the sentence:

~~Because the school board concentrated on English and mathematics as the fundamental cores of education~~, ~~rather than supplementing the curriculum with a music program~~, many students ~~from East Lake High~~ were robbed ~~of an opportunity to apply for the Lake County Scholarship~~, ~~as it was awarded to those who excelled in orchestra~~.

Put them all together:

~~Because the school board concentrated on English and mathematics as the fundamental cores of education~~, ~~rather than supplementing the curriculum with a music program~~, many students ~~from East Lake High~~ were robbed ~~of an opportunity to apply for the Lake County Scholarship~~, ~~as it was awarded to those who excelled in orchestra~~.

The verb, *were robbed*, appears, and you do not even need to ask "Who were robbed?" The only subject left is the subject of the sentence: *students*.

Because the GMAT is a CAT test, you are not able to physically cross out the clauses and phrases that do not contain the main subject and verb. You must practice mentally eliminating unnecessary phrases and clauses. PowerScore carries two GMAT books with real Sentence Correction questions: *The Official Guide for GMAT Review* and *The Official Guide for GMAT Verbal Review*. You can find these books on our website at powerscore.com. We strongly recommend practicing with these real questions before your test.

Do not rewrite the sentence on your noteboard! This wastes valuable time. Instead, practice mentally eliminating phrases and clauses.

One last note about finding subjects: all sentences have a visible subject except for commands, or **imperative sentences**. A command has an implied subject that does not appear in the sentence.

Imperative sentences are commonly used in directions, such as in cookbooks or manuals.

Jump over the hurdle.
[You] jump over the hurdle.

Verb: *jump*
Who jumps? *You* (Implied)

The subject of all commands is implied *you*. Here are some examples of others:

Please pass the potatoes.
[You] please pass the potatoes.

Verb: *pass*
Who passes? *You* (Implied)

Ride your bike next door and borrow some sugar.
[You] Ride your bike next door and borrow some sugar.

Verb: *ride and borrow* (compound)
Who rides and borrows? *You* (Implied)

The GMAT is not known for including commands in the Writing portion, but it is best to be prepared.

Remember that when you encounter a Sentence Correction question, the error might be obvious immediately. If this is the case, do not worry about finding the subject and verb. However, if you are unable to see an error right away, find the subject and verb and begin testing them for agreement, tense, and form, as discussed in the following chapters.

Finding the Subject and Verb Mini-Drill

In the following sentences, underline the simple subject once and the main verb (simple predicate) twice. Insert any implied subjects at the beginning of the sentence. Try to mentally eliminate clauses and phrases without using your pencil. *Answers are provided on page 58.*

1. Still upset by the loss, the captain of the tennis squad, who had lost his own match in three quick sets, refused to comment on his team's poor performance.

2. I argued with the waitress, who refused to acknowledge that my French fries were cold, for over five minutes before the manager approached my table.

3. Dip the dough in the butter before rolling in the flour mixture, and bake for one hour at 350 degrees.

4. Nervous that she might cause her book sales to drop by speaking out against the political leader, thus enabling her rival's book to rise on the list of best sellers, the outspoken author surprised the media by remaining quiet about the topic.

Final Notes

It's a wrap! Our review of basic grammar is complete, and we will now apply what we have learned to questions and concepts specific to the GMAT.

Remember, you can refer back to this chapter at any time.

Remember, you do not need to define vocabulary terms to succeed on the GMAT. We simply present these terms to help you remember past grammar lessons and to facilitate discussion. Also remember that this is not a comprehensive study of basic grammar. We have presented the information needed to understand errors specific to the GMAT.

The remaining chapters of this book look at typical GMAT errors using questions that follow Sentence Correction format. You may need to refer back to this chapter from time to time to review certain parts of speech.

Chapter Three Answer Key

Noun Mini-Drill (page 21)

1. General Washington led the Continental Army across the Delaware River by the cover of darkness. Over one thousand unsuspecting Hessian soldiers were camped out in the homes and businesses of Trenton, where they had just celebrated Christmas far from their German homeland.

Common Nouns		Proper Nouns
cover	darkness	General Washington
soldiers		Continental Army
homes		Delaware River
businesses		Trenton
homeland		Christmas

2. A jazz band is a musical ensemble that consists of two sections. The rhythm section includes a set of drums, the bass, and an instrument capable of playing chords, such as a piano. The horns group contains several trumpets, saxophones, and trombones.

Singular Nouns		Plural Nouns	
band (collective noun)		sections	drums
ensemble	section	chords	trumpets
set	bass	saxophones	trombones
instrument	piano		
group (collective noun)			

3. The moving company bases its prices on the number of pieces of furniture, the weight of the load, and the time spent packing your home. A contract is required, and all money must be paid up front.

Count Nouns		Non-Count Nouns	
company	prices	furniture	weight
number	pieces	time	money
load	home		
contract			

Note that some nouns become adjectives in these passages. In the second passage, the word *jazz* modifies *band* and the word *horns* modifies *group*. These words, *jazz* and *horns*, are often nouns but are acting as adjectives in this passage.

Pronoun Mini-Drill (page 24)

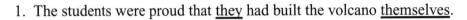

1. The students were proud that <u>they</u> had built the volcano <u>themselves</u>.

    Note: *They* is a personal pronoun; *themselves* is a reflexive pronoun.

2. The new law, <u>which</u> went into effect last month, requires more paperwork.

    Note: *Which* is a relative pronoun.

3. <u>Everyone</u> at the meeting agreed that the resolution would pass.

    Note: *Everyone* is an indefinite pronoun, and the antecedent is inherently understood. *That* is a conjunction in this sentence, rather than a relative pronoun, as it doesn't have a noun in which to relate.

4. Doug <u>himself</u> should make the phone call if <u>he</u> wants to have an impact.

    Note: *Doug* is the antecedent for two pronouns: *himself*, an intensive pronoun, and *he*, a personal pronoun.

5. Daily use of vitamins and moisturizer helps <u>your</u> skin replenish <u>itself</u>.

    Note: *Itself* is a reflexive pronoun. *Your* is a personal pronoun without an antecedent.

6. <u>What</u> is the difference in gas mileage between the SUV and the sedan?

    Note: *What* is an interrogative pronoun (no antecedent).

7. After <u>she</u> retired, Tanya worked part-time for Virgina as <u>her</u> bookkeeper.

    Note: Both pronouns are personal pronouns. The reader must use the context of the sentence to choose the correct antecedent.

<u>Verb Mini-Drill</u> (page 29)

1. The cast of the movie hv. v. <u>is rumored</u> to include several leading celebrities.

    Note: This sentence has one verbal. *To include several leading celebrities* is a phrase based on the infinitive *to include* (called an infinitive phrase).

2. Cheetahs hv. v. <u>can accelerate</u> faster than a Lamborghini and <u>reach</u> speeds of seventy miles and hour.

    Note: This sentence has more than one action verb pertaining to *cheetahs*.

3. Learning to ride a bike lv. <u>is</u> one of the many milestones of childhood.

    Note: *Learning* is a gerund and *to ride* is an infinitive. *Is* is a linking verb because action is not shown.

4. The town council hv.   hv.   v. <u>has been planning</u> to increase taxes and decrease parking fines.

    Note: *To increase taxes* and *[to] decrease parking fines* are infinitive phrases.

5. In the writing class, students v. <u>work</u> in study groups, v. <u>read</u> at home, and v. <u>present</u> projects in class.

    Note: Three verbs refer back to *students*. *Writing* is a participle adjective.

6. Running from the dog, the daring squirrel v. <u>sprinted</u> into the house.

    Note: Running from the dog is an participle phrase that acts as an adjective and modifies squirrel. Daring is a participle adjective.

7. At the time of the incident, the doctor lv. <u>looked</u> guilty of malpractice.

    Note: The doctor is not physically looking at anything, so *looked* is not an action verb. It links the doctor to *guilty*.

8. Dancing hv.   hv.   v. <u>has been voted</u> the campers' favorite activity while sailing hv.   hv.   v. <u>has been elected</u> their least favorite activity.

    Note: This compound sentence has two subjects and thus two verbs. *Dancing* and *sailing* are gerunds.

Preposition Mini-Drill (page 30)

1. I am supposed to meet James <u>at the pool hall</u>.
   ^prep.^ ^n.^

2. <u>On the Oregon Trail</u>, women and children rode <u>in the wagon</u>, while men
   ^prep.^ ^n.^ ^prep.^ ^n.^

   walked <u>alongside the caravan</u> <u>with the livestock</u>.
   ^prep.^ ^n.^ ^prep.^ ^n.^

3. <u>Before Milo</u> left <u>for vacation</u>, he took his dog <u>to the vet</u> <u>for boarding</u>.
   ^prep.^ ^n.^ ^prep.^ ^n.^ ^prep.^ ^n.^ ^prep.^ ^n.^

Adjective and Adverb Mini-Drill (page 33)

1. The <u>angry</u> motorist <u>carelessly</u> wove <u>through four lanes of traffic</u>.
   ^adj.^ ^adv.^ ^adv. phrase^

   Note: *Angry* modifies *motorist*, and both adverbs modify *wove*.

2. The <u>first</u> USS *Allegheny*, <u>named for the Allegheny river</u>, was an

   <u>iron-hulled</u> gunboat <u>that ran on steam</u>.
   ^adj.^ ^adj. phrase^

   Note: *First* and *named for the Allegheny river* modify *USS Allegheny*. The
   remaining adjectives modify *gunboat*.

3. The <u>nervous</u> applicant did not <u>effectively</u> communicate his <u>career</u> goals.
   ^adj.^ ^adv.^ ^adj.^

   Note: *Nervous* modifies *applicant*, *effectively* modifies *communicate*, and
   career modifies *goals*.

4. <u>Frustrated with the new dress code</u>, Kacey <u>openly</u> and <u>defiantly</u> disobeyed
   ^adj. phrase^ ^adv.^ ^adv.^

   her supervisor <u>by wearing jeans to work</u>.
   ^adv. phrase^

   Note: The adjective phrase modifies *Kacey*, while all adverbs and adverb
   phrases modify *disobeyed*.

Conjunction Mini-Drill (page 35)

1. Do you want heads <u>or</u> tails?
   ^cc.^

2. Jeff wants to go to Harvard <u>or</u> Yale, <u>but</u> he is worried about his test scores.
   ^cc.^ ^cc.^

3. <u>Once</u> the immigrants reached Ellis Island, they were subject to medical
   ^sc.^

   examinations <u>and</u> interviews.
   ^cc.^

4. The sociology experiment tests <u>whether</u> people return money they have
   ^twin^

   found <u>or</u> keep it for themselves.
   ^twin^

<u>Subject and Predicate Mini-Drill</u> (page 39)

1. The new office *manager* <u>was *forced*</u> to discipline several employees during his first week of work. [ss. over *manager*, sp. over *was forced*]

2. The playful *puppy*, a terrier and shepherd mix, <u>*pounced* on the flowers and</u> <u>*chased* the birds</u>. [sp. over *chased*]

   Note: This sentence has a compound predicate.

3. <u>There *seems* to be</u> a *problem* with the copier. [sp. over *seems*, ss. over *problem*]

   Note: This sentence is inverted. Rearrange it to be *A problem with the copier seems to be there.*

4. The injured *plaintiff* and the insurance *company* <u>*reached* a settlement</u> <u>which will remain undisclosed</u>. [ss. over *plaintiff*, ss. over *company*, sp. over *reached*]

   Note: A compound subject complicates this sentence.

5. <u>After nearly fifty years of marriage</u>, my *grandparents* <u>*decided* to divorce</u>. [ss. over *grandparents*, sp. over *decided*]

   Note: A split predicate places part of the predicate before the subject and part of the predicate after the subject.

6. <u>Even more important *is*</u> the proper *use* of power <u>in the department</u>. [sp. over *is*, ss. over *use*]

   Note: This sentence is inverted. Rearrange the sentence to say *The proper use of power in the department is even more important.*

7. <u>The most important *point* of the story *is* that a true friend never</u> <u>intentionally hurts you</u>. [ss. over *point*, sp. over *is*]

Direct and Indirect Object Mini-Drill (page 41)

1. The agent sold <u>Mrs. Petty</u> the <u>house</u> by the lake.
   _(io.) (do.)_

   Direct Object: What was sold? The house.
   Indirect Object: Who received the house? Mrs. Petty

2. The city raised <u>the speed limit</u> by 15 miles per hour after conducting a
   traffic study.
   _(do.)_

   Direct Object: What was raised? The speed limit.
   Indirect Object: Who received the speed limit? Not applicable.

3. Gary sent <u>his mother</u> <u>flowers</u> on her birthday.
   _(io.) (do.)_

   Direct Object: What was sent? Flowers.
   Indirect Object: Who received the flowers? His mother.

4. The new intern slept through the staff meeting.

   Direct Object: What was slept? Not applicable.
   This sentence has neither a direct object nor an indirect object.

5. Upon her death, the lonely old woman left <u>her gardener</u> <u>her entire estate</u>,
   causing the neighbors to speculate on their relationship.
   _(io.) (do.)_

   Direct Object: What was left? Her entire estate.
   Indirect Object: Who received her entire estate? Her gardener.

6. While the catcher chased the overthrown ball, one runner easily stole

   <u>third base</u> and another scored.
   _(do.)_

   Direct Object: What was stolen? Third base.
   Indirect Object: Who received third base? Not applicable.

7. As a homework assignment, each student in the school wrote <u>the governor</u>
   _(io.)_

   <u>a letter</u> about the loss of the the statewide music program.
   _(do.)_

   Direct Object: What was written? A letter.
   Indirect Object: Who received the letter? The governor.

Clauses Mini-Drill (page 45)

1. (Unless you ace the exam,) <u>your biology grade looks dismal</u>.

2. <u>Trey purchased a new computer</u>, but <u>it didn't come with a monitor</u>.

3. <u>Leticia wanted to become an oncologist</u> (because she had experienced cancer firsthand).

4. (If the new dress code is enacted), <u>I won't be able to wear shorts to school</u>.

5. <u>Jose threw his first strike</u> (following a six game slump).

6. <u>Anna Maria is going to attend culinary school in France</u>, and <u>her brother hopes to visit her often</u>.

7. <u>My daughter doesn't know about the purse</u> (that I bought yesterday).

8. (Despite the published dangers of smoking), <u>millions of teenagers become addicted to cigarettes every year</u>.

Finding the Subject and Verb Mini-Drill (page 50)

1. Still upset by the loss, the <u>captain</u> of the tennis squad, who had lost his own match in three quick sets, <u>refused</u> to comment on his team's poor performance.

2. <u>I</u> <u>argued</u> with the waitress, who refused to acknowledge that my French fries were cold, for over five minutes before the manager approached my table.

3. [<u>You</u>] <u>Dip</u> the dough in the butter before rolling in the flour mixture, and <u>bake</u> for one hour at 350 degrees.

4. Nervous that she might cause her book sales to drop by speaking out against the political leader, thus enabling her rival's book to rise on the list of best sellers, the outspoken <u>author</u> <u>surprised</u> the media by remaining quiet about the topic.

CHAPTER FOUR: ERRORS INVOLVING VERBS

Subject and Verb Agreement ████████████

The subject of a sentence and its corresponding verb must agree with each other. Similarly, the subject of a clause and its verb must be in agreement. This simply means that singular subjects need singular verbs, and plural subjects need plural verbs:

	CORRECT	INCORRECT
Singular Subject	The *boy* <u>plays</u> cards. A *cat* <u>catches</u> mice. The *computer* <u>whirs</u>. *She* <u>needs</u> a haircut.	The *boy* <u>play</u> cards. A *cat* <u>catch</u> mice. The *computer* <u>whir</u>. *She* <u>need</u> a haircut.
Plural Subject	The *boys* <u>play</u> cards. *Cats* <u>catch</u> mice. The *computers* <u>whir</u>. *They* <u>need</u> a haircut.	The *boys* <u>plays</u> cards. *Cats* <u>catches</u> mice. The *computers* <u>whirs</u>. *They* <u>needs</u> a haircut.

Many singular verbs end in *-s* or *-es*, such as *plays, catches, whirs,* and *needs.* This is especially true for action verbs.

The test will also feature agreement mistakes with the verb *to be* (*am, is, are, was, were, being, been, be*) used both as a linking verb and a helping verb:

	CORRECT	INCORRECT
Singular Subject	*Sam* <u>is</u> tired	*Sam* <u>are</u> tired.
Plural Subject	The *plans* <u>were made</u>.	The *plans* <u>was made</u>.

Most native English speakers should be able to quickly spot problems with Subject Verb Agreement in simple sentences, like the examples above, because they sound alien to the ear and feel funny on the tongue. However, ETS will make sure that sentences are not simple on the GMAT, and will use four types of sentence constructions to confuse you regarding the agreement of the subject and verb.

1. Phrases between the Subject and the Verb

The most common trick used by GMAC is to insert long phrases between the main subject and verb in an already lengthy sentence. The test makers hope you'll lose track of any agreement issues when other nouns and verbs are present. An example follows:

Notice that the example sentence is labeled "incorrect." We do not want you to mistake faulty grammar for valid sentence construction.

> The feline leukemia virus, characterized by a loss of appetite, weight loss, poor coat condition, and other debilitating losses, are rampant among cats on the island. [*Incorrect*]

In this sentence, *virus* is the subject and *are* is the verb. However, there is a long phrase in between listing symptoms of the disease, all of which are in noun format. Note that the last item in the list is plural (*losses*), which makes *are* seem correct: *losses are*. However, the subject is the singular *virus*, and *virus are* creates an agreement problem. In order for the sentence to agree, it must read *virus is*. Remember, a subject is never in a dependent clause, a prepositional phrase, or a phrase separated by commas. Thus, we can mentally eliminate the problem-causing phrase:

> The feline leukemia virus, ~~characterized by a loss of appetite, weight loss, poor coat condition, and other debilitating losses~~, are rampant among cats on the island.   [*Incorrect*]

If needed, you can also eliminate the two prepositional phrases (*among cats* and *on the island*) at the end of the sentence:

Memorizing the preposition list in the appendix of this book can help you quickly remove prepositional phrases from the subject and verb.

> The feline leukemia virus, ~~characterized by a loss of appetite, weight loss, poor coat condition, and other debilitating losses~~, are rampant ~~among cats on the island~~.   [*Incorrect*]

To correct this sentence, change the plural *are* to the singular *is*:

> The feline leukemia <u>virus</u>, characterized by a loss of appetite, weight loss, poor coat condition, and other debilitating losses, <u>is</u> rampant among cats on the island. [*Correct*]

Be prepared for the reverse problem, in which the subject is plural, and the offending singular verb sits next to a singular noun in a phrase:

> The Supreme Court's rulings on assisted suicide, which overturned two previous decisions by a United States Circuit Court, dictates that any health care official involved can be held responsible. [*Incorrect*]

In this sentence, the verb *dictates* is situated next to *Court*, so it may appear to be in agreement: *court dictates*. However, *rulings* is the subject, as you can see if you remove the phrases and dependent clauses:

> The Supreme Court's rulings ~~on assisted suicide, which overturned two previous decisions by a United States Circuit Court~~, dictates ~~that any health care official involved can be held responsible~~. [*Incorrect*]

> Dependent clause: *that any health care official involved can be held responsible*
> Prepositional phrase: *on assisted suicide*
> Phrase separated by commas: *which overturned two previous decisions by a United States Circuit Court*

The correct Subject Verb agreement is *rulings dictate*:

> The Supreme Court's <u>rulings</u> on assisted suicide, which overturned two previous decisions by a United States Circuit Court, <u>dictate</u> that any health care official involved can be held responsible. [*Correct*]

You should also be aware that phrases are sometimes separated by dashes rather than commas:

> The Tony award-winning plays—*Sunset Boulevard, Rent, The Lion King*, and *The Producers*—was performed by the local theater throughout the summer and autumn seasons. [*Incorrect*]

The titles of the four plays divide the subject *plays* from the verb *was performed*:

> The Tony award-winning plays—~~*Sunset Boulevard, Rent, The Lion King, and The Producers*~~—was performed by the local theater throughout the summer and autumn seasons.

> Prepositional phrases: *by the local theater, throughout the summer and autumn seasons*
> Phrase separated by dashes: *Sunset Boulevard, Rent, The Lion King, and The Producers*

The correct agreement is *plays were performed*:

> The Tony award-winning <u>plays</u>—*Sunset Boulevard, Rent, The Lion King*, and *The Producers*—<u>were performed</u> by the local theater throughout the summer and autumn seasons. [*Correct*]

Subject and verb agreement errors can involve a singular subject and a plural verb, or a plural subject and a singular verb.

Even short prepositional phrases can disguise the real subject:

> The scent of apples and cinnamon sticks permeate throughout the cider mill, causing most visitors to purchase snacks while on the tour. [*Incorrect*]

The preposition "of" causes a lot of errors on the GMAT. Beware of the use of "of" in expressions such as "the number of...," and "the thought of...."

This sentence would be perfect if apples and cinnamon sticks permeate throughout the mill. However, it is the *scent* that is permeating, and since *scent* is singular, the verb must be *permeates*. Remove the phrases and clauses and look again:

> The scent ~~of apples and cinnamon sticks~~ permeate ~~throughout the cider mill, causing most visitors to purchase snacks while on the tour~~. [*Incorrect*]

The sentence should appear as follows:

> The <u>scent</u> of apples and cinnamon sticks <u>permeates</u> throughout the cider mill, causing most visitors to purchase snacks while on the tour. [*Correct*]

Furthermore, beware of GMAC combining short prepositional phrases with long phrases to complicate the sentence even more:

> The number of car accidents involving deer, up seventeen percent from ten years ago and continuing to rise throughout the country, have decreased in Michigan's Upper Peninsula due to the increased use of car-mounted deer whistles by residents. [*Incorrect*]

Can you find the subject and the verb? Are they in agreement? Maybe this will help:

> The number ~~of car accidents~~ involving deer, ~~up seventeen percent from ten years ago and continuing to rise throughout the country~~, have decreased ~~in Michigan's Upper Peninsula due to the increased use of car-mounted deer whistles by residents~~. [*Incorrect*]

> Prepositional phrase: *of car accidents, in Michigan's Upper Peninsula, due to the increased use, of car-mounted deer whistles, by residents*
> Phrase separated by commas: *up seventeen percent from ten years ago and continuing to rise throughout the country*

This one is especially tricky. *Accidents* is not the subject, as most people believe. The subject is *number*, because *accidents* is in the prepositional phrase *of car accidents*. In order for *number* to agree with the verb, it must be *has decreased*, not *have decreased*. GMAC is known to use Sentence Correction questions beginning with *The number of…*, which almost always have Subject Verb agreement problems. The correct sentence is:

The <u>number</u> of car accidents involving deer, up seventeen percent from ten years ago and continuing to rise throughout the country, <u>has decreased</u> in Michigan's Upper Peninsula due to the increased use of car-mounted deer whistles by residents.   [*Correct*]

2. The Subject Follows the Verb

Most sentences in the English language are arranged so that the main subject comes before the verb.

> subj.   vb..
> She ‖ smiled.

>   subj.   vb.
> The seat cushion ‖ can be reupholstered.

>   subj.   vb.
> The wedding ‖ was held outdoors, despite the threat of rain.

The makers of the GMAT know that this is customary sentence construction, which is why sentences with inverted subjects and verbs make perfect fodder for your test.

An expletive construction on the GMAT is nothing to curse about once you learn how to monitor subject-verb agreement. Expletive constructions occur when a sentence begins with *there*, *here*, or *it*, and they invert the order of the subject and verb:

>   vb.   subj.
> There are many reasons for the tax increase.

>   vb.   subj.
> Here is the map.

>   vb.   subj.
> It has come to my attention that you failed to file the paperwork correctly.

If you are unable to see the true subject in an expletive construction, rearrange the sentence so that the subject comes before the verb:

>   subj.   vb.
> Many reasons for the tax increase are there.

>   subj. vb.
> The map is here.

>   subj.   vb.
> That you failed to file the paperwork correctly has come to my attention.

In the last sentence, the subject is a noun clause (*that you have failed to file the paperwork correctly*) acting as a noun.

Of course, expletive constructions on the GMAT will not be this brazenly obvious. They will likely be hidden between clauses and phrases. However, if you follow the subject rule and remove the clauses and phrases, expletive constructions become easier to see:

> According to the latest census, which was released in 2002, there is two television sets per home for every family in America, a statistic that nearly doubled in the last ten years.   [*Incorrect*]

Sentences containing "there is" or "here is" should cause you to immediately confirm subject and verb agreement.

Mentally delete the phrases:

> ~~According to the latest census, which was released in 2002~~, there is two television sets ~~per home for every family in America, a statistic that nearly doubled in the last ten years~~.   [*Incorrect*]

We are left with *there is two television sets*, but the expletive construction can be rearranged:

> Two television sets is there.

It becomes immediately apparent that the verb, *is*, does not agree with the subject, *sets*. The verb should be plural: *Two television sets are there*. Thus, the corrected sentence looks like:

> According to the latest census, which was released in 2002, there <u>are</u> two television <u>sets</u> per home for every family in America, a statistic that nearly doubled in the last ten years.   [*Correct*]

Try this one:

> Once the contract is signed, by either the borrower or the co-signer, there is few, if any, exceptions which will free the borrower from the debt. [*Incorrect*]

Not sure if the subject and verb agree? Remove the phrases and clauses:

> ~~Once the contract is signed, by either the borrower or the co-signer~~, there is few, ~~if any~~, exceptions ~~which will free the borrower from the debt~~. [*Incorrect*]

Rearrange the expletive construction, *there is few exceptions*:

> Few exceptions is there.   [*Incorrect*]

The verb should be *are*:

> Few exceptions *are* there.   [*Correct*]

The final sentence:

> Once the contract is signed, by either the borrower or the co-signer, there <u>are</u> few, if any, <u>exceptions</u> which will free the borrower from the debt. [*Correct*]

Expletive constructions can also appear in a dependent clause, which we will examine later in this chapter.

Rearranging sentences is a tactic used by great test takers. Putting the contents into a more-easily recognized form can help you pinpoint errors.

3. Compound Subject

Compound subjects are plural and receive plural verbs:

> Erin and Kara <u>sing</u> together.
> Baseball and apple pie <u>are</u> American traditions.
> He and I <u>do not agree</u>.
> A GMAT score, an essay, and a letter of recommendation <u>are required</u> for admission.
> The boy and four others <u>were recognized</u> for their heroic actions during the earthquake.

On the GMAT, look for longer sentences with a compound subject paired with a singular verb:

> Ernest Hemingway and his contemporaries, all of whom were authors born at the turn of century, was revered for describing the sense of aimlessness felt by their generation.   [*Incorrect*]

The sentence has a compound subject: *Ernest Hemingway and his contemporaries*. Remove the phrases:

> Ernest Hemingway and his contemporaries, ~~all of whom were authors born at the turn of century~~, was revered ~~for describing the sense of aimlessness felt by their generation~~.   [*Incorrect*]

The verb must be plural: *Ernest Hemingway and his contemporaries were revered*:

> <u>Ernest Hemingway and his contemporaries</u>, all of whom were authors born at the turn of century, <u>were revered</u> for describing the sense of aimlessness felt by their generation.   [*Correct*]

Compound subjects on the GMAT will often consist of one singular subject and one plural subject, so that either form of the verb seems plausible.

An exception to this rule occurs when the compound subject is joined by *or* or *nor*. The noun or pronoun closest to the verb determines the form of the verb; if the nearest noun is singular, the verb is singular. If the closest noun is plural, the verb is plural.

> singular
> A napkin or *paper towel* <u>is</u> fine.

> plural
> Either a slice of toast or *eggs* <u>are</u> what I will eat for breakfast.

> plural
> Neither the driver nor the *passengers* <u>were</u> aware of the seat belt law.

With the use of phrases between the subject and verb, recognizing an error in the correct verb form with a compound subject connected by *or* or *nor* can be daunting:

> Once the flight landed, neither the flight attendants nor the captain, who even tried using a hammer, were able to open the emergency exit door. [*Incorrect*]

Once again, remove phrases and dependent clauses:

> ~~Once the flight landed~~, neither the flight attendants nor the captain, ~~who even tried using a hammer~~, were able to open the emergency exit door. [*Incorrect*]

Now you can see that singular *captain* is next to the plural *were*, a violation in subject verb agreement. The sentence may sound correct with a plural verb because it is obvious there is more than one person attempting to open the door. However, *captain*, a singular noun, is closest to the verb, so it must have a singular verb: neither the flight attendants nor the *captain was*:

> Once the flight landed, neither the flight attendants nor the captain, who even tried using a hammer, was able to open the emergency exit door. [*Correct*]

Another exception to the rule occurs when *each* and *every* are attached to the compound subject. In this case, each and every are acting as an adjective, modifying the nouns in the compound subject:

> *Each* child, teenager, and adult
> *Every* nook and cranny
> *Each* skirt, *each* shirt, and even *each* scarf

Sentences with *each* and *every* in front of a compound subject must have a singular verb because *each* and *every* are singular. Their use indicates that the subject is referring to a string of individual items, rather than to the items as a group:

> *Each* child, teenager, and adult was wearing a seat belt on the bus.
> *Every* nook and cranny is a possible hiding spot.
> *Each* skirt, *each* shirt, and even *each* scarf hangs on its own padded hanger in her closet.

Look for *each* and *every* to be used on the GMAT, separated from their verb by a phrase:

> At the Springfield Museum of Art, each painting and sculpture, some purchased for millions of dollars and others found discarded at garage sales, have their history displayed on a board beside the piece. [*Incorrect*]

Mentally remove the phrases and clauses:

> ~~At the Springfield Museum of Art~~, each painting and sculpture, ~~some purchased for millions of dollars and others found discarded at garage sales~~, have their history displayed ~~on a board beside the piece~~. [*Incorrect*]

Remember the exception words: the conjunctions *or* and *nor*, and the indefinite adjectives *each* and *every*.

Because *each* is attached to the compound subject, the verb must be the singular *has* rather than the plural *have*. The plural pronoun *their* must also be changed it *its*: *each painting and sculpture has its history displayed*:

> At the Springfield Museum of Art, <u>each painting and sculpture</u>, some purchased for millions of dollars and others found discarded at garage sales, <u>has</u> its history <u>displayed</u> on a board beside the piece. [*Correct*]

4. Indefinite Pronouns as the Subject

A pronoun that does not refer to any one person or thing in particular, such as *someone*, *many*, or *everybody*, is an **indefinite pronoun**. Most indefinite pronouns have a verb form assigned to their usage, but there are a handful that can be singular or plural:

SINGULAR	PLURAL	BOTH
anybody	both	all
anyone	few	any
each	many	more
either	several	most
everybody		none
everyone		some
neither		
nobody		
no one		
somebody		
someone		

Use the verbs "is" and "are" to test these indefinite pronouns. For example, is the correct usage "Anybody is welcome," or "Anybody are welcome?"

Most indefinite pronouns have widely-recognized subject verb agreement forms. Take *someone*, for example. You always say "*Someone is home*," rather than "*Someone are home*."

Everybody and *everyone* often give writers a difficult time. The use of *every* might lead one to think that the reference is to more than one noun. However, the second part of each word is singular: *body* and *one*. *Everybody* and *every-one* are always singular:

Everybody is invited to the party.
Everyone claps at the end of the movie.

The most troublesome indefinite pronoun, and the one most likely to be tested on the GMAT, is *each*. It is always singular (just as it is singular when used as a adjective to modify a compound subject). When used without a reference, its agreement is clear:

Each is going to attend.

However, when *each* is coupled with a prepositional phrase ending in a plural noun, it gives the test taker more trouble:

Each *of the members* is going to attend.

Many might be tempted to choose *are* as the correct verb because *members* is plural. However, *members* is in a prepositional phrase, thus it is not part of the subject. The subject is *each*, and it must have the singular verb *is*.

Try a more difficult example:

> At the beginning of the play, each of King Lear's daughters—Goneril, Regan, and Cordelia—appear to be jealous, treacherous, and immoral, but it is soon discovered that Cordelia is virtuous and loyal.   [*Incorrect*]

Remove the phrases and clauses to find the subject and verb:

> ~~At the beginning of the play~~, each of King Lear's daughters—~~Goneril, Regan, and Cordelia~~—appear to be jealous, treacherous, and immoral, but it is soon discovered ~~that Cordelia is virtuous and loyal~~.   [*Incorrect*]

The subject is *each*, so the verb must be singular:

> <u>Each</u> <u>appears</u> to be jealous, treacherous, and immoral.

Plug the correct verb into the original sentence:

> At the beginning of the play, <u>each</u> of King Lear's daughters—Goneril, Regan, and Cordelia—<u>appears</u> to be jealous, treacherous, and immoral, but it is soon discovered that Cordelia is virtuous and loyal.   [*Correct*]

Examine another:

> Each of the fossils, some more than ten thousand years old and admired by archeologists around the globe, were destroyed by the fire that engulfed the science laboratory.   [*Incorrect*]

Can you spot the subject and the verb? Do they agree? Mentally remove phrases and clauses:

> Each of the fossils, ~~some more than ten thousand years old and admired by archeologists around the globe~~, were destroyed ~~by the fire that engulfed the science laboratory~~.   [*Incorrect*]

The subject and verb do not agree. *Each*, the subject, needs the singular verb, *was destroyed*:

> <u>Each</u> <u>was destroyed</u>.

Remember: *Each* is ALWAYS singular!

While the verb form assignment of most indefinite pronouns is easily determined, it is best to memorize that *each* is always singular.

> <u>Each</u> of the fossils, some more than ten thousand years old and admired by archeologists around the globe, <u>was destroyed</u> by the fire that engulfed the science laboratory.   [*Correct*]

Subject-Verb Agreement in Dependent Clauses

The errors in the Sentence Correction questions will not be limited to one type of sentence construction. GMAC is just not that nice. Instead, you may experience a Subject Verb agreement problem in a sentence with an expletive construction, a long phrase between the subject and the verb, and an indefinite pronoun as the subject. And all of this may be mixed with another grammatical error, such as wordiness or an illogical comparison!

Similarly, errors in subject and verb agreement are not always limited to the main subject and main verb. You may also find an agreement error in a dependent clause:

> Because a hive of European honeybees produce much more honey than the bees can consume, beekeepers harvest the excess for human consumption.   [*Incorrect*]

If we were to mentally cross out the phrases and clauses, we'd see that the main subject and verb are in agreement:

> ~~Because a hive of European honeybees produce much more honey than the bees can consume~~, beekeepers harvest the excess ~~for human consumption~~.

The subject, *beekeepers*, is in agreement with the verb, *harvest*. If you find that the main subject and verb are in agreement, return to the dependent clause to check its subject and verb agreement:

> Because a hive of European honeybees produce much more honey than
>   the bees can consume

The subject of a dependent clause will never occur in a prepositional phrase.

If we remove the prepositional phrase *of European honeybees*, the subject and verb of the dependent clause become clearer, and their non-agreement is apparent:

> *hive produce*

The subject is singular (*hive*), so the verb must be singular (*produces*).

> Because a *hive* of European honeybees *produces* much more honey than the bees can consume, beekeepers harvest the excess for human consumption.   [*Correct*]

The GMAT is more prone to test your knowledge of subject verb agreement among the main parts of the sentence. However, as questions become more difficult, you may see similar errors in dependent clauses. Expect five to ten percent of your questions to test Subject and Verb Agreement.

Subject and Verb Agreement Problem Set

Please complete the problem set and review the answer key and explanations. Answers on pages 74-76.

1. According to a study by the American Education Bureau, the average number of calendar days in a school year across the fifty states have increased by nearly twenty five percent since 1950.

   (A) the average number of calendar days in a school year across the fifty states have increased
   (B) across the fifty states, the average number of calendar days in a school year have increased
   (C) the average number of calendar days, across the fifty states, in a school year have increased
   (D) the average number of calendar days in a school year across the fifty states has increased
   (E) the average numbers of calendar days in a school year across the fifty states has increased

2. Information for travelers, such as road maps, hotel directions, or rest area locations, are provided free of charge from the automotive club, long known for its roadside assistance plan.

   (A) are provided free of charge from the automotive club, long known for its
   (B) is provided free of charge from the automotive club, long known for its
   (C) are provided free of charge from the automotive club, long known for their
   (D) is provided free of charge from the automotive club, long known for their
   (E) is to be provided free of charge from the automotive club, long known for their

3. The reasons for the budget cuts, of which there is dozens, will be revealed at tonight's city council meeting by the mayor and the council members.

   (A) The reasons for the budget cuts, of which there is dozens
   (B) The reason for the budget cuts, of which there is dozens
   (C) The reasons for the budget cut, of which there is dozens
   (D) The reason for the budget cuts, of which there are dozens
   (E) The reasons for the budget cuts, of which there are dozens

4. Tear gas, launched in the form of grenades or aerosol cans, are irritants used by police to calm rioting crowds and unruly mobs.

   (A) are irritants used by police
   (B) used by police, are irritants
   (C) is an irritant used by police
   (D) is an irritants to be used by police
   (E) are irritants for use by police

5. During the debate in October 1992, each of the candidates—George Bush, Bill Clinton, and Ross Perot—<u>was allowed to ask one question of each of his opponents</u>.

    (A) was allowed to ask one question of each of his
        opponents
    (B) were allowed to ask one question of each of his
        opponents
    (C) was allowed to ask one question of every one of
        his opponents
    (D) were allowed to ask one question of each of
        their
        opponents
    (E) were allowed one question of each of his
        opponents

6. The causes of the American Revolution and the reasons for the colonists' victory—including home field advantage and more strategic generals—<u>is firmly rooted in a citizen's sense of</u> patriotic duty and belonging.

    (A) is firmly rooted in a citizen's sense of
    (B) is rooted firmly in a citizen's sense of
    (C) are a citizen's sense firmly rooted in
    (D) are firmly rooted in a citizen's sense for
    (E) are firmly rooted in a citizen's sense of

7. According to the Constitution, neither those senators under 35 years of age <u>nor the representative born outside of the United States are able to run for the position of President</u>.

    (A) nor the representative born outside of the United
        States are able to run for the position of
        President
    (B) nor the representative born outside of the United
        States is running for the position of President
    (C) nor the representative born outside of the United
        States are running for the position of President
    (D) nor the representative born outside of the United
        States is not able to run for the position of
        President
    (E) nor the representative born outside of the
        United States is able to run for the position of
        President

8. <u>Once each vote and piece of paper are burned</u>, the cardinals in the conclave are given time to reflect before casting their next vote.

    (A) Once each vote and piece of paper are burned
    (B) Once each vote and piece of paper is burned
    (C) Once each vote and piece of paper is burning
    (D) Once each vote and pieces of paper are burned
    (E) Once each votes and pieces of paper are burned

Subject Verb and Agreement Problem Set Answer Key

Correct answers are in bold.

1. According to a study by the American Education Bureau, <u>the average number of calendar days in a school year across the fifty states have increased</u> by nearly twenty five percent since 1950.

   (A)   the average number of calendar days in a school year across the fifty states have increased
   (B)   across the fifty states, the average number of calendar days in a school year have increased
   (C)   the average number of calendar days, across the fifty states, in a school year have increased
   (D)   the average number of calendar days in a school year across the fifty states has increased
   (E)   the average numbers of calendar days in a school year across the fifty states has increased

The sentence has an agreement problem between the subject, *number*, and the verb, *have increased*. Choice (D) puts the singular verb, *has increased*, with the singular subject, *number*. The two prepositional phrases between the subject and the verb—*of calendar days* and *across the fifty states*—are meant to throw off the novice test taker.

2. Information for travelers, such as road maps, hotel directions, or rest area locations, <u>are provided free of charge from the automotive club, long known for its</u> roadside assistance plan.

   (A)   are provided free of charge from the automotive club, long known for its
   (B)   is provided free of charge from the automotive club, long known for its
   (C)   are provided free of charge from the automotive club, long known for their
   (D)   is provided free of charge from the automotive club, long known for their
   (E)   is to be provided free of charge from the automotive club, long known for their

The sentence has an agreement problem between the subject, *information*, and the verb, *are provided*. Choice (B) puts the singular verb, *is provided*, with the singular subject, *information*. Choice (D) also does this, but it has changed the pronoun *its* to *their*. The word *club* is not plural, thus *their* is an incorrect pronoun. It must stay *its*. Choice (E) changed the entire verb form, consequently changing the timing (tense) of the sentence.

3. <u>The reasons for the budget cuts, of which there is dozens,</u> will be revealed at tonight's city council meeting by the mayor and the council members.

   (A)   The reasons for the budget cuts, of which there is dozens
   (B)   The reason for the budget cuts, of which there is dozens
   (C)   The reasons for the budget cut, of which there is dozens
   (D)   The reason for the budget cuts, of which there are dozens
   (E)   The reasons for the budget cuts, of which there are dozens

The sentence has an agreement problem in the dependent clause, *of which there are dozens*. The dependent clause is an expletive construction, so the subject, *dozens*, does not agree with the verb, *is*. The verb must be *are*. Choice (D) also changes *is* to *are*, but it makes *reason* a singular noun. This changes the meaning of the sentence, and thus Choice (D) is incorrect.

4. Tear gas, launched in the form of grenades or aerosol cans, <u>are irritants used by police</u> to calm rioting crowds and unruly mobs.

   (A) are irritants used by police
   (B) used by police, are irritants
   (C) is an irritant used by police
   (D) is an irritant to be used by police
   (E) are irritants for use by police

The sentence has an agreement problem between the subject, *tear gas*, and the verb, *are*. *Tear gas* is singular, so the verb must be *is*. This also requires changing *irritants* to the singular form, *an irritant*. Choice (D) also makes this change, but it adds the unnecessary verb *to be*.

5. During the debate, each of the candidates—George Bush, Bill Clinton, and Ross Perot—<u>was allowed to ask one question of each of his opponents</u>.

   (A) was allowed to ask one question of each of his opponents
   (B) were allowed to ask one question of each of his opponents
   (C) was allowed to ask one question of every one of his opponents
   (D) were allowed to ask one question of each of their opponents
   (E) were allowed one question of each of his opponents

Choice (A) is correct. The subject of the sentence is *each*, which is correctly paired with a singular verb, *was*. The only other choice with *was* is Choice (C), but this answer changed the second *each* to *every one*, an unidiomatic expression. The original sentence was grammatically sound.

6. The causes of the American Revolution and the reasons for the colonists' victory—including home field advantage and more strategic generals—<u>is firmly rooted in a citizen's sense of</u> patriotic duty and belonging.

   (A) is firmly rooted in a citizen's sense of
   (B) is rooted firmly in a citizen's sense of
   (C) are a citizen's sense firmly rooted in
   (D) are firmly rooted in a citizen's sense for
   (E) are firmly rooted in a citizen's sense of

The sentence has an agreement problem between the compound subject, *the causes and the reasons*, and the verb, *is firmly rooted*. A compound subject must have a plural verb, *are firmly rooted*. Choice (D) corrects this, but chooses an unidiomatic preposition, *for*. Choice (C) also corrects the subject verb agreement, but rearranges the segment, thus changing the meaning of the sentence.

7. According to the Constitution, neither those senators under 35 years of age <u>nor the representative born outside of the United States are able to run for the position of President</u>.

   (A) nor the representative born outside of the United States are able to run for the position of President
   (B) nor the representative born outside of the United States is running for the position of President
   (C) nor the representative born outside of the United States are running for the position of President
   (D) nor the representative born outside of the United States is not able to run for the position of President
   (E) nor the representative born outside of the United States is able to run for the position of President

The sentence has an agreement problem between the compound subject and the verb *are able to run*. When *neither...nor* is used to create a compound subject, the noun closest to the verb determines the verb's form. The nearest noun in this case is in the form of a noun phrase (*the representative born outside of the United States*) which is singular. Therefore, the verb must be singular, *is able to run*. Choice (B) correctly uses *is*, but changes the verb form to *is running*. Choice (D) adds a negative (*not*) to the verb, thus creating a double negative overall.

8. <u>Once each vote and piece of paper are burned</u>, the cardinals in the conclave are given time to reflect before casting their next vote.

   (A) Once each vote and piece of paper are burned
   (B) Once each vote and piece of paper is burned
   (C) Once each vote and piece of paper is burning
   (D) Once each vote and pieces of paper are burned
   (E) Once each votes and pieces of paper are burned

The sentence has an agreement problem in the dependent clause, *once each vote and piece of paper are burned*. The use of *each* before the compound subject *vote and piece of paper* requires the use of a singular verb, *is burned*. Only Choice (B) and Choice (C) make this required change. However, Choice (C) incorrectly changes the verb from of burned to burning, thus changing the tense of the verb. For more on verb tense, see the next section.

Another common error involving verbs is the incorrect use of tense. Verb tense expresses the point in time, whether in the past, the present, or in the future, that the action, or lack of action, takes place. It helps a reader visualize when the events in the sentence occur. Consider the following example:

> When Shelly's husband was deployed overseas, she *was married* for two months.

Most students could infer the order of events based on the context of the sentence, but what if it were read literally? It says that at the same time her husband was deployed, Shelly participated in a wedding ceremony that lasted for two months. We use different forms of tense to show the sequence of action:

> When Shelly's husband was deployed overseas, she *had been married* for two months.

The English language has three basic tenses to help us determine the point in time in which an action occurs (*past*, *present*, and *future*), and each of these tenses has four forms they can then take to further convey timing (*simple*, *progressive*, *perfect*, and *perfect progressive*).

Tense	Subj.	Simple
Past	he	walked
Present	he	walks
Future	he	will walk

Tense	Subj.	Progressive
Past	he	was walking
Present	he	is walking
Future	he	will be walking

Tense	Subj.	Perfect
Past	he	had walked
Present	he	has walked
Future	he	will have walked

Tense	Subj.	Perfect Progressive
Past	he	had been walking
Present	he	has been walking
Future	he	will have been walking

The GMAT tests all three tenses and all four forms.

SIMPLE TENSES

Tense	Subj.	Simple
Past	he	walked
Present	he	walks
Future	he	will walk

The Official Guide to GMAT Review refers to simple tenses as indicative tenses.

Simple tenses express an action. A plain and simple action, as their name suggests. The action may or may not have been completed at the time the sentence is uttered or written:

He walked to the store.

The example above uses a simple past tense of the infinitive *to walk*. Did he walk to the store two years ago, or did he leave two minutes ago? Is he back from his walk to the store? This cannot be answered by the simple tense. The purpose of the simple past tense verb is to show that at some point in the past he walked to the store.

Simple Past

As we just saw int he example above, this form simply shows that the action occurred at some point in the past.

I *walked* two miles.
He *walked* over to the woman.
They *walked* away from the fight.

Simple Present

Present tense shows what happens right now, at the moment the sentence is spoken or written. It is also used to state a general fact or truth, or in discussing literature or art.

I *walk* the path every day.
He *walks* the reader through the complexities of the character's mind.
They *walk* around the locker room.

Simple Future

The simple form of future tense shows what will or what may happen at some point in the future. Simple future tenses need *shall* or *will*, which are helping verbs, to convey that the events will occur in the future.

Note that adverbs 'such as "not" and "never" come between the helping verb and the verb, as in the third sentence.

I *will walk* to school tomorrow.
He *shall walk* you home.
They *will not walk* on the grass.

PROGRESSIVE TENSES

Tense	Subj.	Progressive
Past	he	was walking
Present	he	is walking
Future	he	will be walking

The progressive tenses are aptly named because they are showing progress. With the use of helping verbs, they indicate something happening or being.

Past Progressive

This form shows that the action occurred at a specific time in the past. The ongoing action occurred in the past and has been completed by the time the sentence is spoken or written.

> I *was walking* to the beach when you called.
> She *was not walking* in the crosswalk when the light changed.
> They *were walking* through the parking lot at midnight.

Present Progressive

Present progressive tense shows what is happening now. It is sometimes used interchangeably with the simple present tense, but present progressive indicates a continuation of the action or event.

> I *am walking* to the store to get milk.
> She *is walking* off the plane right now.
> They *are walking* away from the car with their hands above their heads.

Future Progressive

The progressive form of future tense shows what will continue to happen in the future.

> I *will still be walking* to the party when you get there.
> She *will be walking* down the street when he appears out of nowhere.
> They *will not be walking* ten miles a day once winter arrives.

PERFECT TENSES

Tense	Subj.	Perfect
Past	he	had walked
Present	he	has walked
Future	he	will have walked

The perfect tense describes a finished action.

Past Perfect

The incorrect use of past perfect test is one of the most common GMAT verb tense errors, which we will cover later in this chapter.

The past perfect verb tense is used to show action that was started and completed in the past. It is often used in a sentence that discusses two past events that occurred at different times; past perfect is assigned to the first event to distinguish the time of its occurrence from the more recent event. This form shows that the action occurred at some point in the past before another event in the past, so sentences with past perfect tense will have two verbs.

> I *had walked* to the store and back by the time you *got* off the phone.
> He *had walked* to the car before she *sped* out of the parking lot.
> They *had walked* into the backyard when everyone *yelled* "Surprise!"

Present Perfect

Present perfect tense shows something that has happened in the past, that may or may not yet be completed. It often suggests that the past action is influencing events in the present. Present perfect tenses cannot be used in association with words like *yesterday* or *one day*, but can be used with less specific words like *once* or *before*.

> I *have walked* to work for over six years.
> He *has walked* in your shoes.
> They *have walked* around the track ten times.

Future Perfect

The perfect form of future tense shows an action or event that will be completed sometime in the future before another action or event occurs.

> I *will have walked* six miles by the time you get out of bed tomorrow.
> He *will have walked* with a limp for three years this March.
> They *will have walked* for over three hours when the charity relay is over.

PERFECT PROGRESSIVE TENSES

Tense	Subj.	Perfect Progressive
Past	he	had been walking
Present	he	has been walking
Future	he	will have been walking

Past Perfect Progressive

The past perfect progressive tense shows that an action started at some point in the past, continued for a period of time, and was eventually interrupted or stopped by another event in the past.

I *had been walking* to school for months before I got my new car.
She *had been walking* in the woods for an hour when she spotted a deer.
They *hadn't been walking* long when he ran out of breath.

Present Perfect Progressive

Like the present perfect tense, present perfect progressive tense shows an action that started at some point in the past and has continued. However, this tense stresses that the action has continued and is not completed.

I *have been walking* with you since we moved into the neighborhood.
She *has been walking* around the mall for hours.
They *have been walking* past the house every day for ten years.

Future Perfect Progressive

The progressive form of future tense shows an action that began in the past, but will continue until a particular point in the future.

In ten minutes, I *will have been walking* on the treadmill for an hour.
She *will have been walking* to the laundry mat for three years by the time she buys a car.
They *will have been walking* together for six years next May.

Incorrect Verb Tense

On the GMAT, the most common verb tense error is an incorrect use of tense. Look at an example:

> A recent survey has revealed that within the last ten years, many working mothers had chosen to work part time, rather than place their children in daycare full time. [*Incorrect*]

If you find a Sentence Correction question containing the word "had," immediately check the verb tenses in the sentence.

The verb *had chosen* is in past perfect tense, which indicates that the action was started and ended in the past. However, the sentence describes a situation that is continuing into the present, and possibly the future. Therefore, the present perfect tense, *have chosen*, is required:

> A recent survey has revealed that within the last ten years, many working mothers *have chosen* to work part time, rather than place their children in daycare full time. [*Correct*]

This example required a switch between past and present, but stayed in the perfect form. Some sentences will stay in the same tense, but require you to change form:

> Never before had the author used as much sarcasm as he had used in his fifth novel. [*Incorrect*]

In this sentence, we have two events occurring in the past:
    1. The use of little sarcasm in books 1, 2, 3, and 4
    2. The use of a lot of sarcasm in book 5

However, both verbs are in the past perfect form (*had [the author] used* and *had used*), indicating that the two events are happening at the same time. We know that this is not true, thanks to the phrase *never before* and our knowledge of numbers; the first four books were written prior to the fifth. In a sentence with two separate past events occurring at different times, the past perfect tense is assigned to the first event to distinguish the time of its occurrence from the more recent event. The more recent event receives a simple past tense verb:

> Never before *had the author used* as much sarcasm as he *used* in his fifth novel. [*Correct*]

The majority of tense errors will occur with the improper use of present and past tense in both simple and perfect forms. However, you would be wise to prepare for errors in future tense, and study the progressive forms as well:

> By the time scientists discover a way to stop the ozone layer from deteriorating, global temperatures will be rising for over two hundred years, causing the polar ice caps to gradually melt.   [*Incorrect*]

The use of the future progressive tense (*will be rising*) in the sentence above indicates that the event will continue to occur. However, the dependent clause lets us know that the scientists are going to discover a way to stop the event at some point in the future. Therefore, the sentence needs the future perfect progressive form of *to rise*:

> By the time scientists discover a way to stop the ozone layer from deteriorating, global temperatures *will have been rising* for over two hundred years, causing the polar ice caps to gradually melt.   [*Correct*]

By changing the tense, the sentence now indicates that the rising temperatures will stop in the future when scientists stop the ozone layer from deteriorating.

Shift in Verb Tense

In a sentence with two events occurring at two different times, it is imperative to use two verb tenses to show the order in which the action takes place. However, in sentences with two events happening simultaneously, the verbs must share the same tense. The second most common verb tense error occurs when there is a shift in verb tense in a sentence with simultaneous events. Here is an example:

> While Paul Revere rode from Lexington to Concord on the last leg of his famous journey, John Hancock and Sam Adams, wanted for their treacherous comments against the British monarchy, had escaped Lexington by foot.   [*Incorrect*]

Two events are happening at the same time:
1. Revere rode from Lexington to Concord
2. Hancock and Adams escaped Lexington

However, there are two verb tenses present. *Rode* is in simple past tense, and *had escaped* is in past perfect tense, thus indicating that the escape took place before Revere rode from Lexington to Concord. The very first word of the sentence, *while*, reveals that this is not true. Both events occurred at the same time so they both need the same verb tense:

> While Paul Revere *rode* from Lexington to Concord on the last leg of his famous journey, John Hancock and Sam Adams, wanted for their treacherous comments against the British monarchy, *escaped* Lexington by foot.   [*Correct*]

See if you can spot the error in the next example:

Referring to the current teacher shortage on the west coast, education graduates from Midwestern and Northeastern colleges had cited distance from their families as the main reason for not leaving the only two regions with teacher surpluses.   [*Incorrect*]

There are two events in this sentence:
1. Graduates are referring to the teacher shortage
2. Graduates are citing a reason for not moving

These events are happening at the same time. As indicated by the introductory phrase, the graduates are currently referring to the shortage, which means the verbs must be in the present tense. Since *had cited* is in the past perfect tense, it is incorrect. The sentence shifted tense halfway through, and must be corrected with a present tense verb:

Referring to the current teacher shortage on the west coast, education graduates from Midwestern and Northeastern colleges *cite* distance from their families as the main reason for not leaving the only two regions with teacher surpluses.   [*Correct*]

In sentences with two events taking place, evaluate whether the events are simultaneous or separated by time. Then, check the verbs to make sure that the tenses convey the accurate sequence of events.

Notice that the word "had" appeared incorrectly in both of these examples.

Conditional Verbs

The GMAT may also require knowledge of verb tenses in conditional situations. However, this concept is typically only tested in higher-level difficulty questions. If you are just beginning to understand subject-verb agreement, skip to the problem set on page 90. You can come back to this section when you are confident in your ability to find subject and verb agreement errors.

A **conditional statement** uses the word *if* in a dependent clause to state an outcome in an independent clause:

> *If the doctors are wrong*, the experimental treatment will have adverse effects.

Or:

> The experimental treatment will have adverse effects *if the doctors are wrong*.
>
> Conditional clause: *if the doctors are wrong*
> Independent clause: <u>the experimental treatment will have adverse effects</u>

Most conditional statements appear in two types of construction using the word *if*: *If x occurs, then y occurs* and *y occurs if x occurs*.

However, conditionals can also place the subject after the verb in the dependent clause. In this case, the word *if* is not needed:

> *Had the doctors been wrong*, the experimental treatment would have had adverse effects.

Or:

> The experimental treatment would have had adverse effects, *had the doctors been wrong.*
>
> Conditional clause: *had the doctors been wrong*
>   Subject: *the doctors*
>   Verb: *had been wrong*
> Independent clause: <u>the experimental treatment would have had adverse effects</u>

In order to determine the proper tenses of the two verbs in a conditional statement, you must first determine whether the sentence is factual or hypothetical. We will look first at factual statements. They can be made in the past, present, or future tense and state an event that is possible or even likely to happen.

Conditional sentences and conditional reasoning are covered thoroughly in the PowerScore Critical Reasoning Bible.

Factual Past Tense

Factual conditional statements in the past receive a past tense verb in both the conditional clause and the main clause:

If we *were* in town for Labor Day, we always *went* to the Rossi's party.

Factual Present Tense

Present tense factual conditionals use a present tense verb in both clauses:

If the grill *turns* off, the bratwurst *gets* cold.

Factual Future Tense

Real conditionals in the future use a present tense verb in the conditional clause, and a simple future tense verb in the independent clause:

If I *play* horseshoes, I *will call* you.

It gets a little more complicated when you examine hypothetical statements that use a conditional. A hypothetical statement allows us to look at unlikely or impossible situations. Using the conditional in a hypothetical statement expresses our desire for how things could have been different in the past, could be different in the present, or could be different in the future. And to do so, we make the verb in the conditional clause take a step back in time, and make the main verb adopt a form of *will*, *can*, *shall*, or *might*.

Hypothetical Past Tense

Past tense hypothetical conditional statements take a step further back in the past and use a past perfect verb in the conditional clause:

If he *had gone* to the party, he *would have had* a great time.

Hypothetical Present Tense

Present tense hypothetical conditionals step back and use a past tense verb in the conditional:

If they *played* better, we *might win* this game.

Hypothetical Future Tense

And finally, the future hypothetical conditional turns back the clock two steps and uses a past tense verb in the conditional clause and the word *would* with the verb in the independent clause:

If unicorns *came* out of that forest, I *would faint*.

The conditional clause should never receive the *will*, *can*, *shall*, or *might*— these words are always in the main clause.

We've just reviewed the basics of conditional statements, but how will they come into play on the GMAT? Look at the following sentence:

If the botanist was right, the plant's failure to produce buds is caused by something other than the placement of the seeds and the moisture level of the soil.   [*Incorrect*]

Conditional clause: *if the botanist was right*
Independent clause: the plant's failure to produce buds is caused by some
                    thing other than the placement of the seeds and
                    moisture level of the soil

The sentence is a factual conditional in the present tense. Therefore, both of the verbs must be in the present tense. To correct this, the past tense verb in the conditional clause (*was*) must be changed to present tense (*is*):

If the botanist *is* right, the plant's failure to produce buds is caused by something other than the placement of the seeds and the moisture level of the soil.   [*Correct*]

Let's try another:

Scientists have predicted that the sea level will have risen 50 centimeters by the year 2100 if the polar ice caps continue to melt at the rate they are melting now.   [*Incorrect*]

Conditional clause: *if the polar ice caps continue to melt at the rate they
                    are melting now*
Independent clause: Scientists have predicted that the sea level will have
                    risen 50 centimeters by the year 2100

How do you know when to use a factual future tense, and when to use a hypothetical future tense? Save the hypothetical for far-fetched or impossible events, like pigs flying or winning the lottery. The events in the previous sentence are entirely possible because they are predicted by scientific experts, so use the factual future tense.

In the factual future tense, the verb in the conditional clause must be in simple present form. This sentence meets this requirement: *continue* is in simple present form. The second rule is that the verb in the independent clause must be in simple future tense. *Will have risen* is the perfect future tense, not the simple future tense. Change this verb to correct the sentence:

Scientists have predicted that the sea level *will rise* 50 centimeters by the year 2100 if the polar ice caps continue to melt at the rate they are melting now.   [*Correct*]

You may also find GMAT errors in hypothetical statements:

> Most literary critics believe that had her father not died during her childhood, Sylvia Plath was less prone to depression and suicide. [*Incorrect*]

> Conditional clause: *had her father not died during her childhood*
> Independent clause: <u>Sylvia Plath was less prone to depression and suicide</u>

The statement presents a hypothetical condition from the past. It is impossible to change the fact that Plath's father died during her childhood, but that is what the literary critics are imagining. Therefore, the verb in the conditional clause must take a step back in time by using the perfect past tense, and the verb in the main clause must use a form of *will, can, shall, or might* with the future perfect tense.

When you check the verbs to see if they follow the correct pattern, you will see that this sentence presents a more complicated verb in the conditional clause. The subject of the clause, *her father*, is inserted between the verb *had not died*. By separating the subject from the verb, you can see that *had not died* is in the perfect past tense, so it is correct. The error lies in the independent clause. The verb there is in simple past tense (*was*), but because the statement is conditional, it needs a form of *will, can, shall, or might* with the future perfect tense:

> Most literary critics believe that had her father not died during her childhood, Sylvia Plath *would have been* less prone to depression and suicide.   [*Incorrect*]

Think you've got it? Try your knowledge of verb tenses on the following problem set.

Verb Tense Problem Set

Please complete the problem set and review the answer key and explanations. Answers on pages 92-94.

1. While most educators believe that the SAT is an accurate indication of a student's future performance in college, others feel that the test score should be used for admissions <u>only if it would be statistically equivalent to the student's GPA</u>.

   (A) only if it would be statistically equivalent to the student's GPA
   (B) only if it had been statistically equivalent to the student's GPA
   (C) only if it will be statistically equivalent to the student's GPA
   (D) only if it will have been statistically equivalent to the student's GPA
   (E) only if it is statistically equivalent to the student's GPA

2. Today, because of public education and government breeding programs, the state of Michigan reports three times <u>as many peregrine falcon nests than it has</u> in 1970.

   (A) as many peregrine falcon nests than it has
   (B) as many peregrine falcon nests than it had
   (C) as many peregrine falcon nests than it did
   (D) as many peregrine falcon nests than it had been reporting
   (E) as many peregrine falcon nests than it does

3. Scientists <u>believe that the great white shark has evolved</u> from the megalodon, a prehistoric shark measuring over 50 feet in length.

   (A) believe that the great white shark has evolved
   (B) believe that the great white shark evolved
   (C) believed that the great white shark has evolved
   (D) are believing that the great white shark has evolved
   (E) have believed that the great white shark has evolved

4. The state's transportation engineer believes that the planned overpasses <u>would not relieve traffic congestion if access roads are not built</u> along the highway.

   (A) would not relieve traffic congestion if access roads are not built
   (B) will not relieve traffic congestion if access roads are not built
   (C) would not relieve traffic congestion if access roads were not built
   (D) will not relieve traffic congestion if access roads were not built
   (E) would not relieve traffic congestion if access roads are not being built

5. At the time of the Great Depression, the government <u>was more involved in the regulation of the economy than it ever was before</u>, which is why it is often blamed for the economic collapse.

    (A)   was more involved in the regulation of the economy than it ever was before

    (B)   was more involved in the regulation of the economy than it ever would have been before

    (C)   having been more involved in the regulation of the economy than it ever was before

    (D)   was more involved in the regulation of the economy than it ever had been before

    (E)   was to be more involved in the regulation of the economy than it ever will have been before

6. If the actress wins the Emmy Award, <u>she is joining a short list of performers</u>—including Mel Brooks, Rita Moreno, and Audrey Hepburn—who have won an Oscar, a Tony, a Grammy, and an Emmy.

    (A)   she is joining a short list of performers

    (B)   she would have joined a short list of performers

    (C)   she has been joining a short list of performers

    (D)   she will join a short list of performers

    (E)   she joined a short list of performers

7. Beginning as an NBC radio program in 1937, the soap opera *Guiding Light* <u>moved to CBS television in 1952 and is</u> currently the longest running drama in broadcast history.

    (A)   moved to CBS television in 1952 and is

    (B)   had moved to CBS television in 1952 and is

    (C)   had been moved to CBS television in 1952 and is

    (D)   moved to CBS television in 1952 and was

    (E)   moved to CBS television in 1952 and will be

8. <u>The Goodyear Blimp will provide aerial footage of the car race</u>, which occurs just fifteen miles from its airbase in Ohio, for as long as the race is sponsored by the tire company.

    (A)   The Goodyear Blimp will provide aerial footage of the car race

    (B)   The Goodyear Blimp has provided aerial footage of the car race

    (C)   The Goodyear Blimp will have been providing aerial footage of the car race

    (D)   The Goodyear Blimp will have provided aerial footage of the car race

    (E)   The Goodyear Blimp will be providing aerial footage of the car race

Verb Tense Problem Set

Correct answers are in bold.

1. While most educators believe that the SAT is an accurate indication of a student's future performance in college, others feel that the test score should be used for admissions <u>only if it would be statistically equivalent to the student's GPA</u>.

   (A)   only if it would be statistically equivalent to the student's GPA
   (B)   only if it had been statistically equivalent to the student's GPA
   (C)   only if it will be statistically equivalent to the student's GPA
   (D)   only if it will have been statistically equivalent to the student's GPA
   (E)   only if it is statistically equivalent to the student's GPA

The sentence has a verb tense error in the conditional clause. If you rearrange the independent clause, you'll see it creates its own conditional statement: *If the test score would be statistically equivalent to the student's GPA, it should be used for admissions.* The conditional clause contains *would be*, and present tense factual conditionals use a present tense verb in both clauses. Therefore, the correct verb is in Answer (E).

2. Today, because of public education and government breeding programs, the state of Michigan reports three times <u>as many peregrine falcon nests than it has</u> in 1970.

   (A)   as many peregrine falcon nests than it has
   (B)   as many peregrine falcon nests than it had
   (C)   as many peregrine falcon nests than it did
   (D   as many peregrine falcon nests than it had been reporting
   (E)   as many peregrine falcon nests than it does

This sentence not only has a verb tense error, but it has the wrong verb as well. Because Michigan made the report in 1970, the sentence needs a past tense verb in the underlined portion. *Has* is present tense. *Had* is past test, but we need a verb that mirrors *reports*: *reports three times as many as it had* or *reports three times as many as it did*. *Did* is the correct word choice. Choice (D) used the past perfect progressive, and Choice (E), although using the correct verb, uses the present tense.

3. Scientists <u>believe that the great white shark has evolved</u> from the megalodon, a prehistoric shark measuring over 50 feet in length.

   (A)   believe that the great white shark has evolved
   (B)   believe that the great white shark evolved
   (C)   believed that the great white shark has evolved
   (D)   are believing that the great white shark has evolved
   (E)   have believed that the great white shark has evolved

There are two events occurring in this sentence; *scientists believe*, which is occurring in the present, and *the great white shark evolved*, which happened in the past. Therefore, the verb in the past should be simple past, not past perfect as in Choice (A). Choice (B) is the only answer that offers the simple past tense of to evolve (*evolved*), and does not change the tense of *to believe*.

Verb Tense Problem Set

4. The state's transportation engineer believes that the planned overpasses <u>would not relieve traffic congestion if access roads are not built</u> along the highway.

   (A)   would not relieve traffic congestion if access roads are not built
   (B)   will not relieve traffic congestion if access roads are not built
   (C)   would not relieve traffic congestion if access roads were not built
   (D)   will not relieve traffic congestion if access roads were not built
   (E)   would not relieve traffic congestion if access roads are not being built

This sentence experiences an illegal shift in tense (and happens to be a conditional statement, too). All of the action occurs at the same time, in the present: *believes*, *will not relieve*, and *are*. However, the underlined portion used *would not relieve*, a past tense verb. Only Choice (B) keeps all of the verbs in the same tense.

5. At the time of the Great Depression, the government <u>was more involved in the regulation of the economy than it ever was before</u>, which is why it is often blamed for the economic collapse.

   (A)   was more involved in the regulation of the economy than it ever was before
   (B)   was more involved in the regulation of the economy than it ever would have been before
   (C)   having been more involved in the regulation of the economy than it ever was before
   (D)   was more involved in the regulation of the economy than it ever had been before
   (E)   was to be more involved in the regulation of the economy than it ever will have been before

There are two events in the sentence: 1.) *the government's involvement at the time of the Great Depression*, and 2.) *the government's involvement prior to the Great Depression*. However, the same past tense verb, *was*, is used to convey the action for both events. The earlier action needs the past perfect form of the verb: *had been*. Answer (D) is the only choice to use *had been*.

6. If the actress wins the Emmy Award, <u>she is joining a short list of performers</u>—including Mel Brooks, Rita Moreno, and Audrey Hepburn—who have won an Oscar, a Tony, a Grammy, and an Emmy.

   (A) she is joining a short list of performers
   (B) she would have joined a short list of performers
   (C) she has been joining a short list of performers
   (D) she will join a short list of performers
   (E) she joined a short list of performers

Based on the conditional clause, we know that the actress has not won the award yet but there is a possibility she might, so this is a future factual conditional sentence. This means the verb in the independent clause (*to join*) must be in the simple future tense (*will join*) and the verb in the conditional clause is simple present (*wins*). In this case, that verb, *wins*, is already in the present tense. Therefore the independent clause must be corrected.

7. Beginning as an NBC radio program in 1937, the soap opera *Guiding Light* moved to CBS television in 1952 and is currently the longest running drama in broadcast history.

    (A) **moved to CBS television in 1952 and is**
    (B) had moved to CBS television in 1952 and is
    (C) had been moved to CBS television in 1952 and is
    (D) moved to CBS television in 1952 and was
    (E) moved to CBS television in 1952 and will be

This sentence contains two actions: 1.) *the soap moved to CBS in 1952* and 2.) *the soap is the longest running show in the present*. Therefore, the verb tenses are correct. The past action receives the simple past verb moved, and the present action receives the simple present form of *to be*. Choice (B) uses the past perfect *had moved*, Choice (C) uses a past perfect form with another helping verb (*had been moved*), Choice (D) incorrectly uses the past tense (*was*) for the current action, and Choice (E) uses the future tense (*will be*) for a present action.

8. The Goodyear Blimp will provide aerial footage of the car race, which occurs just fifteen miles from its airbase in Ohio, for as long as the race is sponsored by the tire company.

    (A) The Goodyear Blimp will provide aerial footage of the car race
    (B) The Goodyear Blimp has provided aerial footage of the car race
    (C) The Goodyear Blimp will have been providing aerial footage of the car race
    (D) The Goodyear Blimp will have provided aerial footage of the car race
    (E) **The Goodyear Blimp will be providing aerial footage of the car race**

This sentence indicates that the aerial coverage will continue into the future until an unknown point. This sort of statement requires a future progressive verb (*will be providing*). Choice (B) uses a past tense. Choices (A), (C), and (D) use a future tense, but they are not simple progressive.

Irregular verbs are rare on the GMAT. They are like the elusive giant squid; although they are seldom seen, marine biologists know that they exist and that it is best to be carrying a camera should one go swimming by their boat. Similarly, you should be carrying a working knowledge of irregular verbs, in case one swims up onto your computer screen.

Most of the verbs you encounter on the GMAT are regular verbs, meaning that you simply add *–ed* to the verb in order to create its past and past participle forms.

Present	Past	Past Participle
walk	walked	had walked
continue	continued	had continued
disappear	disappeared	had disappeared
create	created	had created

However, the GMAT may use irregular verbs to test your knowledge of the English language. Irregular verbs are any verbs that do not add *–ed* to create the past form and part participle form. Take, for example, the word *arise*. You wouldn't say:

The dog *arised* at daybreak.   [*Incorrect*]

Instead you would say:

The dog *arose* at daybreak.   [*Correct*]

Or:

The dog *had arisen* at daybreak.   [*Correct*]

Present	Past	Past Participle
arise	arose	had arisen

Notice that some verbs have a different word for all three forms, while some verbs have identical forms:

Present	Past	Past Participle
bend	bent	bent
drink	drank	drunk
fly	flew	flown
let	let	let
take	took	taken

If you find an error with an irregular verb on the GMAT, chances are it will not be as easy to spot as *the dog had arised*, *he bited*, or *the bite had stinged*. The GMAT might attempt to throw you off by separating the helping verb (*had*, *has*, or *have*) from the past participle. Look at an example:

If you see the words *had*, *has*, or *have* in a Sentence Correction question, beware of verb tense errors with both regular and irregular verbs!

> Once the chorus line has danced across the stage and sang the final lyrics, the hero and heroine walk off into the sunset and the curtain drops. [*Incorrect*]

To confuse you, this sentence uses a compound verb in the dependent clause. The complete verb is *has danced and sang*. However, the prepositional phrase, *across the stage*, is inserted between the two verbs to make you forget that *sang* should be in the past participle form (*sung*). The verb is essentially *has danced and has sang*—but the past participle of to *sing* is *sung*. The correct sentence should look like this:

> Once the chorus line has danced across the stage and *sung* the final lyrics, the hero and heroine walk off into the sunset and the curtain drops. [*Correct*]

Try one more:

> The woman was furious to learn that the network had began filming a made-for-television movie about her experience even before she was rescued. [*Incorrect*]

As evidenced by the word *had*, this sentence is attempting to use the past participle form of *to begin*. Although the helping verb and verb are situated next to each other, *to begin* is one of the irregular verbs that catch many students off guard. Is it *had began* or *had begun*? The correct answer is *had begun*:

> The woman was furious to learn that the network *had begun* filming a made-for-television movie about her experience even before she was rescued. [*Correct*]

As this question demonstrates, much of your success with irregular verb forms depends on your ability to memorize past tense and past participle forms. The appendix of this book contains the conjugations of hundreds of verbs. Although irregular verbs are not common on the GMAT, the smart test taker will have at least memorized the most troublesome irregular verbs on that list.

Irregular Verbs Problem Set

Please complete the problem set and review the answer key and explanations. Answers on page 98.

1. The lawyer informed the jurors that the defendant was on trial for three crimes; she had embezzled thousands of dollars from her employer, <u>stolen merchandise from the company, and misleaded detectives by attempting to blame coworkers</u>.

   (A) stolen merchandise from the company, and misleaded detectives by attempting to blame coworkers
   (B) stole merchandise from the company, and misled detectives by attempting to blame coworkers
   (C) stole merchandise from the company, and misleaded detectives by attempting blaming coworkers
   (D) stealed merchandise from the company, and misleaded detectives by attempting to blame coworkers
   (E) stolen merchandise from the company, and misled detectives by attempting to blame coworkers

2. In addition to negotiating the North American Free Trade Agreement, Mexican President Carlos Salinas <u>reformed the Clerical Laws, which had forbidden priests to vote and had kept</u> the Catholic church from owning land.

   (A) reformed the Clerical Laws, which had forbidden priests to vote and had kept
   (B) had reformed the Clerical Laws, which had forbade priests to vote and had kept
   (C) reformed the Clerical Laws, which had forbade priests to vote and had kept
   (D) reformed the Clerical Laws, which had forbade priests to vote and had kept
   (E) was reforming the Clerical Laws, which forbade priests to vote and kept

1. The lawyer informed the jurors that the defendant was on trial for three crimes; she had embezzled thousands of dollars from her employer, <u>stolen merchandise from the company, and misleaded detectives by attempting to blame coworkers</u>.

    (A)   stolen merchandise from the company, and misleaded detectives by attempting to blame coworkers
    (B)   stole merchandise from the company, and misled detectives by attempting to blame coworkers
    (C)   stole merchandise from the company, and misleaded detectives by attempting blaming coworkers
    (D)   stealed merchandise from the company, and misleaded detectives by attempting to blame co-workers
    (E)   stolen merchandise from the company, and misled detectives by attempting to blame coworkers

The question contains two irregular verbs—*to steal* and *to mislead*—and one of them has an error. The verbs should all be in past participle from, to match *had embezzled*. So the defendant *had embezzled*, *had stolen*, and *had misled*. The only answer choice with the correct form of both verbs is (E).

2. In addition to negotiating the North American Free Trade Agreement, Mexican President Carlos Salinas <u>reformed the Clerical Laws, which had forbidden priests to vote and had kept</u> the Catholic church from owning land.

    (A) reformed the Clerical Laws, which had forbidden priests to vote and had kept
    (B) had reformed the Clerical Laws, which had forbade priests to vote and had kept
    (C) reformed the Clerical Laws, which had forbade priests to vote and had kept
    (D) reformed the Clerical Laws, which had forbade priests to vote and had kept
    (E) was reforming the Clerical Laws, which forbade priests to vote and kept

The irregular verb in this question is *to forbid*. The past tense form is *forbade*, and the past participle is *had forbidden*. There are two events in the sentence: 1.) the Clerical Laws forbade priests to vote and kept the church from owning land and 2.) Salinas reformed these Laws. Therefore, the priests had been forbidden before the second event, so the past perfect of *to forbid* is required: *had forbidden*. The sentence is grammatically correct as it stands. Note that many of the incorrect answer choices tempt you with the grammatically incorrect *had forbade*.

Verb Voice

Verbs that take a direct object are called **transitive verbs**. Examples include the verbs *set*, *commanded*, and *drives* in the following sentences:

> vb. do.
> I set the *table*.

> vb. do.
> She commanded the *army*.

> vb. do.
> He drives a *tractor*.

Some verbs cannot take a direct object, such as *sleep* or *smile*. While you can *set* or *drive* something, you cannot *smile* or *sleep* something. Verbs that do not take a direct object are called **intransitive verbs**. They are often followed by an adverb or a phrase that acts as an adverb.

> vb. adv.
> She smiles often.

> vb. prep. phrase
> I sleep on a futon.

Transitive verbs, those that take a direct object, can be constructed in the active or passive voice. In an **active voice**, the subject of the sentence completes the action of the verb:

> Joan of Arc commanded the French army.

Joan of Arc, the subject, is responsible for the action of the sentence. She *commanded*.

In the **passive voice**, the subject does not perform the action of the sentence; rather, the action is done to the subject:

> Joan of Arc was burned at the stake by *the Duke of Bedford*.

In this sentence, the Duke of Bedford completes the action, and Joan receives the action (ouch!). Sentences in the passive voice might not always identify who or what is responsible for the action:

> Joan of Arc was burned at the stake.

Joan is still receiving the action, but whoever is burning her is unclear.

A direct object is a noun or pronoun in the predicate that receives the action of the verb. Review Chapter Three for more information.

Some verbs can be both transitive and intransitive, such as "collapse."

Transitive:
I collapsed the tent.

Intransitive:
It collapses easily.

Intransitive verbs cannot be used in the passive voice.

The active voice is almost always preferred in writing and on the GMAT. Not only is it more concise, but it gives sentences more snap and zing, and keeps paragraphs more lively. It also accepts responsibility for the action; you'll likely find the passive voice used by politicians, lawyers, schoolyard bullies, and those looking to blame someone else for their actions:

The <u>governor</u> <u>was forced</u> to increase taxes.

Who forced the governor to increase taxes? A sentence in the active voice puts the blame on the governor, where it should have been all along:

The <u>governor</u> <u>increased</u> taxes.

The passive voice is not incorrect or ungrammatical—it's just that the active voice is preferred most of the time. One instance in which the passive voice is favored is when *who* or *what* did the action is not as important as *to whom* or *to what* it was done, such as in describing processes or writing scientific reports:

The molten <u>steel</u> <u>is poured</u> into a cooling vat.

It is not important who pours the molten steel, but it is important to know that the steel is poured.

You can more easily recognize passive verbs by their use of a form of the verb *to be* with a past participle:

am pulled
is teased
was convicted
has been sighted
will be monitored

Look at the following sentence in the passive voice:

subj.   vb.   object of the preposition
A <u>bald eagle</u> <u>has been sighted</u> by the *Department of Natural Resources*.

To make the verb active, simply flip the positions of the subject and the object of the preposition:

subj.   vb.   do.
The <u>Department of Natural Resources</u> <u>sighted</u> a *bald eagle*.

On the GMAT, the use of passive voice is typically a secondary error. For example, a sentence might be written in the passive voice, but it also has a blatant pronoun error. The correct answer choice will be the only answer with the acceptable correction of the pronoun error, but it might also change the verb to the active voice in the process. Consider the following example:

By the time a way to stop the ozone layer from deteriorating is discovered by scientists, global temperatures will be rising for over two hundred years, causing the polar ice caps to gradually melt.

(A) By the time a way to stop the ozone layer from deteriorating is discovered by scientists, global temperatures will be rising
(B) By the time scientists discover a way to stop the ozone layer from deteriorating, global temperatures will be rising
(C) By the time a way to stop the ozone later from deteriorating is discovered by scientists, global temperatures would have been rising
(D) By the time scientists discover a way to stop the ozone layer from deteriorating, global temperatures will have been rising
(E) By the time a way to stop the ozone layer from deteriorating is discovered by scientists, global temperatures will rise

The sentence has a grammatically incorrect verb. *Will be rising* should be in the perfect progressive form: *will have been rising*. The only answer choice to make this correction also switches from passive voice to active voice. Since an active construction is always preferred, choice (D) is correct. Note that choice (B) also uses the active voice, but it fails to correct the verb error.

The use of active voice and passive voice should never be mixed in the same sentence, and this type of grammatically incorrect sentence is individually tested on the GMAT. Look at an example:

After last month's Board of Directors' meeting, the airline released plans to revamp flight plans and the new policy concerning aircraft weight limits was approved.   [*Incorrect*]

This sentence illegally switches from the active voice (*the airline released plans to revamp flight plans*) to the passive voice (*the new policy concerning aircraft weight limits was approved [by the airline]*).

The sentence must stay completely active or passive, and since the active voice is preferred, switch the passive portion of the sentence:

After last month's Board of Directors' meeting, the airline released plans to revamp flight plans and *approved the new policy concerning aircraft weight limits*.   [*Correct*]

Remember, choose answer choices that use the active voice while correcting grammatical errors.

Verb Voice Problem Set

Please complete the problem set and review the answer key and explanations. Answers on page 104.

1. France's longest-ruling monarch, Louis XIV, <u>inherited the throne at the age of four and the country was ruled by him for 72 years</u>.

   (A) inherited the throne at the age of four and the country was ruled by him for 72 years
   (B) had inherited the throne at the age of four and the country was ruled by him for 72 years
   (C) inherited the throne at the age of four and ruled the country for 72 years
   (D) inherited the throne at the age of four and the country had been ruled by him for 72 years
   (E) had inherited the throne at the age of four and he ruled the country for 72 years

2. Al Pacino had already turned down the role of Han Solo <u>when Harrison Ford was casted by George Lucas in 1975</u>.

   (A) when Harrison Ford was casted by George Lucas in 1975
   (B) when George Lucas cast Harrison Ford in 1975
   (C) when Harrison Ford had been cast by George Lucas in 1975
   (D) when George Lucas casted Harrison Ford in 1975
   (E) when Harrison Ford would be cast by George Lucas in 1975

The GMAT tests a verb's agreement, tense, form, and voice.

AGREEMENT

First person singular:	I type
Second person singular:	You type
Third person singular:	he types, she types, it types
First person plural:	we type
Second person plural	you type
Third person plural	they type

TENSE

<u>Past</u>

Simple past:	I typed
Past progressive:	I was typing
Past perfect:	I had typed
Past perfect progressive:	I had been typing

<u>Present</u>

Simple present:	I type
Present progressive:	I am typing
Present perfect:	I have typed
Present perfect progressive:	I have been typing

<u>Future</u>

Simple future:	I will type
Future progressive:	I will be typing
Future perfect:	I will have typed
Future perfect progressive:	I will have been typing

FORM

Infinitive:	to type
Past tense:	typed
Past participle:	(has, have, had) typed

VOICE

<u>Active</u>
He typed the letter.

<u>Passive</u>
The letter was typed by him.

Verb Voice Practice Set Answer Key

Correct answers are in bold.

1. France's longest-ruling monarch, Louis XIV, <u>inherited the throne at the age of four and the country</u> <u>was ruled by him for 72 years</u>.

    (A) inherited the throne at the age of four and the country was ruled by him for 72 years
    (B) had inherited the throne at the age of four and the country was ruled by him for 72 years
    (C) inherited the throne at the age of four and ruled the country for 72 years
    (D) inherited the throne at the age of four and the country had been ruled by him for 72 years
    (E) had inherited the throne at the age of four and he ruled the country for 72 years

The sentence has two actions completed by Louis XIV, but one is in the active voice (*Louis inherited the throne*) and the other is in the passive voice (*the country was ruled by Louis*). A sentence cannot switch between active and passive voice. In order for the sentence to have matching construction, the passive portion must become active (*Louis ruled the country*). Choice (C) correctly fixes this problem.

2. Al Pacino had already turned down the role of Han Solo <u>when Harrison Ford was casted by George</u> <u>Lucas in 1975</u>.

    (A) when Harrison Ford was casted by George Lucas in 1975
    (B) when George Lucas cast Harrison Ford in 1975
    (C) when Harrison Ford had been cast by George Lucas in 1975
    (D) when George Lucas casted Harrison Ford in 1975
    (E) when Harrison Ford would be cast by George Lucas in 1975

The main error in this sentence is the incorrect form of the verb *to cast*. Because it is an irregular verb, the past tense is *cast,* not *casted*. The only answer choices that use the correct form are (B), (C), and (E). Choice (C) creates a tense problem in the dependent clause; Ford was offered the role after Pacino passed, but (C) makes these two actions simultaneous. Choice (E) uses a helping verb (*would*) that is reserved for conditional hypothetical statements. Choice (B) not only corrects the past tense of *to cast*, but it makes the passive clause an active construction.

CHAPTER FIVE: ERRORS WITH NOUNS AND PRONOUNS

Noun Agreement

Nouns must agree in number to the nouns they are referencing. This means that singular nouns must be used to refer to singular nouns, and plural nouns must be used to refer to plural nouns. Errors often occur when the nouns are far apart in the sentence, causing the reader to forget that the second noun is referring to the first. Look at the faulty noun reference below:

> *Bill and Lissy* believed that if they were coached every day and dedicated themselves to practice, their dream of becoming *a professional skater* could someday be a reality.   [*Incorrect*]

How are Bill and Lissy, two people, going to combine together to be ONE professional skater? If they have a fantastic plastic surgeon, this sentence might be grammatically correct. But the GMAT does not deal with possibilities unless they are acknowledged in a conditional statement. *Bill and Lissy*, two people, dream of becoming two *skaters*. A plural noun is needed to agree with the subject it is referencing.

> *Bill and Lissy* believed that if they were coached every day and dedicated themselves to practice, their dream of becoming *professional skaters* could someday be a reality.   [*Correct*]

The nouns do not always have to be at opposite ends of the sentence, however, to trip up the unprepared test taker:

> *Hospitals* have always been thought of as a *place* for the sick and dying so many people avoid *them*, even for preventative medicine.   [*Incorrect*]

In this sentence, there are two shifts in number (*hospitals* to *place* and *place* to *them*), and the sentence needs to be consistent:

> *Hospitals* have always been thought of as *places* for the sick and dying so many people avoid *them*, even for preventative medicine.   [*Correct*]

Noun agreement errors occur in a small fraction of the questions in *The Official Guide to GMAT Review*, but are closely related to Pronoun and Antecedent errors, covered in the next section.

Noun Agreement Problem Set

Please complete the problem set and review the answer key and explanations. Answers on page 108-109.

1. The three Supreme Court Justices appointed by the current President <u>were judged on their trial records as an attorney and as an elected judge</u>.

   (A) were judged on their trial records as an attorney and as an elected judge
   (B) were judged, as attorneys and as elected judges, on their trial records
   (C) were judged, as an attorney and as an elected judge, on their trial records
   (D) were judged on their trial record as an attorney and as an elected judge
   (E) were judged on their trial records as attorneys and as elected judges

2. When *War of the Worlds* was read on air by Orson Welles in 1938, <u>many radio listeners believed that the play was an actual broadcast</u>, creating a panic in an already-tense America.

   (A) many radio listeners believed that the play was an actual broadcast
   (B) many radio listeners believed that the play was actual broadcasts
   (C) many radio listeners believed that the plays were an actual broadcast
   (D) a radio listener believed that the play was an actual broadcast
   (E) many radio listeners believed that the plays were actual broadcasts

Noun Agreement Problem Set

Please complete the problem set and review the answer key and explanations. Answers on page 108-109.

3. Despite their cute and cuddly image, <u>hippopotamuses—Africa's most feared animal— account</u> for more human deaths than any other African creature.

    (A) hippopotamuses—Africa's most feared animal—account
    (B) hippopotamus—Africa's most feared animal—account
    (C) hippopotamus—Africa's most feared animal—accounts
    (D) hippopotamuses—Africa's most feared animals—account
    (E) hippopotamuses—Africa's most feared animals—accounts

4. <u>For Romanian farmers, rain dances called *paparudas* are an important ritual</u>, used to invoke rain and guarantee a successful harvest.

    (A) For Romanian farmers, rain dances called *paparudas* are an important ritual
    (B) For Romanian farmers, a rain dance called *paparudas* are an important ritual
    (C) For a Romanian farmer, rain dances called *paparudas* are an important ritual
    (D) For Romanian farmers, a rain dance called *paparudas* are important rituals
    (E) For Romanian farmers, rain dances called *paparudas* are important rituals

Noun Agreement Problem Set Answer Key

Correct answers are in bold.

1. The three Supreme Court Justices appointed by the current President <u>were judged on their trial records as an attorney and as an elected judge</u>.

   (A) were judged on their trial records as an attorney and as an elected judge
   (B) were judged, as attorneys and as elected judges, on their trial records
   (C) were judged, as an attorney and as an elected judge, on their trial records
   (D) were judged on their trial record as an attorney and as an elected judge
   (E) were judged on their trial records as attorneys and as elected judges

There are three *justices*, so other nouns referring to them must be plural. Thus, they were judged as *attorneys* and *judges*. Choice (B) is incorrect because it moves a phrase away from the *records* it is modifying (more about errors with modifiers in the next chapter).

2. When *War of the Worlds* was read on air by Orson Welles in 1938, <u>many radio listeners believed that the play was an actual broadcast</u>, creating a panic in an already-tense America.

   (A) many radio listeners believed that the play was an actual broadcast
   (B) many radio listeners believed that the play was actual broadcasts
   (C) many radio listeners believed that the plays were an actual broadcast
   (D) a radio listener believed that the play was an actual broadcast
   (E) many radio listeners believed that the plays were actual broadcasts

This sentence is grammatically correct, and all of the nouns are in agreement.

3. Despite their cute and cuddly image, <u>hippopotamuses—Africa's most feared animal—account</u> for more human deaths than any other African creature.

   (A) hippopotamuses—Africa's most feared animal—account
   (B) hippopotamus—Africa's most feared animal—account
   (C) hippopotamus—Africa's most feared animal—accounts
   (D) hippopotamuses—Africa's most feared animals—account
   (E) hippopotamuses—Africa's most feared animals—accounts

The subject of the sentence, *hippopotamuses*, is plural, as is evidenced by the plural noun and the use of a plural pronoun (*their*). So *hippopotamuses* must be Africa's most feared *animals*, also plural. While Choice (E) also makes this correction, it ruins the subject verb agreement by using the singular *accounts*, rather than the plural *account*.

4. <u>For Romanian farmers, rain dances called *paparudas* are an important ritual</u>, used to invoke rain and guarantee a successful harvest.

(A) For Romanian farmers, rain dances called *paparudas* are an important ritual
(B) For Romanian farmers, a rain dance called *paparudas* are an important ritual
(C) For a Romanian farmer, rain dances called *paparudas* are an important ritual
(D) For Romanian farmers, a rain dance called *paparudas* are important rituals
(E) For Romanian farmers, rain dances called *paparudas* are important rituals

The subject, *rain dances*, is plural, so all referring nouns should also be plural. The name of the dance is plural (*paparudas*), but the word *ritual* is singular. It must match the plural referents. Choice (D) makes this correction, but changes the subject to a singular noun, thus it is incorrect. Choice (E) is best.

Pronouns

As we discussed in the introduction, pronouns take the place of nouns and refer to people or things previously mentioned in the sentence or surrounding sentences. A list of the most common pronouns follows:

all	everything	its	nothing	something	we
another	few	itself	one	that	what
any	he	many	others	their	which
anybody	her	me	our	theirs	who
anyone	hers	mine	ours	them	whom
anything	herself	my	ourselves	themselves	whose
both	him	myself	several	these	you
each	himself	neither	she	they	your
either	his	nobody	some	this	yours
everybody	I	none	somebody	those	yourself
everyone	it	no one	someone	us	yourselves

An antecedent is the word a pronoun stands for in the sentence. In the following passage, buttons is an antecedent for *several*:

> Do you need some extra buttons? I have *several* over here.

Some pronouns, like *several*, can serve as other parts of speech as well. Look at *several* in the next sentence:

> I have *several* extra buttons over here.

In this sentence, *several* is an adjective, describing the number of buttons.

Personal pronouns are those that refer to particular people or things, such as *I, you, he, her, we, they, me*, and *yourself*.

Indefinite pronouns are just the opposite. They do not refer to any particular people or things, and include words such as *all, everyone, each, somebody*, and *something*.

Refer back to Chapter Two for a more in-depth discussion of the seven types of pronouns.

Relative pronouns are used to introduce a clause and will be discussed in detail later in this section. They include words like *who, which*, and *that*.

While searching for errors on the GMAT, look for three specific pronoun errors—pronoun and antecedent agreement, unclear pronoun reference, and incorrect pronoun choice—all of which are covered on the following pages.

Pronoun and Antecedent Agreement

Like subjects that agree with verbs and nouns that agree with other nouns, pronouns must agree in gender, person, and number with their antecedent. Gender agreement (*the <u>man</u> lost <u>his</u> wallet*) and person agreement (*If <u>one</u> is hungry, <u>one</u> may eat*) are not tested on the GMAT, but number agreement is a common error, appearing in many questions in *The Official Guide to GMAT Review.*

A singular antecedent must employ a singular pronoun:

The <u>girl</u> mailed <u>her</u> application.
<u>Owen</u> thought <u>he</u> deserved a raise.
The <u>dog</u> chases <u>its</u> tail.

A plural antecedent must use a plural pronoun:

The <u>girls</u> won <u>their</u> game.
The <u>children</u> wonder what <u>they</u> might be when <u>they</u> grow up.

Compound antecedents must also receive plural pronouns:

<u>Grace and Hakim</u> are proud of <u>themselves</u>.
Although <u>Harry, Ron, and Hermione</u> are fictional, <u>they</u> come to life in the book.

As with other areas of agreement, GMAC will put distance between the antecedent and the pronoun so that you might fail to notice that they don't agree. The test makers will also use singular and plural nouns in between, hoping you'll incorrectly choose one of them as the antecedent. Look at an example:

While the definition of Generation X is hotly debated concerning the age ranges of its members, culturists generally agree that they describe a group of adults that are self-focused, cynical, and skeptical.   [*Incorrect*]

In this sentence, there are five nouns—*definition, Generation X, age ranges, members,* and *culturists*—preceding the word *they*, so it is hard to spot the real antecedent, which is *definition*. To paraphrase, the sentence states "*The definition is hotly debated but it describes a group.*" Since definition is singular, it needs the pronoun *it*, rather than *they*. Notice that the correction of the pronoun also means a correction to the verb *describe*, in order to achieve subject verb agreement with the new pronoun:

While the *definition* of Generation X is hotly debated concerning the age ranges of its members, culturists generally agree that *it describes* a group of adults that are self-focused, cynical, and skeptical.   [*Correct*]

> If you find a pronoun in a sentence, immediately identify the antecedent.

The GMAT has two other pronoun agreement tricks up its computer-generated sleeve: indefinite pronouns and misleading words used as antecedents. These sentences will test your ability to determine what sounds correct versus what is correct.

Just as indefinite pronouns can cause havoc with subject and verb agreement, they also meddle with pronoun and antecedent agreement. The indefinite pronouns *anyone, anybody, each, everyone, everybody, someone, somebody, no one*, and *nobody* are always singular antecedents on the GMAT. This is often confusing to students who think of *everybody* and *everyone* as a large group of people. However, look at the roots of the words: *body* and *one*. They are singular. Look for errors with these words and a plural pronoun on the GMAT:

> Everyone of the soldiers reported that they had completed the training exercise prior to the incident, although the lieutenant claimed several members of the squadron were not present.   [*Incorrect*]

In this sentence, *everyone* is the antecedent, thus it is singular. However, the pronoun reference, *they*, is plural. Look at the correction:

> *Everyone* of the soldiers reported that *he or she* had completed the training exercise prior to the incident, although the lieutenant claimed several members of the squadron were not present.   [*Correct*]

Similarly, *few, many,* and *several* are plural antecedents, so watch for singular pronouns which do not agree with them:

> A few of the nurses from the emergency room were disgruntled to learn that he or she had been moved to another area of the hospital due to the budget crisis.   [*Incorrect*]

The word *few* is always plural, so its pronoun stand-in must also be plural:

> A *few* of the nurses from the emergency room were disgruntled to learn that *they* had been moved to another area of the hospital due to the budget crisis.   [*Correct*]

The final pronoun agreement error occurs with the use of misleading words. The makers of the GMAT will use singular antecedents that sound plural, such as *army* or *citrus*, and plural antecedents that sound singular, such as *cacti* or *persons*. Combine one of these misleading words with an improper pronoun, and you have a perfect GMAT sentence:

> With the release of their fifth album, *Hotel California*, the band explored the pursuit of the American dream when accompanied by the loss of innocence and the presence of temptations.   [*Incorrect*]

This sentence might sound acceptable to you. However, *band* is a singular antecedent, so *their* is incorrectly used. The sentence can be amended two ways:

> With the release of *their* fifth album, *Hotel California*, the *members* of the band explored the pursuit of the American dream when accompanied by the loss of innocence and the presence of temptations.   [*Correct*]

Or:

> With the release of *its* fifth album, *Hotel California*, the *band* explored the pursuit of the American dream when accompanied by the loss of innocence and the presence of temptations.   [*Correct*]

On test day, if you are given a sentence containing a pronoun, immediately identify the antecedent and look for agreement between the two. If they are in agreement, look for another error in the sentence. However, if they disagree, begin searching for the answer choices that correct the error—this can save you valuable time!

Pronoun and Antecedent Agreement Problem Set

Please complete the problem set and review the answer key and explanations. Answers on page 116-117.

1. Counting each of the nine planets and their many moons, there is 162 known and accepted celestial bodies in our solar system.

   (A) Counting each of the nine planets and their many moons, there is
   (B) Counting each of the nine planets and their many moons, there are
   (C) Counting each of the nine planets and its many moons, there is
   (D) Counting each of the nine planets and its many moons, there are
   (E) Counting everyone of the nine planets and their many moons, there are

2. The bank has offered so many convenient services, such as checking by phone and online banking, that many of their customers no longer visit the bank itself.

   (A) that many of their customers no longer visit the bank itself
   (B) that each of its customers no longer visit the bank itself
   (C) that many of their customers no longer visit the bank themselves
   (D) that many of its customers no longer visit the bank itself
   (E) that many of its customers no longer visit the bank him or herself.

Pronoun and Antecedent Agreement Problem Set

Please complete the problem set and review the answer key and explanations. Answers on page 116-117.

3. After Ben Franklin returned from his visit to the Iroquois Nation, <u>the founding fathers created a constitution that resembled those of the Native Americans</u>.

    (A) the founding fathers created a constitution that resembled those of the Native Americans
    (B) the founding fathers created a constitution resembling the Native Americans'
    (C) the founding fathers created a constitution that resembled these of the Native Americans
    (D) the founding fathers created a constitution that those of the Native Americans resembled
    (E) the founding fathers, resembling the Native Americans, created a constitution

4. Upon hearing of the chairman's illness, the committee motioned <u>to postpone their next meeting until after he was released</u> from the hospital.

    (A) to postpone their next meeting until after he was released
    (B) to postpone its next meeting until after he was released
    (C) to postpone their next meeting until after he or she was released
    (D) to postpone their next meeting until after they were released
    (E) to postpone its next meeting until after each was released

Pronoun and Antecedent Agreement Problem Set Answer Key

Correct answers are in bold.

1. <u>Counting each of the nine planets and their many moons, there is</u> 162 known and accepted celestial bodies in our solar system.

   (A) Counting each of the nine planets and their many moons, there is
   (B) Counting each of the nine planets and their many moons, there are
   (C) Counting each of the nine planets and its many moons, there is
   (D) Counting each of the nine planets and its many moons, there are
   (E) Counting everyone of the nine planets and their many moons, there are

This sentence contains two errors: pronoun antecedent agreement and subject verb agreement in an expletive construction. Deal with the pronoun error first. *Each* is a singular antecedent, so *their* does not agree. Choices (C) and (D) change *their* to *its*. Choice (D), though, goes an extra step and corrects the subject verb agreement between *celestial bodies* and *is* – it should be *there are 162 celestial bodies*. Choice (D) is correct.

2. The bank has offered so many convenient services, such as checking by phone and online banking, <u>that many of their customers no longer visit the bank itself</u>.

   (A) that many of their customers no longer visit the bank itself
   (B) that each of its customers no longer visit the bank itself
   (C) that many of their customers no longer visit the bank themselves
   (D) that many of its customers no longer visit the bank itself
   (E) that many of its customers no longer visit the bank him or herself.

Bank is a misleading word. We think of the people working there, not the singular structure itself. However, it is singular, so it needs a singular pronoun. *Their* should be *its*. Choice (D) is the only one that makes this change without incorrectly changing another part of the sentence.

3. After Ben Franklin returned from his visit to the Iroquois Nation, <u>the founding fathers created a constitution that resembled those of the Native Americans</u>.

   (A) the founding fathers created a constitution that resembled those of the Native Americans
   (B) the founding fathers created a constitution resembling the Native Americans'
   (C) the founding fathers created a constitution that resembled these of the Native Americans
   (D) the founding fathers created a constitution that those of the Native Americans resembled
   (E) the founding fathers, resembling the Native Americans, created a constitution

The plural pronoun *those* is referring to the singular noun *constitution*. Choice (C) incorrectly substitutes another plural pronoun (*these*) for *those*. Choice (D) simply rearranged word order, but did not correct the plural pronoun. Choice (E) also rearranged words and in the process changed the meaning of the sentence. Choice (B) is correct because it removes the offending pronoun and concisely conveys the comparison between the two constitutions.

4. Upon hearing of the chairman's illness, the committee motioned <u>to postpone their next meeting until after he was released</u> from the hospital.

    (A) to postpone their next meeting until after he was released
    (B) to postpone its next meeting until after he was released
    (C) to postpone their next meeting until after he or she was released
    (D) to postpone their next meeting until after they were released
    (E) to postpone its next meeting until after each was released

The word *committee* is misleading. It takes more than one person to make a committee, so you might think it is plural when in fact it is singular. Therefore, the pronoun *their* is incorrect—it should be *its*. Only Choice (B) makes this change without changing another part of the sentence.

Relative Pronouns

Relative pronouns are appropriately named because they *relate* groups of words to another noun or pronoun. Relative pronouns include *who, whom, that, which, whoever, whomever,* and *whichever.* Look at the following example:

> In Major League Baseball, the All-Star game, *which* is held halfway through the season, determines home field advantage for the World Series. [*Correct*]

In this sentence, the relative pronoun appears in a clause (*which is held halfway through the season*) and relates to the antecedent *game.* They may also appear in a phrase:

> The league *that* wins will play four of seven games at its championship team's home stadium.   [*Correct*]

The pronoun *that*, in the phrase *that wins*, relates to *league.*

It is easy to identify relative pronouns; you can remove them and their accompanying clauses or phrases and the sentence will still make sense. However, the meaning might be slightly altered:

> In Major League Baseball, the All-Star game determines home field advantage for the World Series.
>
> Removed: *which is held halfway through the season*

> The league will play four of seven games at its championship team's home stadium.
>
> Removed: *that wins*

When referring to people, use *who, whom, whoever,* and *whomever.* When referring to a place, a thing, or an idea, use *that, which,* and *whichever.* Failure to follow these rules is the most common relative pronoun error on the GMAT. Look at the example:

> The team who I follow just signed a multi-million dollar contract with the best home run hitter since Mark McGuire.   [*Incorrect*]

While the *team* is made up of people, the *team* itself is a thing. Therefore, *who* is an incorrect relative pronoun used to refer to it. The correct pronoun is *that*:

> The team *that* I follow just signed a multi-million dollar contract with the best home run hitter since Mark McGuire.   [*Correct*]

Side notes:

A clause beginning with a relative pronoun should be positioned as close as possible to the noun it is modifying. Look at how a sentence's meaning can be changed when its relative clause is moved:

"The All Star game determines home field advantage for the World Series, which is held halfway through the season."

Read more about misplaced modifiers in the next chapter.

The most common relative pronoun errors on the GMAT occur when a pronoun used to refer to a person is used to refer to a thing, or when a pronoun used to refer to a thing is used to refer to a person.

Handwritten notes: Important read this; Place — that; thing — which; idea — whichever

Be on the lookout for the reverse error, as well:

> The obnoxious fan *that* threw the cup into left field was thrown out of the stadium. [*Incorrect*]

If the sentence is referring to a fan that circulates air, than *that* is correct because it is referring to a thing. But the context of the sentence tells us that *fan* is referring to a person who roots for a team, so *that* must be replaced with *who*:

> The obnoxious fan *who* threw the cup into left field was thrown out of the stadium. [*Correct*]

There is good news and bad news about the remaining relative pronoun errors on the GMAT. The good news: you do not need to know when to use *which* and when to use *that*, a common grammatical error. The explanation is long and boring and littered with vocabulary terms. But now for the bad news: you do need to know when to use *who* and when to use *whom*. Fortunately, there are two easy tricks to help you keep the two words straight.

Trick #1: Use *whom* when it follows a preposition:

> He threw the ball <u>at</u> *whom*?

> Mr. Kobiyashi, <u>with</u> *whom* I am attending the game, is well-known for his stance on inter-league play.

Trick #2: Substitute *he* or *him* for *who* or *whom* in the clause or in the sentence. If *he* makes sense, the answer is *who*. If *him* makes sense, the answer is *whom*:

> The manager yelled at the umpire, *whom* had called the pitch a strike, before throwing first base into the dugout. [*Incorrect*]

To test if *whom* is correct in this sentence, begin by separating the clause it appears in from the rest of the sentence:

> *whom* had called the pitch a strike

Then, substitute both *he* and *him* for *whom*. Which one makes sense?

> *he* had called the pitch a strike   OR   *him* had called the pitch a strike

Because *he* makes sense, the correct relative pronoun should be *who*:

> The manager yelled at the umpire, *who* had called the pitch a strike, before throwing first base into the dugout. [*Correct*]

Sometimes you might have to rearrange the clause or the sentence in order for either one to make sense:

> With such a large score deficit, the game seems lost, no matter *who* they send in to relieve the pitcher.   [*Incorrect*]

Begin by separating the clause containing the relative pronoun:

> no matter *who* they send in to relieve the pitcher

Substituting *he* or *him* for who does not make sense, so rearrange the sentence:

> they send *who* in to relieve the pitcher

Now substitute:

> they send *he* in   OR   they send *him* in

Him is correct, so *whom* is the correct relative pronoun:

> With such a large score deficit, the game seems lost, no matter *whom* they send in to relieve the pitcher.   [*Correct*]

Relative pronoun errors such as these occur in a small percentage of the questions in *The Official Guide to GMAT Review*. However, as you'll see in the next section, relative pronouns are often ambiguous or implied, leading to an entirely different set of errors.

You may need to delete phrases while rearranging sentences. Notice how "no matter" was dropped here.

Relative Pronoun Problem Set

Please complete the problem set and review the answer key and explanations. Answers on page 122-123.

1. As a result of reality television shows such as American Idol, <u>many aspiring rock stars that would never have had the means to pursue their dreams</u> now have become major celebrities.

    (A) many aspiring rock stars that would never have had the means to pursue their dreams
    (B) many aspiring rock stars which would never have had the means to pursue their dreams
    (C) many aspiring rock stars whom would never have had the means to pursue their dreams
    (D) many aspiring rock stars who would never have had the means to pursue their dreams
    (E) many aspiring rock stars so that would never have had the means to pursue their dreams

2. <u>The distance between the two runners, which is over 50 meters</u>, cannot be made up with only three laps to go in the race.

    (A) The distance between the two runners, which is over 50 meters
    (B) The distance between the two runners, who is over 50 meters
    (C) The distance between the two runners, whom is over 50 meters
    (D) The distance between the two runners, that is over 50 meters
    (E) The distance between the two runners, whoever is over 50 meters

3. At the conclusion of the space shuttle launch, <u>everyone whom attended agreed that it was a spectacular sight</u>.

    (A) everyone whom attended agreed that it was a spectacular sight
    (B) everyone who attended agreed that it was a spectacular sight
    (C) everyone whom attended agreed whom it was a spectacular sight
    (D) everyone who attended agreed as to it being a spectacular sight
    (E) everyone whom attended agreed which it was a spectacular sight

4. It was extremely discouraging to learn <u>that the bank, with whom I have had a savings account for over twenty years</u>, could not open a checking account for me because I did not have proper identification.

    (A) that the bank, with whom I have had a savings account for over twenty years
    (B) that the bank, with which I have had a savings account for over twenty years
    (C) that the bank, with who I have had a savings account for over twenty years
    (D) that the bank, with that I have had a savings account for over twenty years
    (E) that the bank, where I have had a savings account for over twenty years

Relative Pronoun Problem Set Answer Key

Correct answers are in bold.

1. As a result of reality television shows such as *American Idol*, <u>many aspiring rock stars that would never have had the means to pursue their dreams</u> now have become major celebrities.

   (A) many aspiring rock stars that would never have had the means to pursue their dreams
   (B) many aspiring rock stars which would never have had the means to pursue their dreams
   (C) many aspiring rock stars whom would never have had the means to pursue their dreams
   (D) many aspiring rock stars who would never have had the means to pursue their dreams
   (E) many aspiring rock stars so that would never have had the means to pursue their dreams

Rock stars are people, not things, so the correct relative pronoun is *who*. If you follow Trick #2 from the section, you would see that *whom* is incorrect when *him* is substituted into *him would never have had the means*.

2. <u>The distance between the two runners, which is over 50 meters,</u> cannot be made up with only three laps to go in the race.

   (A) The distance between the two runners, which is over 50 meters
   (B) The distance between the two runners, who is over 50 meters
   (C) The distance between the two runners, whom is over 50 meters
   (D) The distance between the two runners, that is over 50 meters
   (E) The distance between the two runners, whoever is over 50 meters

The sentence is correct as is. The relative pronoun *which* is referring to *the distance*, a thing. Some test takers might be thrown off by its placement in the sentence; thinking it is referring to *runners*, they might mistakenly select *who* or *whom*.

3. At the conclusion of the space shuttle launch, <u>everyone whom attended agreed that it was a spectacular sight.</u>

   (A) everyone whom attended agreed that it was a spectacular sight
   (B) everyone who attended agreed that it was a spectacular sight
   (C) everyone whom attended agreed whom it was a spectacular sight
   (D) everyone who attended agreed as to it being a spectacular sight
   (E) everyone whom attended agreed which it was a spectacular sight

To test the relative pronoun, *whom*, insert *he* and *him* into the clause *whom attended*: *he attended* or *him attended*? Since *he* is correct, *who* is the correct relative pronoun. Choices (B) and (D) both offer this correction. (D), however, changes *that* to *as to it being*, a wordy and awkward expression. (B) is correct.

4. It was extremely discouraging to learn <u>that the bank, with whom I have had a savings account for over twenty years</u>, could not open a checking account for me because I did not have proper identification.

   (A) that the bank, with whom I have had a savings account for over twenty years
   (B) that the bank, with which I have had a savings account for over twenty years
   (C) that the bank, with who I have had a savings account for over twenty years
   (D) that the bank, with that I have had a savings account for over twenty years
   (E) that the bank, where I have had a savings account for over twenty years

The bank is an object, not a person, so the correct relative pronoun is *which* (or *that* if you removed *with*). Some may be tempted by Choice (E). *Where* can be used as a relative pronoun, but when used in this sentence *where I have had a savings account for over twenty years* becomes an adjective phrase, modifying *bank*, and the commas are no longer needed.

The most common pronoun errors on the GMAT are ambiguous and implied pronouns, occurring in a large number of the questions in *The Official Guide to GMAT Review*.

Ambiguous pronoun errors occur when the proper antecedent is unclear, leaving the reader to wonder whom or what the pronoun is referencing. Ambiguous pronouns most often occur when the pronoun can refer to more than one antecedent:

> After Ryan called Seth, *he* went to visit Katina.

Who went to see Katina? Ryan or Seth? The sentence needs to be rewritten:

> Solution 1: After Ryan called Seth, Ryan went to visit Katina.

> Solution 2: Ryan went to visit Katina after he called Seth.

Sometimes you can replace the pronoun with a noun, as in the first example. In some instances, though, this solution can create an awkward sentence, and you must rearrange the sentence entirely, as was done in the second example.

Unfortunately, ambiguous pronouns might be harder to spot on the GMAT:

> Looking at written warnings, actual citations, and even arrest records, it is evident that releasing tagged fish is still a driving force behind the DNR's monitoring of the waterways, like that of other state agencies. [*Incorrect*]

This sentence lacks a clear antecedent for *that (of other state agencies)*. Do other state agencies have similar warnings, citations, and arrests? Or do they always release tagged fish? Or do they share the same driving force? Or do they monitor the water in the same fashion? The context of the sentence and our prior knowledge tell us that other state agencies have the same driving force, but this must be made clear in the sentence:

> Looking at written warnings, actual citations, and even arrest records, it is evident that releasing tagged fish is still a driving force behind the DNR's monitoring of the waterways, *as it is for* other state agencies. [*Correct*]

To correct the sentence, we added a conjunction and a verb and changed the pronoun and its antecedent. The new antecedent, *releasing tagged fish*, is the reference for *it*. Now the comparison is more clear; *X is a driving force for Y as X is for Z.*

Look at another:

By adding a value menu and allowing customers to choose side orders such as salads and baked potatoes, Wendy's has not only lured customers away from Burger King and McDonald's, but has enticed them to choose fast-food over meals prepared by finer dining establishments.   [*Incorrect*]

The pronoun *them* can have several antecedents: *salads and baked potatoes*, *customers*, or *Burger King and McDonald's*. In order to make the sentence clearer, remove the pronoun:

By adding a value menu and allowing customers to choose side orders, such as salads and baked potatoes, Wendy's has not only lured customers away from Burger King and McDonald's, but has enticed *these customers* to choose fast-food over meals prepared by finer dining establishments. [*Correct*]

Similar to ambiguous pronouns, but much more prominent on the GMAT, are implied pronouns. These are pronouns that do not have an antecedent in the sentence; the antecedent is implied by the reader. They are used so often in speech that they are difficult to spot in sentences. Look at the following:

Last night on the news, they said that pilot error caused the air show collision.   [*Incorrect*]

Implied pronouns appear frequently on the GMAT.

Who are *they*? We can infer that the writer meant the news anchor or the reporter made this statement. Because our speech is informal, we make similar statements every day. But because we are preparing for a test of standard English, we must provide an antecedent for every pronoun!

Last night on the news, *the anchor* said that pilot error caused the air show collision.   [*Correct*]

Here is another example of an implied pronoun:

Although I own the band's album, I have never seen them in concert. [*Incorrect*]

We have never seen an *album* in concert, either! But that is exactly what this sentence is saying. The intended antecedent is the noun *the band*. In this sentence, however, the possessive noun *band's* is used as an adjective to describe *the album*. An antecedent must be a noun or pronoun:

Possessive nouns can never be an antecedent. If you find a apostrophe s ('s) in a sentence, immediately verify that all pronouns have clear antecedents.

Although I own their album, I have never seen *the band* in concert. [*Correct*]

Of course, GMAC will attempt to hide implied pronouns in more complex sentences, often containing other pronouns:

> During World War II, the French strategy for protection was a wall of staggered forts and lookout points called the Maginot Line, but its weakest section ultimately led to their invasion.   [*Incorrect*]

This sentence has two pronouns but one of them lacks an antecedent. The antecedent for *its* is *wall*; this is correct. However, there is no logical noun referent for *their*. We know that *their* is referring to the French, but in the sentence, *French* is an adjective used to modify *strategy*. *France* does not appear as a noun in the sentence, and pronouns must refer to nouns or other pronouns. The sentence must be changed:

> During World War II, the French strategy for protection was a wall of staggered forts and lookout points called the Maginot Line, but its weakest section ultimately led to France's invasion.   [*Correct*]

Look at another example involving a relative pronoun:

> Real estate analysts have found home prices have nearly doubled in the last ten years in the Southern California market, which is consistent with the increases in population and inflation there.   [*Incorrect*]

This sentence contains two implied pronouns. The first is the relative pronoun *which*. Not only does *which* look like it's referring to the *market*, but it is missing an antecedent such as *results*, *findings*, or *research*. The other implied pronoun is *there*. As in the previous example, we can infer that *there* is *Southern California*. But *Southern California* appears as an adjective modifying *market*, rather than as a noun needed for the antecedent. Here is one possible correction:

> Real estate analysts have found home prices have nearly doubled in the last ten years in the Southern California market, research consistent with the increases in population and inflation in the area.   [*Correct*]

One out of every ten or eleven questions in *The Official Guide to GMAT Review* contains an error involving a pronoun, and the majority of these errors are ambiguous and implied pronouns. You would be wise to locate and confirm the antecedent for any pronoun on the GMAT.

Ambiguous and Implied Pronoun Problem Set

Please complete the problem set and review the answer key and explanations. Answers on page 129-131.

1. The company, known for its benevolence and community-involvement, has donated over $100,000 to charity over the last twenty years and <u>will continue to do it as long as it is</u> financially able.

    (A) will continue to do it as long as it is
    (B) will continue to do that as long as it is
    (C) will continue to do so as long as it is
    (D) will continue to do it as long as the
    (E) will continue to do it as long as they are

2. Because her mother was unable to support a family, Marilyn Monroe spent the first seven years of <u>her life with a couple who became foster parents to supplement their income.</u>

    (A) her life with a couple who became foster parents to supplement their income
    (B) their life with a couple who became foster parents to supplement their income
    (C) her life with a couple who became foster parents to supplement Marilyn's income
    (D) her mother's life with a couple who became foster parents to supplement their income
    (E) the child's life with a couple who became foster parents to supplement the couple's income

3. A manatee differs from its relative, the dugong, in both size and shape; the largest difference is the dugong's tail, <u>which is forked, unlike their paddle-shaped tail.</u>

    (A) which is forked, unlike their paddle-shaped tail
    (B) which the dugong's is forked, unlike their paddle-shaped tail
    (C) which being forked, unlike their paddle-shaped tail
    (D) which is forked, unlike its paddle-shaped tail
    (E) which is forked, unlike the manatee's paddle-shaped tail

4. While most Americans have heard of and have used Microsoft products, <u>few people know that its name is actually short for "microcomputer software."</u>

    (A) few people know that its name is actually short for "microcomputer software."
    (B) few people know that their name is actually short for "microcomputer software."
    (C) few of them know that its name is actually short for "microcomputer software."
    (D) only a handful of them know that its name is actually short for "microcomputer software."
    (E) few people know that the company's name is actually short for "microcomputer software."

Ambiguous and Implied Pronoun Problem Set

Please complete the problem set and review the answer key and explanations. Answers on page 129-131.

5. <u>Student admissions to medical school are not accepted solely based on their MCAT scores</u>; other considerations include their undergraduate grade point averages and extracurricular activities.

(A) Student admissions to medical school are not accepted solely based on their MCAT scores

(B) Students seeking admission to medical school are not accepted solely based on their MCAT scores

(C) Student admissions to medical school are not accepted solely based on the schools' MCAT scores

(D) Student admissions to medical school are not accepted solely based on MCAT scores

(E) Students seeking admission to medical school are not accepted solely based on its MCAT scores

6. Hippies, rebellious youth of the 1960s and 1970s, expressed <u>their desire for pacifism and tolerance through peace movements, which included</u> marches and protests.

(A) their desire for pacifism and tolerance through peace movements, which included

(B) its desire for pacifism and tolerance through peace movements, which included

(C) their desire for pacifism and tolerance through peace movements, that were to include

(D) such desire for pacifism and tolerance through peace movements, which included

(E) its desire for pacifism and tolerance through peace movements, including

7. From 1995 to 1999, the posted speed limit on Montana's highways was "reasonable and prudent," <u>meaning their drivers could travel</u> at speeds in excess of 80 mph when road conditions were good.

(A) meaning their drivers could travel

(B) meaning its drivers could travel

(C) meaning that their drivers could travel

(D) meaning drivers could travel

(E) which meant their drivers could travel

8. Marco Polo's <u>travels are documented in his book, *Il Milione*, which took him over seventeen years</u>.

(A) travels are documented in his book, *Il Milione*, which took him over seventeen years

(B) travels are documented in his book, *Il Milione*, which took over seventeen years to travel

(C) travels, which took him over seventeen years to complete, are documented in his book, *Il Milione*

(D) travels are documented in his book, *Il Milione*, which took the explorer over seventeen years

(E) travels, which having taken him over seventeen years, are documented in the book, *Il Milione*

Ambiguous and Implied Pronoun Problem Set Answer Key

Correct answers are in bold.

1. The company, known for its benevolence and community-involvement, has donated over $100,000 to charity over the last twenty years and <u>will continue to do it as long as it is financially able</u>.

   (A) will continue to do it as long as it is financially able
   (B) will continue to do that as long as it is financially able
   (C) will continue to do so as long as it is financially able
   (D) will continue to do it as long as the company is financially able
   (E) will continue to do it as long as they are financially able

The pronoun *it* appears twice in the sentence, but only one is implied. The second *it* refers to the company, so it is correct, making Choices (D) and (E) incorrect. The first *it* refers to a verb, *has donated*. Pronouns must refer to nouns or other pronouns. Choice (B) just changes the pronoun, so that the word *that* is now referring to a verb. Choice (C), the right answer, removes the pronoun and adds an adverb, *so*, to modify the verb.

2. Because her mother was unable to support a family, Marilyn Monroe spent the first seven years of <u>her life with a couple who became foster parents to supplement their income</u>.

   (A) her life with a couple who became foster parents to supplement their income
   (B) their life with a couple who became foster parents to supplement their income
   (C) her life with a couple who became foster parents to supplement Marilyn's income
   (D) her mother's life with a couple who became foster parents to supplement their income
   (E) the child's life with a couple who became foster parents to supplement the couple's income

The sentence is grammatically correct. All of the pronouns have clear antecedents: both *hers* refer to *Marilyn*, *who* refers to the *couple*, and *their* refers to the *couple*.

3. A manatee differs from its relative, the dugong, in both size and shape; the largest difference is the dugong's tail, <u>which is forked, unlike their paddle-shaped tail</u>.

   (A) which is forked, unlike their paddle-shaped tail
   (B) which the dugong's is forked, unlike their paddle-shaped tail
   (C) which being forked, unlike their paddle-shaped tail
   (D) which is forked, unlike its paddle-shaped tail
   (E) which is forked, unlike the manatee's paddle-shaped tail

This sentence presents an ambiguous pronoun, *their*, which also happens to disagree in number with its antecedents. It is unclear whether *their* is referring to manatees or to dugongs. Only Choice (E) clears up the ambiguity.

4. While most Americans have heard of and have used Microsoft products, <u>few people know that its name is actually short for "microcomputer software."</u>

    (A) few people know that its name is actually short for "microcomputer software."
    (B) few people know that their name is actually short for "microcomputer software."
    (C) few of them know that its name is actually short for "microcomputer software."
    (D) only a handful of them know that its name is actually short for "microcomputer software."
    (E) few people know that the company's name is actually short for "microcomputer software."

Most readers will infer that the antecedent for *its* is Microsoft. However, *Microsoft* is used as an adjective, to modify software. It is not used as a noun in the sentence, so *its* must be removed. Only Choice (E) clears up the sentence.

5. <u>Student admissions to medical school are not accepted solely based on their MCAT scores;</u> other considerations include their undergraduate grade point averages and extracurricular activities.

    (A) Student admissions to medical school are not accepted solely based on their MCAT scores
    (B) Students seeking admission to medical school are not accepted solely based on their MCAT scores
    (C) Student admissions to medical school are not accepted solely based on the schools' MCAT scores
    (D) Student admissions to medical school are not accepted solely based on MCAT scores
    (E) Students seeking admission to medical school are not accepted solely based on its MCAT scores

This sentence has two implied pronouns, *their* and *their*, only one of which is in the underlined portion of the sentence. Therefore, the correction must create an antecedent for the second *their*. Begin by looking at the first *their*. It is implied that *their* refers to the *students*. However, *student* is used as an adjective to modify *admissions*, and is not in the noun form that is needed for an antecedent. Choice (B) corrects this error, and gives the second *their* a clear antecedent. Choice (C) states that medical schools take the MCAT. Choice (D) removes the first offending pronoun, but does not provide an antecedent for the second *their*. Choice (E), like (C), states that the medical school takes the MCAT.

6. Hippies, rebellious youth of the 1960s and 1970s, expressed <u>their desire for pacifism and tolerance through peace movements, which included</u> marches and protests.

    (A) their desire for pacifism and tolerance through peace movements, which included
    (B) its desire for pacifism and tolerance through peace movements, which included
    (C) their desire for pacifism and tolerance through peace movements, that were to include
    (D) such desire for pacifism and tolerance through peace movements, which included
    (E) its desire for pacifism and tolerance through peace movements, including

The two pronouns in the sentence, *their* and *which*, have clear antecedents: *hippies* and *movements*. The sentence is grammatically correct.

7. From 1995 to 1999, the posted speed limit on Montana's highways was "reasonable and prudent," <u>meaning their drivers could travel</u> at speeds in excess of 80 mph when road conditions were good.

    (A) meaning their drivers could travel
    (B) meaning its drivers could travel
    (C) meaning that their drivers could travel
    (D) meaning drivers could travel
    (E) which meant their drivers could travel

The sentence has an ambiguous pronoun: *their*. Is *their* referring to Montana or to highways? If it is referring to Montana, the possessive noun is functioning as an adjective. Therefore, replacing *their* with *its* in Choice (B) creates an agreement problem with *its* and the antecedent *highways*. Choices (C) and (E) still contain *their*. Choice (D) is correct.

8. Marco Polo's <u>travels are documented in his book, *Il Milione*, which took him over seventeen years</u>.

    (A) travels are documented in his book, *Il Milione*, which took him over seventeen years
    (B) travels are documented in his book, *Il Milione*, which took over seventeen years to travel
    (C) travels, which took him over seventeen years to complete, are documented in his book, *Il Milione*
    (D) travels are documented in his book, *Il Milione*, which took the explorer over seventeen years
    (E) travels, which having taken him over seventeen years, are documented in the book, *Il Milione*

The offending pronoun in this sentence is a relative pronoun: *which*. It is unclear whether *which* refers to *travels* or to *book*. Did his travels take 17 years to complete, or did the book take 17 years to complete? Currently, the pronoun is situated next to the name of the book, so it appears to be referencing the book. However, the infinitive *to complete* is needed on the end of the relative clause, and only Choice (C) makes this correction. It also moves the relative clause to correctly refer to *travels*.

THE POWERSCORE GMAT SENTENCE CORRECTION BIBLE

CHAPTER SIX: ERRORS INVOLVING MODIFIERS

Adjectives Versus Adverbs

An adjective is a word that describes or modifies a noun or a pronoun. *Skinny* is an adjective. You can have a *skinny* <u>horse</u>, *skinny* <u>children</u>, and a *skinny* <u>file</u>. <u>She</u> can be *skinny*, <u>it</u> can be *skinny*, <u>they</u> can be *skinny*.

An adverb is a word that describes or modifies a verb, adjective, or other adverb. *Quickly* is an adverb used to modify a verb. You can <u>skip</u> *quickly*, <u>count</u> *quickly*, and <u>brush</u> *quickly*. *Extremely* is an adverb used to modify adjectives or other adverbs. You can be *extremely* <u>skinny</u> or lose weight *extremely* <u>quickly</u>.

For a review of adjectives and adverbs, see Chapter Three.

The GMAT may test your knowledge of when to use an adjective versus when to use an adverb. Look at an example:

> The main tourist attraction in Dorchester-on-Thames, a rather tiny village west of London, is the surprising large abbey; built in the seventh century, it remains one of the largest churches in Oxfordshire.   *[Incorrect]*

The sentence contains several adjectives and adverbs. *Rather*, an adverb, correctly modifies the adjective *tiny*. However, look at *surprising*. Is the abbey surprising, or is the size of the abbey surprising? The second part of the sentence references the vast size, so *surprising*, an adjective, is not modifying *abbey*—it is modifying *large*, and thus must be made into an adverb. By adding an *–ly*, we can correct this error:

> The main tourist attraction in Dorchester-on-Thames, a rather tiny village west of London, is the *surprisingly* large abbey; built in the seventh century, it remains of one of the largest churches in Oxfordshire. *[Correct]*

Try another:

> Studies have shown that first-born children learn speech faster, but speak quieter, than children born later to the same parents.   *[Incorrect]*

Quieter is an adjective, and should only modify nouns or pronouns *quieter* dog, *quieter* night, *quieter* sound. *Quietly* is an adverb, and should be used to modify the verb *speak*:

> Studies have shown that first born children learn speech faster, but speak *more quietly*, than children born later to the same parents. *[Correct]*

The incorrect use of an adjective or an adverb occurs less frequently than errors with verbs and pronouns. If another error is not immediately apparent in a GMAT sentence, find the adjectives and adverbs. Check that each adjective modifies a noun or pronoun, and that each adverb modifies a verb, adjective, or other adverb.

Adjectives Versus Adverbs Problem Set

Please complete the problem set and review the answer key and explanations. Answers on page 136.

1. Patrons reported that they would visit the restaurant more <u>frequent than they currently do, provided the management hired an efficient waitstaff and offered more nightly specials</u>.

    (A) frequent than they currently do, provided the management hired an efficient waitstaff and offered more nightly specials

    (B) frequent than they currently do, provided the management hired an efficient waitstaff and offered more night specials

    (C) frequent than they currently do, provided the management hired a more efficient waitstaff and offered more nightly specials

    (D) frequently than they currently do, provided the management hired an efficient waitstaff and offered more nightly specials

    (E) frequent than they current dine, provided the management hired an efficient waitstaff and offered more nightly specials

2. Many celebrities, such as Britney Spears, Tom Cruise, and Jessica Simpson, <u>have secretly vacationed on Turtle Island in Fiji, an exclusively tropical resort known for its privacy and beauty</u>.

    (A) have secretly vacationed on Turtle Island in Fiji, an exclusively tropical resort known for its privacy and beauty

    (B) have secretly vacationed on Turtle Island in Fiji, an exclusive, tropical resort known for its privacy and beauty

    (C) have vacationed in secret on Turtle Island in Fiji, an exclusively tropical resort known for its privacy and beauty

    (D) have secretly vacationed on Turtle Island in Fiji, an tropically exclusive resort known for its privacy and beauty

    (E) have secretly vacationed on Turtle Island in Fiji, an exclusively tropical, private, beautiful resort

Adjectives Versus Adverbs Problem Set Answer Key

Correct answers are in bold.

1. Patrons reported that they would visit the restaurant more <u>frequent than they currently do, provided the management hired an efficient waitstaff and offered more nightly specials</u>.

    (A) frequent than they currently do, provided the management hired an efficient waitstaff and offered more nightly specials
    (B) frequent than they currently do, provided the management hired an efficient waitstaff and offered more night specials
    (C) frequent than they currently do, provided the management hired a more efficient waitstaff and offered more nightly specials
    (D) frequently than they currently do, provided the management hired an efficient waitstaff and offered more nightly specials
    (E) frequent than they current dine, provided the management hired an efficient waitstaff and offered more nightly specials

Frequent, an adjective, is modifying *visit*, a verb, therefore it must be changed into an adverb, *frequently*. Only Choice (D) makes this correction.

2. Many celebrities, such as Britney Spears, Tom Cruise, and Jessica Simpson, <u>have secretly vacationed on Turtle Island in Fiji, an exclusively tropical resort known for its privacy and beauty</u>.

    (A) have secretly vacationed on Turtle Island in Fiji , an exclusively tropical resort known for its privacy and beauty
    (B) have secretly vacationed on Turtle Island in Fiji , an exclusive, tropical resort known for its privacy and beauty
    (C) have vacationed in secret on Turtle Island in Fiji, an exclusively tropical resort known for its privacy and beauty
    (D) have secretly vacationed on Turtle Island in Fiji , an tropically exclusive resort known for its privacy and beauty
    (E) have secretly vacationed on Turtle Island in Fiji , an exclusively tropical, private, beautiful resort

The issue in this sentence is the adverb *exclusively*. Should it stay an adverb, and modify *tropical*, or should it become an adjective, and modify *resort*? The phrase *exclusively tropical* is redundant—a climate cannot be both tropical and arid or both tropical and polar. Plus, the context of the sentence indicates that the resort is exclusive; celebrities *secretly* stay there because it is *private*. Only Choice (B) makes this correction.

Quantifiers

Nouns can be divided into two categories—count nouns and non-count nouns.

Count nouns are aptly named; they are objects that you can count:

> five *dogs*
> a million *ideas*
> two dozen *donuts*
> a *window*
> seven *students*

Non-count nouns, sometimes referred to as mass nouns, are not so easy to count:

> some *water* (five water?)
> a little *sunshine* (a million sunshine?)
> most of the *applause* (two dozen applause?)
> a good deal of *wood* (a wood?)
> no *harm* (seven harm?)

Quantifiers are the modifying words that come before the noun and tell how many or how much. They are underlined below:

> <u>five</u> dogs
> <u>some</u> water
> <u>two dozen</u> donuts
> <u>most of the</u> applause
> <u>no</u> harm

The following quantifiers can only be used with count nouns (such as *flowers*):

> <u>many</u> flowers
> <u>both</u> flowers
> <u>a few</u> flowers
> <u>few</u> flowers
> <u>several</u> flowers
> <u>a couple of</u> flowers
> <u>none of the</u> flowers
> <u>numerous</u> flowers
> <u>a number of</u> flowers

Some quantifiers can only be used with non-count nouns (such as *talking*):

The biggest offenders on the GMAT are *many/much* and *few/little*.

<u>much</u> talking
<u>a little</u> talking
<u>little</u> talking
<u>a bit of</u> talking
<u>a good deal of</u> talking
<u>no</u> talking
<u>an amount of</u> talking

And other quantifiers can be used with both count nouns and non-count nouns:

<u>all of the</u> flowers   <u>all of the</u> talking
<u>some</u> flowers   <u>some</u> talking
<u>most</u> flowers   <u>most</u> talking
<u>a lot of</u> flowers   <u>a lot of</u> talking
<u>plenty of</u> flowers   <u>plenty of</u> talking
<u>a lack of</u> flowers   <u>a lack of</u> talking

So if *much* cannot be used with *flowers*, doesn't it seem likely that GMAC will use this type of error on the GMAT? Absolutely! Unfortunately, it will not be as easy to spot as *Much of the flowers are blooming*. As in all other GMAT questions, there will likely be words or phrases between the offending quantifier and its noun:

The botanist was pleased to see that much of the recently planted and heavily fertilized flowers were in bloom.   [*Incorrect*]

Flowers are count nouns, and must be used with *many*:

The botanist was pleased to see that *many* of the recently planted and heavily fertilized flowers were in bloom.   [*Correct*]

The presence of a quantifier in a GMAT sentence should cause you to check that the correct quantifier is in use.

Quantifier Problem Set

Please complete the problem set and review the answer key and explanations. Answers on page 140.

1. <u>Although the area had little traffic and pedestrians, the developers were convinced that</u> the restaurant should be opened in the district; it was only a matter of time before urban sprawl would bring residents and visitors alike.

   (A) Although the area had little traffic and pedestrians, the developers were convinced that

   (B) Although the area had few traffic and pedestrians, the developers were convinced that

   (C) Although the area had little traffic and few pedestrians, the developers were convinced that

   (D) Although the area had few traffic and little pedestrians, the developers were convinced that

   (E) Although the area had a little traffic and pedestrians, the developers were convinced that

2. <u>The volume of the aquarium, when made with glass, is not as numerous as the volume of the plastic aquarium.</u>

   (A) The volume of the aquarium, when made with glass, is not as numerous as the volume of the plastic aquarium

   (B) The volume of the aquarium, which is made with glass, is not as numerous as the volume of the plastic aquarium

   (C) The volume of the aquarium, which is made with glass, is greater than the volume of the plastic aquarium

   (D) Made of glass, the volume of the aquarium is lesser than the volume of the plastic aquarium

   (E) When the aquarium is made of glass, the volume is less than the volume of the plastic aquarium

Quantifier Problem Set Answer Key

Correct answers are in bold.

1. <u>Although the area had little traffic and pedestrians, the developers were convinced that</u> the restaurant should be opened in the district; it was only a matter of time before urban sprawl would bring residents and visitors alike.

   (A) Although the area had little traffic and pedestrians, the developers were convinced that
   (B) Although the area had few traffic and pedestrians, the developers were convinced that
   (C) Although the area had little traffic and few pedestrians, the developers were convinced that
   (D) Although the area had few traffic and little pedestrians, the developers were convinced that
   (E) Although the area had a little traffic and pedestrians, the developers were convinced that

As the sentence appears now, the quantifier *little* applies to both *traffic* and *pedestrians*; the area had *little traffic* and *little pedestrians*. *Little* should only be used with non-count nouns, so it is correctly placed with *traffic*. However, when placed with *pedestrians*, it appears as if the area has the presence of *small pedestrians*. *Few* should be placed with *pedestrians*, as in Choice (C).

2. <u>The volume of the aquarium, when made with glass, is not as numerous as the volume of the plastic aquarium.</u>

   (A) The volume of the aquarium, when made with glass, is not as numerous as the volume of the plastic aquarium
   (B) The volume of the aquarium, which is made with glass, is not as numerous as the volume of the plastic aquarium
   (C) The volume of the aquarium, which is made with glass, is greater than the volume of the plastic aquarium
   (D) Made of glass, the volume of the aquarium is lesser than the volume of the plastic aquarium
   (E) When the aquarium is made of glass, the volume is less than the volume of the plastic aquarium

This sentence pairs *numerous*, a quantifier for a count noun, with *volume*, a non-count noun. Only Choice (E) uses *less than*.

Modifier Placement

Adjective and adverbs are always modifiers, which are words or phrases used to tell something about another word or phrase in the sentence. The adjectives and adverbs in italics below modify the underlined words in the following sentences:

I want the *blue* necklace for my birthday.
He *barely* passed the test.
Your home is *very beautiful*.
She *nervously* tapped her *long* fingers.

As discussed in Chapter Three, modifiers can be phrases and clauses, too:

Matt drove the go-cart *that wouldn't go over ten miles an hour*.
Unable to control her temper, the customer threw down her purse and demanded a refund.
My uncle, *who once played on the professional tour*, gives golf lessons on the weekend.
It is important to take a calcium supplement, *which helps prevent osteoporosis*.

All of the modifiers above are adjective phrases; they each modify a noun or a pronoun. Similarly, adverb phrases often modify verbs:

Lynne made hamburgers *while I sliced vegetables*.
In the movie, the actor plays an innocent banker accused of stealing.
You must finish your dinner *before you are allowed to go outside*.
Because she was her grandmother's favorite grandchild, Mardy received most of the estate.

Modifiers, both as individual words and as phrases, are like leeches. They have the bad habit of attaching themselves to any words with which they come in contact, and some writers have the bad habit of putting modifiers next to the wrong word, creating a misplaced modifier. Look at the following example:

He *nearly* fell ten feet.

Nearly, an adverb, is the modifier in this sentence. It is in the correct location if the sentence means:

He almost fell but he didn't but it would have been a ten foot fall if he did.

In the original sentence, *nearly* is placed next to *fell*, so it has leeched on to modify that word. In this position in the sentence, it can only mean *almost fell*.

But what if the modifier changed positions and leeched onto the adjective *ten feet*?

He fell *nearly* <u>ten feet</u>.

Now the sentence has a completely different meaning:

He did fall, and he fell almost ten feet before hitting the ground.

GMAC may test you on a single misplaced adjective or adverb, especially with *barely*, *nearly*, *only*, and *just* because they often leech on to the wrong word. A single-word misplaced modifier such as these will likely occur in a sentence containing a more blatant grammatical error. However, the most common modifier error occurs when a phrase or clause is misplaced in a sentence:

Short on money, <u>the action figure</u> was the best present Marsha could find. [*Incorrect*]

In this sentence, most readers will deduce that Marsha is short on money. However, because of the placement of the modifying phrase next to the wrong noun, the sentence is seriously flawed. As it reads now, the action figure was short on money (as if little GI Joes were out shopping at the mall). To correct these types of sentences, rearrange them and/or add words to convey the true meaning:

Short on money, <u>Marsha</u> felt that the action figure was the best present she could find.   [*Correct*]

Or:

The action figure was the best present Marsha could find based on the money she had left.   [*Correct*]

When an introductory phrase or clause is a modifier, the word immediately after the phrase or clause must be the referent:

Preparing for the picnic, <u>Mom</u> made potato salad.
Scavengers of the ocean, <u>blue crabs</u> will feast on most anything on the sea floor.
Seldom found outside of Germany, <u>the Biewer</u> is a rare breed of toy dog.
A teacher and an astronaut, <u>Christa McAuliffe</u> held the hopes of millions of children.

Many questions in *The Official Guide to GMAT Review* have a misplaced modifier in the introductory clause of the sentence. Look at another:

> Produced in London, Alfred Hitchcock directed his first film, *The Pleasure Garden*, for Gainsborough Pictures.   [*Incorrect*]

While it is true that Hitchcock was born in London, the sentence currently reads that Hitchcock himself was produced in London. The sentence is attempting to convey that the film was produced in London. Rearrange the sentence:

> *The Pleasure Garden*, Alfred Hitchcock's first film, was produced in London for Gainsborough Pictures.   [*Correct*]

Note that we have completely changed the modifier; *Alfred Hitchcock's first film* now modifies the title of the film, *The Pleasure Garden*.

A similar problem is the **dangling modifier**. A dangling modifier, which usually occurs in the introductory phrase or clause, doesn't seem to have a logical connection to any word or phrase in the sentence:

> *Driving to Florida*, <u>the dog</u> needed to stop often.   [*Incorrect*]

In this sentence, the dog is driving to Florida. The last time we checked, a dog license did not give canines the right to drive. Who was driving to Florida? The answer is obviously people, but the noun or pronoun that is meant to be modified is completely missing from the sentence and must be added:

> *Driving to Florida*, <u>we</u> needed to stop often because of the dog.
> [*Correct*]

Try a more difficult version:

> Using the Fujita Scale, a tornado's intensity can be rated on a scale of zero to six in order to predict possible damage and warn people in its path.
> [*Incorrect*]

Who is using the Fujita Scale? The way the sentence stands now, the *intensity* is using the scale. The proper referent, be it *scientists* or *researchers* or *stormchasers*, is not identified, thus creating a dangling modifier. To correct the sentence, add the noun being modified:

> *Using the Fujita Scale*, <u>scientists</u> can rate a tornado's intensity on a scale of zero to six in order to predict possible damage and warn people in its path.   [*Correct*]

Misplaced and dangling modifiers create absurd sentences when read literally.

Misplaced modifiers often occur with relative clauses, which are clauses that begin with a relative pronoun such as *that* and *which*. Relative clauses should occur immediately after the word or phrase they are modifying:

> Yogi Rock, *which is a rock on Mars*, was named for its resemblance to Yogi Bear.
> Applications *that are incomplete* will be thrown away.
> The biology professor, *who is visiting from Harvard*, was honored at a banquet.
> There were many mistakes in the newspaper story, *which was written last week.*

Notice that the relative clauses are placed just after the noun to which they are referring. Look at how the meaning of the first sentence from the examples above is changed when the relative clause is moved:

> Yogi Rock was named for its resemblance to Yogi Bear, which is a rock on Mars. [*Incorrect*]

The sentence now reads that Yogi Bear is a rock on Mars. We know that this is wrong; Yogi Bear is a cartoon character, and Yogi Rock is the rock on Mars. The placement of modifiers is crucial to the meaning of the sentence.

Look at one more:

> According to the Georgia Lottery Corporation, lottery tickets will be disqualified that do not contain the store number, state seal, and encoded ink strip. [*Incorrect*]

The relative clause, *that do not contain the store number, state seal, and encoded ink strip*, has latched onto disqualified, when it should be placed immediately behind the referent, tickets:

> According to the Georgia Lottery Corporation, lottery tickets *that do not contain the store number, state seal, and encoded ink strip* will be disqualified. [*Correct*]

Errors with modifiers, including misplaced words, misplaced phrases and clauses, and dangling modifiers, occur on a large percentage of the questions in *The Official Guide to GMAT Review*. It is extremely important to have a firm understanding of their proper placement.

Modifier Placement Problem Set

Please complete the problem set and review the answer key and explanations. Answers on page 147-148.

1. Created by the Pennsylvania Committee of Safety on July 6, 1775, the Pennsylvania Navy served America from the Revolutionary War until the formation of the U.S. Navy in 1798.

    (A) the Pennsylvania Navy served America from the Revolutionary War
    (B) Pennsylvania's Navy served America from the Revolutionary War
    (C) the Revolutionary War was served by the Pennsylvania Navy
    (D) America was served by the Pennsylvania Navy from the Revolutionary War
    (E) the Pennsylvania Navy served the Revolutionary War for American

2. Known for her compassion and commitment, International Nurses' Day is celebrated each year on Florence Nightingale's date of birth to honor her career in nursing.

    (A) International Nurses' Day is celebrated each year on Florence Nightingale's date of birth to honor her career in nursing
    (B) Florence Nightingale's date of birth to honor celebrated each year on International Nurse' Day to honor her career in nursing
    (C) Florence Nightingale's career in nursing is honored each year on International Nurses' Day, which is celebrated on the date of her birth
    (D) International Nurses' Day, celebrated each year on Florence Nightingale's date of birth, honors her career in nursing
    (E) Florence Nightingale is honored for her career in nursing each year on International Nurses' Day, which is celebrated on the date of her birth

3. Although the Wright Brothers' first plane only flew 120 feet, it was an instrumental moment in aviation history.

    (A) plane only flew 120 feet, it was an instrumental moment in aviation history
    (B) plane flew only 120 feet, the event was an instrumental moment in aviation history
    (C) plane only flew 120 feet, aviation history was an instrumental moment
    (D) plane flew only 120 feet, an instrumental moment in aviation history
    (E) plane only flew 120 feet, the plane was an instrumental moment in aviation history

4. The schedule for the skate park's construction, which will serve skateboarders, rollerbladers, and bikers, was detailed at the city council meeting.

    (A) The schedule for the skate park's construction, which will serve
    (B) The schedule for the skate park's construction, that which will serve
    (C) The schedule for the skate park's construction, planned to serve
    (D) The skate park's construction schedule, which will serve
    (E) The construction schedule for the skate park, which will serve

Modifier Placement Problem Set

Please complete the problem set and review the answer key and explanations. Answers on page 147-148.

5. Choreographer George Balanchine founded the School of American Ballet, <u>which enrolled many famous dancers, that included Mikhail Baryshnikov and Suzanne Farrell</u>.

   (A) which enrolled many famous dancers, that included Mikhail Baryshnikov and Suzanne Farrell
   (B) enrolled many famous dancers, that included Mikhail Baryshnikov and Suzanne Farrell
   (C) which enrolled many famous dancers, including Mikhail Baryshnikov and Suzanne Farrell
   (D) that enrolled many famous dancers, that included Mikhail Baryshnikov and Suzanne Farrell
   (E) who enrolled many famous dancers, including Mikhail Baryshnikov and Suzanne Farrell

6. Excited at the prospect of receiving the pair of Giant Pandas, <u>it was decided by the zookeeper to start building a habitat modeled after the mountains of Tibet</u>.

   (A) it was decided by the zookeeper to start building a habitat modeled after the mountains of Tibet
   (B) a habitat modeled after the mountains of Tibet was built by the zookeeper
   (C) it was decided to start building a habitat modeled after the mountains of Tibet by the zookeeper
   (D) the zookeeper decided to start building a habitat modeled after the mountains of Tibet
   (E) and modeled after the mountains of Tibet, the zookeeper decided to start building a habitat

Modifier Placement Problem Set Answer Key

Correct answers are in bold.

1. Created by the Pennsylvania Committee of Safety on July 6, 1775, <u>the Pennsylvania Navy served America from the Revolutionary War</u> until the formation of the U.S. Navy in 1798.

    (A) the Pennsylvania Navy served America from the Revolutionary War
    (B) Pennsylvania's Navy served America from the Revolutionary War
    (C) the Revolutionary War was served by the Pennsylvania Navy
    (D) America was served by the Pennsylvania Navy from the Revolutionary War
    (E) the Pennsylvania Navy served the Revolutionary War for American

This sentence is correct. The introductory clause modifies *the Pennsylvania Navy* correctly.

2. Known for her compassion and commitment, <u>International Nurses' Day is celebrated each year on Florence Nightingale's date of birth to honor her career in nursing</u>.

    (A) International Nurses' Day is celebrated each year on Florence Nightingale's date of birth to honor her career in nursing
    (B) Florence Nightingale's date of birth to honor celebrated each year on International Nurses' Day to honor her career in nursing
    (C) Florence Nightingale's career in nursing is honored each year on International Nurses' Day, which is celebrated on the date of her birth
    (D) International Nurses' Day, celebrated each year on Florence Nightingale's date of birth, honors her career in nursing
    (E) Florence Nightingale is honored for her career in nursing each year on International Nurses' Day, which is celebrated on the date of her birth

Currently, the sentence states that International Nurses' Day, rather than Florence Nightingale, is known for its compassion and commitment. Since the introductory clause is not underlined, it cannot be moved; we know that the noun *Florence Nightingale* must be the first word to follow the clause. Only Choice (E) makes this correction. Choices (B) and (C) are not correct, because *Florence Nightingale* is used as an adjective (rather than a noun) to modify *date of birth* and *career in nursing*.

3. Although the Wright Brothers' first <u>plane only flew 120 feet, it was an instrumental moment in aviation history</u>.

    (A) plane only flew 120 feet, it was an instrumental moment in aviation history
    (B) plane flew only 120 feet, the event was an instrumental moment in aviation history
    (C) plane only flew 120 feet, aviation history was an instrumental moment
    (D) plane flew only 120 feet, an instrumental moment in aviation history
    (E) plane only flew 120 feet, the plane was an instrumental moment in aviation history

It is difficult to find the misplaced modifier in this sentence, and if you do not read all of the answer choices, you might incorrectly choose (A), thinking there is no error. However, Choices (B) and (D) should tip you off that the adverb *only* is in the wrong place. As it reads now, the plane *only* <u>flew</u> (as opposed to <u>swam</u>, <u>ran</u>, or <u>drove</u>). But it should read that it flew *only* <u>120 feet</u> (as opposed to <u>200 feet</u>, <u>1 mile</u>, or <u>cross country</u>). Choice (B) is also correct because it eliminates the ambiguous pronoun *it*.

4. The schedule for the skate park's construction, which will serve skateboarders, rollerbladers, and bikers, was detailed at the city council meeting.

   (A) The schedule for the skate park's construction, which will serve
   (B) The schedule for the skate park's construction, that which will serve
   (C) The schedule for the skate park's construction, planned to serve
   (D) The skate park's construction schedule, which will serve
   (E) The construction schedule for the skate park, which will serve

The relative clause is currently modifying construction: construction *which will serve skateboarders, rollerbladers, and bikers*. It is actually the *park* that that will serve these three groups of people. Only Choice (E) puts *park* immediately before its modifying clause.

5. Choreographer George Balanchine founded the School of American Ballet, which enrolled many famous dancers, that included Mikhail Baryshnikov and Suzanne Farrell.

   (A) which enrolled many famous dancers, that included Mikhail Baryshnikov and Suzanne Farrell
   (B) enrolled many famous dancers, who included Mikhail Baryshnikov and Suzanne Farrell
   (C) which enrolled many famous dancers, including Mikhail Baryshnikov and Suzanne Farrell
   (D) that enrolled many famous dancers, that included Mikhail Baryshnikov and Suzanne Farrell
   (E) who enrolled many famous dancers, including Mikhail Baryshnikov and Suzanne Farrell

This sentence has a modifying clause (*which enrolled many famous dancers*), which correctly refers to to the School of American Ballet. But it also has a modifying phrase referring to *dancers*: *that included Mikhail Baryshnikov and Suzanne Farrell*. *That* improperly modifies *dancers*. The correct answer is (C).

6. Excited at the prospect of receiving the pair of Giant Pandas, it was decided by the zookeeper to start building a habitat modeled after the mountains of Tibet.

   (A) it was decided by the zookeeper to start building a habitat modeled after the mountains of Tibet
   (B) a habitat modeled after the mountains of Tibet was built by the zookeeper
   (C) it was decided to start building a habitat modeled after the mountains of Tibet by the zookeeper
   (D) the zookeeper decided to start building a habitat modeled after the mountains of Tibet
   (E) and modeled after the mountains of Tibet, the zookeeper decided to start building a habitat

The introductory clause is not underlined, thus it cannot be moved. This means that the next word must be the referent of the clause. Who is excited? The zookeeper. Only Choice (D) makes this correction (and puts the sentence in the active voice in the process).

A verb **infinitive** is the word *to* combined with the root form of the verb:

to cook   to think   to be   to dance   to smile

Although infinitives look like verbs, they are actually noun phrases, adjective phrases, and adverb phrases:

As a noun: Maria loves *to cook.*

In the previous sentence, *to cook* is the direct object because it modifies the verb *loves*. Thus *to cook* is a noun. The next sentence shows how it can be used as an adjective:

As a adjective: Her dream *to cook* with Emeril came true.

The noun, *dream,* is being modified by *to cook with Emeril,* making *to cook* an adjective. Finally, look at *to cook* as an adverb:

As an adverb: She was hired *to cook* for the President.

In this sentence, to cook modifies the verb, *was hired.* It is acting as an adverb.

A present infinitive is used with another verb to describe a present situation:

I like *to cook.*
He is waiting for the hamburger *to cook.*

A perfect infinitive describes a time that occurred before the verb in the sentence:

She was proud *to have cooked* for Elvis.
I would like *to have cooked* for you before you left.

Similarly, participles are not verbs, either. They are also modifiers. Present participles work with the verb to describe the action:

I am *cooking.*
We are *cooking* a turkey for Thanksgiving dinner.

Past participles use a form of the helping verb *has* to describe past action:

I had *cooked* a casserole that day.
We have *cooked* a turkey every Thanksgiving.

Errors in verb form on the GMAT typically occur when an infinitive or participle is missing. Look at the following sentence:

> Although most Americans believe that the Emancipation Proclamation was enacted to end slavery, Abraham Lincoln truly intended for the document should preserve the Union.   [*Incorrect*]

The independent clause in this sentence (*Abraham Lincoln truly intended for the document should preserve the Union*) violates grammatical rules. It has two uncompounded verbs: *intended* and *should preserve*. Instead, *preserve* should be in its infinitive form as an adverb, modifying the real verb, *intended*:

> Although most Americans believe that the Emancipation Proclamation was enacted to end slavery, Abraham Lincoln truly <u>intended</u> for the document *to preserve* the Union.   [*Correct*]

You may also find an error in which the participle form of a verb can correct the sentence by acting as modifier:

> For the Stegosaurus, a dinosaur from the late Jurassic Period, the seventeen bony plates embedded in its back were necessary elements for survival, to regulate its temperature throughout its bus-sized body and to protect it from much larger carnivores.   [*Incorrect*]

In this sentence, the infinitives *to regulate* and *to protect* have nothing to modify. There are two ways to fix this sentence. One, we can add a verb such as *used* before the first infinitive. This gives *to regulate* and *to protect* a verb to modify:

> For the Stegosaurus, a dinosaur from the late Jurassic Period, the seventeen bony plates embedded in its back were necessary elements for survival, <u>used</u> *to regulate* its temperature throughout its bus-sized body and *to protect* it from much larger carnivores.   [*Correct*]

The other solution involves using the participle form of the verbs *to regulate* and *to protect*:

> For the Stegosaurus, a dinosaur from the late Jurassic Period, the seventeen bony plates embedded in its back were necessary elements for survival, *regulating* its temperature throughout its bus-sized body and *protecting* it from much larger carnivores.   [*Correct*]

By changing *to regulate* to *regulating* and *to protect* to *protecting*, the entire phrase now acts correctly as an adjective to modify *elements for survival*.

These modifier errors are less common than misplaced and dangling modifiers, and are often confused with verb errors.

Verb Forms as Modifiers Problem Set

Please complete the problem set and review the answer key and explanations. Answers on page 152.

1. Despite winning multiple Grammys for his jazz recordings, Harry Connick, Jr. <u>decided to experiment with funk in the mid-nineties, before returning to jazz</u> later that decade.

   (A) decided to experiment with funk in the mid-nineties, before returning to jazz
   (B) decided experimenting with funk in the mid-nineties, before returning to jazz
   (C) decided to experiment with funk in the mid-nineties, before to return to jazz
   (D) deciding to experiment with funk in the mid-nineties, before returning to jazz
   (E) decided that he would experiment with funk in the mid-nineties, before returning to jazz

2. During the Roman Republic, a slave's testimony in judicial hearings was admissible only if it was obtained by torture, <u>as officials believed that slaves could not be trusted telling the truth otherwise</u>.

   (A) as officials believed that slaves could not be trusted telling the truth otherwise
   (B) as officials believed that slaves could not be trusted having told the truth otherwise
   (C) as officials believed that slaves could not be trusted to tell the truth otherwise
   (D) as officials believing that slaves could not be trusted telling the truth otherwise
   (E) as officials had believed that slaves could not be trusted telling the truth otherwise

3. The most important piece of educational legislation to be enacted in the 1970's was the Individual Education Plan (IEP), <u>to ensure that</u> both gifted and learning disabled children receive instruction appropriate to their level and abilities.

   (A) to ensure that
   (B) having ensured that
   (C) to ensuring that
   (D) having been ensured that
   (E) implemented to ensure that

Verb Forms as Modifiers Problem Set Answer Key

Correct answers are in bold.

1. Despite winning multiple Grammys for his jazz recordings, Harry Connick, Jr. <u>decided to experiment with funk in the mid-nineties, before returning to jazz</u> later that decade.

    (A) decided to experiment with funk in the mid-nineties, before returning to jazz
    (B) decided experimenting with funk in the mid-nineties, before returning to jazz
    (C) decided to experiment with funk in the mid-nineties, before to return to jazz
    (D) deciding to experiment with funk in the mid-nineties, before returning to jazz
    (E) decided that he would experiment with funk in the mid-nineties, before returning to jazz

This sentence is grammatically correct. The infinitive *to experiment* correctly modifies *decided*, and *returning to jazz*, a participle form of *to return*, modifies *Harry Connick, Jr.* The other answer choices incorrectly modify *decided* and *Harry Connick, Jr.* or they use an actual verb as a modifier.

2. During the Roman Republic, a slave's testimony in judicial hearings was admissible only if it was obtained by torture, <u>as officials believed that slaves could not be trusted telling the truth otherwise</u>.

    (A) as officials believed that slaves could not be trusted telling the truth otherwise
    (B) as officials believed that slaves could not be trusted having told the truth otherwise
    (C) as officials believed that slaves could not be trusted to tell the truth otherwise
    (D) as officials believing that slaves could not be trusted telling the truth otherwise
    (E) as officials had believed that slaves could not be trusted telling the truth otherwise

The sentence incorrectly uses a participle form (*telling*) of the verb *to tell*, when the infinitive is needed to modify the verb *trusted*.

3. The most important piece of educational legislation to be enacted in the 1970's was the Individual Education Plan (IEP), <u>to ensure that</u> both gifted and learning disabled children receive instruction appropriate to their level and abilities.

    (A) to ensure that
    (B) having ensured that
    (C) to ensuring that
    (D) having been ensured that
    (E) implemented to ensure that

The sentence has an infinitive, *to ensure*, that does not modify anything. It needs the verb, *implemented*, to serve its purpose. Choice (E) is best.

CHAPTER SEVEN: ERRORS INVOLVING CONJUNCTIONS

Coordinating Conjunctions

As discussed in Chapter Three, coordinating conjunctions are used to join nouns, pronouns, verbs, prepositional phrases, adjectives, and even adverbs. There are seven coordinating conjunctions:

| and | but | or | yet | for | nor | so |

The most basic conjunction error on the GMAT is the use of the incorrect conjunction:

> The Battle of Gettysburg, considered the turning point of the Civil War, saw one-third of its participants killed and injured.   [*Incorrect*]

Logic tells us that a soldier cannot be both *killed* and *injured* at the same time; it is one or the other. The correct conjunction is *or*:

> The Battle of Gettysburg, considered the turning point of the Civil War, saw one-third of its participants killed *or* injured.   [*Correct*]

Easy, right? Unfortunately, only one question in *The Official Guide to GMAT Review* used an incorrect conjunction in this manner.

A larger number of questions test your knowledge of correlating conjunctions, which are pairs of coordinating conjunctions:

| either..or | neither..nor | both..and | not only..but also |
| not..but | whether..or | as..as |

GMAC seems to think they can trip you up by using a correlative conjunction without its proper partner:

> The flying buttresses on Notre Dame de Paris not only serve to add embellishment to the cathedral, which many argue is the most beautiful in France, and also to support and protect the structure.   [*Incorrect*]

As you can see, *not only* is partnered with *and also*. The correct correlation is *not only..but also*:

> The flying buttresses on Notre Dame de Paris *not only* serve to add embellishment to the cathedral, which many argue is the most beautiful in France, *but also* to support and protect the structure.   [*Correct*]

If you spot one half of a correlating conjunction on the exam, verify that the other half is present. Otherwise the sentence must be corrected.

Also be on the lookout for incorrect partnering with *either* and *neither*. *Either* must always be with *or*, and *neither* must always be with *nor*:

> Neither Pete Rose, the leader in hits in major league baseball, or Shoeless Joe Jackson, the only rookie to hit over .400, has been admitted to the Hall of Fame.   [*Incorrect*]

Don't forget that *neither..nor* and *either.. or* are also susceptible to subject and verb agreement issues. The presence of these words in a test question should be an instant clue to a possible error.

Neither should never be with *or*, just as *either* should never be with *and* or *nor*. To correct the baseball sentence, use *neither* with *nor*:

> *Neither* Pete Rose, the leader in hits in major league baseball, *nor* Shoeless Joe Jackson, the only rookie to hit over .400, have been admitted to the Hall of Fame.   [*Correct*]

Coordinating conjunctions and correlative conjunctions are also used to link items in a series:

> Neapolitan ice cream has <u>chocolate</u>, <u>vanilla</u>, *and* <u>strawberry</u> sections.
> <u>Saunders</u>, <u>Peterson</u>, *or* <u>Goldsmith</u> will be promoted to the vacant position.

Conjunctions are fairly straightforward when used in series like these. However, the GMAT might present you with a compound predicate (two verbs) that contains a series; both situations should receive a conjunction, but only one is given, creating a perfect test question:

> Since the teacher introduced the classroom reward system, students have begun paying closer attention, completing homework, following directions, and have stopped causing disruptions during lessons.
> [*Incorrect*]

This sentence is missing a conjunction, causing confusion and a grammatical error. Begin by looking at the compound predicate:

> Students have begun X *and* have stopped Y.

Diagramming sentences is a grammatical technique used to map out the subject and predicate and their parts of speech. The concept is not really needed to help you prepare for the GMAT, but in this instance, it might allow you see that the two verbs in the predicate both connect to the subject:

>   pred.
>   subj.   have begun X
> Students || *and*
>   have stopped Y

Now, notice that X, *what was begun*, is a series. All series must be joined by a conjunction:

> Students have begun paying closer attention, completing homework, *and* following directions

When diagrammed, the solution becomes clearer:

$$
\begin{array}{ll}
 & \text{pred.} \\
 & \text{have begun paying closer attention, completing homework, } \textit{and} \\
 & \text{following directions} \\
\text{subj.} & \\
\text{Students} \quad \| & \textit{and} \\
 & \text{have stopped causing disruptions during lessons}
\end{array}
$$

Put them together in sentence form. There should be two conjunctions in the sentence: one to separate the series, and one to create the compound predicate:

> Since the teacher introduced the classroom reward system, students have begun paying closer attention, completing homework, *and* following directions, *and* have stopped causing disruptions during lessons.
> [*Correct*]

If you encounter a coordinating or correlating conjunction on the GMAT, check first to see if it is used in a comparison. Since comparison errors are more common, look for errors in parallel structure or illogical or incomplete comparisons. If the comparison is correct, then examine the conjunction for proper usage and grammar.

If needed, review coordination and subordination in Chapter Three.

Subordinating conjunctions connect a dependent clause to an independent clause, while stating the relationship between the two clauses. In the following sentences, the independent clause is underlined, the dependent clause is in italics, and the subordination conjunction is in bold:

> I took my umbrella **because** *it was raining.*
> **Despite** *all of the drama,* my office is a great place to work.
> I was shocked **when** *I won the award.*
> **After** *hearing all of the testimony,* the judge ruled in favor of the plaintiff.

The most common subordinating conjunctions are:

after	because	if	so that	till	whenever
although	before	now that	than	unless	where
as	even if	provided	that	until	wherever
as if	even though	since	though	when	while
as though	how				

Errors with subordinating conjunctions can occur when an inappropriate conjunction is used, thus confusing the relationship of the two clauses. Take a simple sentence as an example:

> I cried **although** *I was sad.*   [*Incorrect*]

In this sentence, *although* does not create an effective relationship between the dependent clause and the independent clause. Because is a much better conjunction:

> I cried **because** *I was sad.*   [*Correct*]

You may also have to add a subordinating conjunction to correct a comma splice. A **comma splice** occurs when two complete sentences are only separated by a comma:

> I was sad, I cried.   [*Incorrect*]

On the GMAT, comma splices are never corrected with a two sentence solution.

This sentence can be corrected several ways, and the most obvious is to remove the comma and add a period in its place. However, you will never have a two sentence solution in the GMAT Sentence Correction questions. The easiest way to correct the sentence is to add a subordinating conjunction, making the first sentence a dependent clause:

> **Because** *I was sad,* I cried.   [*Correct*]

This is called **subordination** because we have made one of the sentences subordinate to the main clause. The new dependent clause can no longer stand on its own as a sentence.

Watch for subordinating conjunction errors as secondary errors in sentences. The main errors will likely be much more blatant, such as subject and verb agreement or verb tense. Choosing the right conjunction or adding a conjunction will be an auxiliary correction. Look at an example:

1. <u>Global warming has already made the Hudson River a seeming fragile ecosystem,</u> the introduction of invasive species has the potential to destroy nearly all of the aquatic plants and animals that inhabit the river.

   (A) Global warming has already made the Hudson River a seeming fragile ecosystem
   (B) Global warming has already made the Hudson River a seemingly fragile ecosystem
   (C) While global warming has already made the Hudson River a seemingly fragile ecosystem
   (D) Because global warming has already made the Hudson River a seeming fragile ecosystem;
   (E) Global warming has made the Hudson River a seemingly fragile ecosystem

One error in this sentence is the use of the adjective *seeming*. It is modifying *fragile*, another adjective, so it should be in the form of the adverb *seemingly*. Choices (B), (C), and (E) make this correction. But only Choice (C) addresses the issue of the comma splice. By adding the subordinating conjunction *while*, the relationship between the two clauses is defined and a comma splice is avoided.

Be sure to read every answer choice in case you don't notice a secondary error right away. The answer choices will often clue you in to other errors in the sentence.

"Like" Versus "As"

A specific conjunction error that is tested on the GMAT is the use of the subordinating conjunction *as* versus the use of the preposition *like*.

When *like* is used as a preposition, it must be followed by a noun or pronoun and it must be used to compare two things:

I look *like* my sister.   I = sister
Like a detective, Andrea solved the puzzle.   Andrea = detective
The fountain sounds *like* a bubbling brook.   fountain = brook

As, on the other hand, is a subordinating conjunction. Subordinating conjunctions are used to introduce dependent clauses. *As* should never be used to compare two things:

As I mentioned earlier, the test date has been moved up.
It appears *as* if the St. Louis Cardinals are going to lose again.
My dog is very skittish, *as* you might expect a rescued animal to be.

Problems occur when writers start using *like* for *as* and *as* for *like*, which is easy to do. Just substitute *like* for the word *as* in the three sentences above:

INCORRECT:
Like I mentioned earlier, the test date has been moved up.
It appears *like* the St. Louis Cardinals are going to lose again.
My dog is very skittish, *like* you might expect a rescued animal to be.

Most of us are guilty of making this mistake. Unfortunately, the GMAT is unforgiving and does not allow for error. The test will also make your job more difficult by putting this error in a longer sentence:

The developers of Wembley Stadium claim that the new sliding roof will attract future Olympic Games, provide more comfortable seating for spectators, and close as a retractable dome does to protect players and fans from the elements.   [*Incorrect*]

In this sentence, *as* is used in a subordinate clause: *as a retractable dome does*. However, *as* is used to make a comparison between the new sliding roof and a retractable dome. All comparisons should use the preposition *like*. This also means adding an object of the preposition:

The developers of Wembley Stadium claim that the new sliding roof will attract future Olympic Games, provide more comfortable seating for spectators, and close *like a retractable dome* to protect players and fans from the elements.   [*Correct*]

You must also know the difference between *like* and *such as*. *Like*, as we noted, is a preposition used to compare. *Such as* is a conjunction used to introduce examples:

> *Like* residents of Wisconsin and Ohio, many native Midwesterners have their own unique accent.   [*Correct*]

> Native residents of many Midwestern states, *such as* Wisconsin and Ohio, have their own unique accent.   [*Correct*]

The best rule to remember is that when the word *like* is used as a preposition, it must be used to make a comparison.

Conjunctions Problem Set

Please complete the problem set and review the answer key and explanations. Answers on page 162-163.

1. In *The Matrix*, Neo can choose either the blue pill, which will allow him to forget all that he has learned <u>and return to life as he knew it, and the red pill, which will keep him in reality</u>.

   (A) and return to life as he knew it, and the red pill, which will keep him in reality

   (B) and return to life as he knew it, or the red pill, which will keep him in reality

   (C) or return to life as he knew it, and the red pill, which will keep him in reality

   (D) but also return to life as he knew it, and the red pill, which will keep him in reality

   (E) and return to life as he knew it, for the red pill, which will keep him in reality

2. While a supernova originally causes a star to increase in brilliance, it will eventually cause the star's light to gradually <u>decline and disappear, as a flashlight fading from weakening batteries</u>.

   (A) decline and disappear, as a flashlight fading from weakening batteries

   (B) decline and disappear, like a flashlight fading from weakening batteries

   (C) decline or disappear, as a flashlight fading from weakening batteries

   (D) either decline or disappear, as a flashlight fading from weakening batteries

   (E) decline and disappear, just as a flashlight fading from weakening batteries

Conjunctions Problem Set

Please complete the problem set and review the answer key and explanations. Answers on page 162-163.

3. Plant cell walls not only function to maintain cell shape, which provides <u>structural and mechanical support for the cell and the plant, and they also</u> function to prevent expansion when water enters the cell.

    (A) structural and mechanical support for the cell and the plant, and they also
    (B) structural and mechanical support for the cell and the plant, for they also
    (C) structural and mechanical support for the cell and the plant, but they also
    (D) structural or mechanical support for the cell and the plant, and they also
    (E) structural and mechanical support for the cell or the plant, however they also

4. Edgar Allan Poe attended the University of Virginia and West Point Military Academy <u>and was expelled from both of them; he incurred gambling debts at Virginia and</u> intentionally neglected his duties at West Point.

    (A) and was expelled from both of them; he incurred gambling debts at Virginia and
    (B) as he was expelled from both of them; he incurred gambling debts at Virginia and so
    (C) but was expelled from both of them; he incurred gambling debts at Virginia but also
    (D) and was expelled from both of them; he incurred gambling debts at Virginia but
    (E) but was expelled from both of them; he incurred gambling debts at Virginia and

Conjunctions Problem Set Answer Key

Correct answers are in bold.

1. In *The Matrix*, Neo can choose either the blue pill, which will allow him to forget all that he has learned <u>and return to life as he knew it, and the red pill, which will keep him in reality</u>.

    (A) and return to life as he knew it, and the red pill, which will keep him in reality
    (B) and return to life as he knew it, or the red pill, which will keep him in reality
    (C) or return to life as he knew it, and the red pill, which will keep him in reality
    (D) but also return to life as he knew it, and the red pill, which will keep him in reality
    (E) and return to life as he knew it, for the red pill, which will keep him in reality

Either must always be used with *or*. The confusion might occur in deciding which *and* to replace with *or*. The clause following *the blue pill* tells two things that the pill can do: forget *and* return. *And* is correctly used here. It is incorrectly used to describe Neo's choice: *either* the blue pill *or* the red pill. Choice (B) makes this correction.

2. While a supernova originally causes a star to increase in brilliance, it will eventually cause the star's light to gradually <u>decline and disappear, as a flashlight fading from weakening batteries</u>.

    (A) decline and disappear, as a flashlight fading from weakening batteries
    (B) decline and disappear, like a flashlight fading from weakening batteries
    (C) decline or disappear, as a flashlight fading from weakening batteries
    (D) either decline or disappear, as a flashlight fading from weakening batteries
    (E) decline and disappear, just as a flashlight fading from weakening batteries

The conjunction *and* correctly compounds the verb, so Choices (C) and (D) are eliminated. The error occurs when *as* is used to make a comparison in a simile; the star's light to a flashlight's light. *Like* must be used in comparisons, and (B) makes this correction.

3. Plant cell walls not only function to maintain cell shape, which provides <u>structural and mechanical support for the cell and the plant, and they also</u> function to prevent expansion when water enters the cell.

    (A) structural and mechanical support for the cell and the plant, and they also
    (B) structural and mechanical support for the cell and the plant, for they also
    (C) structural and mechanical support for the cell and the plant, but they also
    (D) structural or mechanical support for the cell and the plant, and they also
    (E) structural and mechanical support for the cell or the plant, however they also

Three conjunctions are contained in the underlined portion of the sentence. Evaluate them one at a time. The first *and* correctly compounds two adjectives describing *support*. Therefore, Choice (D) is incorrect. The second *and* compounds two objects of the preposition *for*. This is also correct, eliminating (E). The last *and* is used in a correlative conjunction: they *not only X, but they also Y. But* is the correct conjunction, so (C) is correct.

4. Edgar Allan Poe attended the University of Virginia and West Point Military Academy <u>and was expelled from both of them; he incurred gambling debts at Virginia and</u> intentionally neglected his duties at West Point.

    (A) and was expelled from both of them; he incurred gambling debts at Virginia and
    (B) as he was expelled from both of them; he incurred gambling debts at Virginia and so
    (C) but was expelled from both of them; he incurred gambling debts at Virginia but also
    (D) and was expelled from both of them; he incurred gambling debts at Virginia but
    (E) but was expelled from both of them; he incurred gambling debts at Virginia and

This sentence has two coordinating conjunctions underlined. The first *and* comes after an independent clause that states that Poe attended two colleges. Which conjunction fits best to then say that he was expelled from both of those colleges? *But*. Only Choices (C) and (E) make this correction. Then look at the second *and*. It compounds the verb; *he incurred and neglected*. It is correct, so Choice (C) is eliminated.

THE POWERSCORE GMAT SENTENCE CORRECTION BIBLE

CHAPTER EIGHT: ERRORS IN CONSTRUCTION

Comparisons

Opinions. Everybody has one. There are opinion polls, opinion pages, opinion reports. We seek expert opinions, the majority opinion, and dissenting opinions. With all of the opinions we hear everyday, it is no wonder that comparisons are so common in our speech and prose:

> I cheered for Magic Johnson more than I cheered for Larry Bird.
> *The Green Mile* is Stephen King's most allegorical book.
> I'd prefer a hamburger over a chicken sandwich.

Written comparisons follow specific rules of Standard English, so they are often tested on the GMAT. You will be asked to identify and correct three types of comparison errors: faulty comparative degree, illogical comparisons, and incomplete comparisons.

Faulty comparisons are common errors in the Sentence Correction section of the GMAT.

Comparative Degree

Comparative degree refers to the three separate degrees of intensity conveyed by adjectives and adverbs. These three levels are called the positive (describes one object), comparative (evaluates two objects), and superlative (ranks three or more objects). Consider the following chart.

	Positive (One Object)	Comparative (Two Objects)	Superlative (Three or More Objects)
adj.	warm	warmer	warmest
adj.	dark	darker	darkest
adj.	dry	drier	driest
adj	sunny	more sunny or sunnier	most sunny or sunniest
adv.	steadily	more steadily	most steadily
adv.	wildly	more wildly	most wildly
adj.	ferocious	more ferocious	most ferocious
adv.	ferociously	more ferociously	most ferociously

In the positive level, adjectives and adverbs appear in their base form. For the comparative degree, we add *–er* to the end of the word or use *more* or *less* before the word. Superlative comparisons need *–est* at the end or *most* or *least* before the word. Most adjectives and adverbs will always follow this pattern. As a general rule, add *–ed* and *–est* to one syllable words, and *more/less* and *most/least* to words with two or more syllables. However, like *sunny* in the chart above, some words can use either form, so trust your ear.

The use of an incorrect degree occurs when the comparative level is used to rank three or more objects, or when the superlative degree is used to rank two objects.

> Mary is the wealthier of the three musicians.   [*Incorrect*]

Wealthier implies that there are only two musicians being compared, but the sentence states that there are three. The sentence should use the superlative degree:

> Mary is the *wealthiest* of the three musicians.   [*Correct*]

Sentences will, of course, be more complex on the GMAT:

> In many respects, George Bush and George W. Bush had the same political agenda, but the younger Bush, who was able to pass more legislation, had the most cooperative Congress.   [*Incorrect*]

Two Presidents and their Congresses are being compared so the comparative degree should be used:

> In many respects, George Bush and George W. Bush had the same political agenda, but the younger Bush, who was able to pass more legislation, had the *more cooperative* Congress.   [*Correct*]

There are several sentences like this one in *The Official Guide to GMAT Review*.

Illogical and Incomplete Comparisons

Illogical comparisons are the most common comparison error on the GMAT.

The most common comparison error is the illogical comparison. When presented with a comparison, be sure that the two objects being compared are alike. For example, you cannot compare a truck to a town, a novel to a thumb tack, or a flashlight to a closet. However, it would be acceptable to compare a truck to a car, a novel to a movie, or a flashlight to a candle. Illogical comparisons often occur as the result of an introductory phrase or clause:

> Like most desks at work, Spence has his laden with pictures of his family.
> [*Incorrect*]

At first glance, it may look and sound correct, but it is completely illogical. Because of the introductory phrase (*like most desks at work*), *desks* are being compared to *Spence*. Instead, Spence's desk needs to be compared to all of the other desks:

> Spence's desk, like most desks at work, is laden with pictures of his family.   [*Correct*]

Or Spence needs to be compared to his coworkers:

> Spence, like most of the employees at work, has his desk laden with pictures of his family.   [*Correct*]

Now try a sentence with more complicated subject matter. Can you spot the illogical comparison?

> Completed sometime between 480 and 450 B.C., the play *Oedipus Rex* by Sophocles is much more foreboding than fourteenth-century William Shakespeare.   [*Incorrect*]

This sentence is comparing a *play* to *William Shakespeare*. It needs to compare Sophocles' *play* to William Shakespeare's *plays*:

> Completed sometime between 480 and 450 B.C., the play *Oedipus Rex* by Sophocles is much more foreboding than the fourteenth-century plays by William Shakespeare.   [*Correct*]

Sometimes a comparison is not parallel, creating an illogical statement:

> While the company insists that its starting salary for a man working in the executive branch of the organization is the same as a woman in equal capacity, the watchdog group found a significant gender wage gap. [*Incorrect*]

The comparison, when broken down and extraneous phrases are removed, *should* be:

> X is the same *for* Y as *for* Z

In other words:

> Salary is the same *for* a man as *for* a woman

Notice that the comparison must be parallel; both parts start with *for*. Without the pronoun *for*, the original sentence is not parallel and is comparing *salary* to *a woman*. To correct the sentence, add the second *for* to create parallelism:

> While the company insists that its starting salary *for* a man working in the executive branch of the organization is the same as *for* a woman in equal capacity, the watchdog group found a significant gender wage gap. [*Correct*]

Parallel structure is discussed further in this chapter.

It is not enough to make sure that all comparisons are made using like objects—sometimes you have to make sure that there are two objects present! Without two objects, you end up with an incomplete comparison, which is less common on the GMAT, but still tested nevertheless. Look at an example:

> The grand champion bulldog, owned by Mrs. Seifert, had a stockier build and more even gait than Mr. Murphy's.   [*Incorrect*]

It does not take a Best of Show judge to figure out that Mrs. Seifert's bulldog is being compared to Mr. Murphy's bulldog, but it must be stated in the sentence. Currently, the sentence is comparing a bulldog's build and gait to something owned by Mr. Murphy, but the something is not stated. Many people would read this sentence and believe the bulldog's build and gait is being compared to Mr. Murphy's build and gait. Add the referent to the sentence to correct this error:

> The grand champion bulldog, owned by Mrs. Seifert, had a stockier build and more even gait than Mr. Murphy's *bulldog.*   [*Correct*]

Comparison errors are responsible for a large portion of the questions in *The Official Guide to GMAT Review*.

Remember, comparison errors are common! Watch for faulty comparative degree, illogical comparisons, and incomplete comparisons.

Comparisons Problem Set

Please complete the problem set and review the answer key and explanations. Answers on page 170-171.

1. Like Mozart's first concerts, Frederic Chopin began performing at age six, both for private parties and public charity events.

    (A) Like Mozart's first concerts, Frederic Chopin began performing at age six
    (B) Like Mozart's young age, Frederic Chopin began performing at age six
    (C) Like Mozart and his first concerts, Frederic Chopin began performing at age six
    (D) Like Mozart, Frederic Chopin began performing at age six
    (E) Like Mozart's first concerts, Frederic Chopin's concerts began performing at age six

2. Of all the celestial bodies in our solar system, Pluto will likely be the more difficult to explore, due to its icy surface and distance from Earth.

    (A) Of all the celestial bodies in our solar system, Pluto will likely be the more difficult to explore
    (B) Of most the celestial bodies in our solar system, Pluto will likely be the more difficult to explore
    (C) Of all the celestial bodies in our solar system, Pluto will likely be the most difficult to explore
    (D) Of all the celestial bodies in our solar system, Pluto will likely be the difficultest to explore
    (E) Of all the celestial bodies in our solar system, Pluto will likely be the more difficult to explore of all

3. Americans have a difficult time understanding the inability to improve one's status under a feudal society, but feudalism's hierarchal system is much more rigid than a democracy.

    (A) than
    (B) than that of
    (C) than is so of
    (D) compared to
    (E) compared to that of

4. The sixth Harry Potter book, by British author J.K. Rowling, sold a record 8.9 million copies in the first 24 hours it was on sale—more than any author to date.

    (A) more than any
    (B) more than any other
    (C) more than are any
    (D) more as are those of any other
    (E) more than those by any other

5. Unlike homophones, which are words with the same sound and spelling but have different meanings, homonyms are words with the same sound but have different spellings and meanings.

    (A) homonyms are words with the same sound
    (B) words called homonyms with the same sound
    (C) the same sound is made by homonyms
    (D) homonyms, same-sounding words,
    (E) the sound is the same for homonyms

Comparisons Problem Set Answer Key

Correct answers are in bold.

1. Like Mozart's first concerts, Frederic Chopin began performing at age six, both for private parties and public charity events.

   (A) Like Mozart's first concerts, Frederic Chopin began performing at age six
   (B) Like Mozart's young age, Frederic Chopin began performing at age six
   (C) Like Mozart and his first concerts, Frederic Chopin began performing at age six
   (D) Like Mozart, Frederic Chopin began performing at age six
   (E) Like Mozart's first concerts, Frederic Chopin's concerts began performing at age six

In the current sentence, *concerts* are being illogically compared to *Chopin*. Mozart must be compared to Chopin, as they are both people and both classical musicians. Only (D) makes this comparison.

2. Of all the celestial bodies in our solar system, Pluto will likely be the more difficult to explore, due to its icy surface and distance from Earth.

   (A) Of all the celestial bodies in our solar system, Pluto will likely be the more difficult to explore
   (B) Of most the celestial bodies in our solar system, Pluto will likely be the more difficult to explore
   (C) Of all the celestial bodies in our solar system, Pluto will likely be the most difficult to explore
   (D) Of all the celestial bodies in our solar system, Pluto will likely be the difficultest to explore
   (E) Of all the celestial bodies in our solar system, Pluto will likely be the more difficult to explore of all

This is an error of comparative degree. There are more than two celestial bodies being referenced, so the superlative form of *difficult* must be used. Pluto is the *most* difficult to explore, Choice (C).

3. Americans have a difficult time understanding the inability to improve one's status under a feudal society, but feudalism's hierarchal system is much more rigid <u>than</u> a democracy.

   (A) than
   (B) than that of
   (C) than is so of
   (D) compared to
   (E) compared to that of

The illogical comparison in this sentence is a *hierarchal system* to a *democracy*, or *rigid* to a *democracy*. It is evident that the author intends to compare feudalism's hierarchal system to democracy's hierarchal system. Choice (B) presents the pronoun, *that*, to go in place of *democracy's hierarchal system*. Many might question why Choice (E) is not correct. It is because of the word *more*. When used in a comparison, it should be coupled with *than*: more...than vs. more...compared to.

4. The sixth Harry Potter book, by British author J.K. Rowling, sold a record 8.9 million copies in the first 24 hours it was on sale—<u>more than any</u> author to date.

    (A) more than any
    (B) more than any other
    (C) more than are any
    (D) more as are those of any other
    (E) more than those by any other

The sentence illogically compares *copies* to *authors*. A pronoun is needed to logically compare *copies by J.K. Rowling*, to *copies by any other author*. The pronoun *those* and preposition *by* create a parallel comparison in Choice (E).

5. Unlike homophones, which are words with the same sound and spelling but have different meanings, <u>homonyms are words with the same sound</u> but have different spellings and meanings.

    (A) homonyms are words with the same sound
    (B) words called homonyms with the same sound
    (C) the same sound is made by homonyms
    (D) homonyms, same-sounding words,
    (E) the sound is the same for homonyms

This sentence is correct. Homophones, types of words, are compared to homonyms, also types of words. Choice (A) is correct.

Parallel Structure

Look around you. Most everything in your office or living room or kitchen is symmetrical, meaning that if we cut an object in half along an imaginary plane, both sides of the object would look exactly the same. People like symmetry; we like symmetrical lamps on symmetrical tables with symmetrical picture frames. Scientists have even proven that we like symmetrical mates— subconsciously, we are more attracted to people with symmetrical faces than those who might have a dimple or freckle on just one side!

The developers of Standard English were no different. They liked symmetrical sentences, meaning that if a sentence had two similar parts linked by a conjunction, the two parts had to be identical in form. They called these properly constructed sentences "parallel." Look at the following parallel sentence:

> The donation might be used *to fund the new playground* or *to replace the old bus*.

Examine the two italicized verb phrases in the sentence, and note that their parts of speech match:

> infinitive   n.
> *to fund the new playground*

> infinitive   n.
> *to replace the old bus*

The pattern is symmetrical: an infinitive verb followed by a noun. This sentence is parallel.

The GMAT will test your ability to recognize this pattern using a sentence such as the following:

> The donation might be used *to fund the new playground* or *replacing the old bus*.   [*Incorrect*]

There are two things the donation may be used to do:

> infinitive   n.
> *to fund the new playground*

> prog. verb   n.
> *replacing the old bus*

The patterns no longer match. The second phrase uses a progressive form of the verb instead of the infinitive form. The sentence now violates parallel structure.

Sometimes sentences have three or more similar parts linked by a conjunction. In these cases, all of the items in the series must follow the same pattern:

The new employee will be responsible for *filing paperwork*, *answering phones*, and *taking new orders*.   [*Correct*]

Look at the three things the new employee will be responsible for:

prog. vb.   n.
filing paperwork

prog. vb.   n.
answering phones

prog. vb.   n.
taking new orders

All three jobs follow the same form: a verb in the progressive form, followed by a noun.

If one of the verbs has a different form than the other two, the sentence is no longer parallel:

The new employee will be responsible for *filing paperwork*, *answering phones*, and *will take new orders*.   [*Incorrect*]

The last phrase does not match the first two:

prog. vb.   n.
filing paperwork

prog. vb.   n.
answering phones

future vb.   n.
will take new orders

It contains a simple future tense form of a verb, which does not match the progressive pattern established by the first two.

Errors in parallel structure occur in dozens of questions in *The Official Guide to GMAT Review*. They may occur with almost any part of speech, including verbs, nouns, and adjectives.

Unparallel construction is a prevalent error on the GMAT because it can occur with almost any part of speech.

Parallel Verbs

Errors in verb form, which we just studied in the two previous examples, are the most common parallelism errors on the test. And why shouldn't they be? Every sentence has to have a verb.

It is sentences with more than one verb that cause problems. Two or more verbs can appear in:

> A compound sentence:
> *I <u>drove</u> the entire trip*, **but** *Bryan <u>claimed</u> to be more tired.*

> A compound predicate:
> *The car <u>rolled</u> down the hill* **and** <u>*crashed*</u> *into the fence.*

> And a relative clause:
> *The class that <u>sold</u> the most cookies* **and** <u>*won*</u> *the prize had a party after school.*

If you encounter a GMAT sentence with two verbs separated by a conjunction, check to ensure that the verbs are parallel in form.

Let's look at an example in a more complex sentence:

> The Department of Motor Vehicles is considering a new paging system that would alleviate lines for walk-in customers renewing their licenses and if employees are overwhelmed they would be assisted.   [*Incorrect*]

This sentence contains two verbs in a relative clause that tells what the new system would do:

> <u>*alleviate*</u> *lines for walk-in customers renewing their licenses* and
> *if employees are overwhelmed they <u>would be assisted</u>*

The verbs in the clause are unparallel in form and tense. The two effects of the paging system are *(it) would alleviate X and (would) assist Y*. The helping verb *would* before *assist* can be omitted, but the main verbs must be parallel:

> <u>*alleviate*</u> *lines for walk-in customers renewing their licenses* and
> <u>*assist*</u> *employees who are overwhelmed*

Rewrite the sentence in this form to create a parallel sentence:

> The Department of Motor Vehicles is considering a new paging system that would alleviate lines for walk-in customers renewing their licenses and assist employees who are overwhelmed.   [*Correct*]

Try another one, this time with a series of verbs:

> The environmental group is asking all boat owners to dispense fuel only into approved containers, throw away all litter generated on the boat, and to avoid disposing of cigarette butts in the water.   [*Incorrect*]

The group is asking boat owners three things:

> *to dispense fuel only into approved containers,*
> *throw away all litter generated on the boat, and,*
> *to avoid disposing of cigarette butts in the water*

Two of the verbals (*to dispense* and *to avoid*) are in infinitive form. When a verb series uses a helping verb or linking verb, such as *am* or *was*, or when a verb series uses an infinitive with the preceding preposition *to*, all of the verbs in the series must use the helping verb and preposition, or only the first verb must use the helping verb and preposition.

So, to correct the sentence, all of the verbs can take *to*:

> *to dispense fuel only into approved containers,*
> *to throw away all litter generated on the boat, and*
> *to avoid disposing of cigarette butts in the water*

> The environmental group is asking all boat owners *to* dispense fuel only into approved containers, *to* throw away all litter generated on the boat, and *to* avoid disposing of cigarette butts in the water.   [*Correct*]

Or only the first verb can take *to*:

> *to dispense fuel only into approved containers,*
> *throw away all litter generated on the boat, and*
> *avoid disposing of cigarette butts in the water*

> The environmental group is asking all boat owners *to* dispense fuel only into approved containers, throw away all litter generated on the boat, and avoid disposing of cigarette butts in the water.   [*Correct*]

Something as simple as one little omitted word can cost you valuable GMAT points!

Read very carefully to avoid missing any errors!

Parallel Nouns

Nearly all nouns are naturally parallel. Problems arise, however, with gerunds, which are verb forms that end in *–ing* and act as a noun. Look at the following verb:

> I <u>am running</u> in circles.

See Chapter Three for a review of gerunds.

In this sentence, *running* is in the present progressive form of the verb, and is coupled with *am*. It is properly functioning as a verb. But look at *running* in another sentence:

> *Running* is my least favorite form of exercise.

In this sentence, *running* is a noun. Verbs that end in *-ing* and act like nouns are gerunds, and when they are used on the GMAT in a compound subject or in a sequence, they must all act as nouns. Examine the following sentence:

> Opened in 1869, the Transcontinental Railroad had immediate and far-reaching effects on America, including a population explosion in the West, the decline of Native Americans, joining of East Coast culture and Western convention, and cultivation of thousands of acres of new farm land. [*Incorrect*]

The sentence lists a series of results due to the railroad, all in noun form: *explosion, decline, joining,* and *cultivation*. However, look at the gerund *joining*. Without an article to precede it, a reader may mistake the noun for a verb. To correct the error, use *the*:

> Opened in 1869, the Transcontinental Railroad had immediate and far-reaching effects on America, including a population explosion in the West, the decline of Native Americans, *the joining* of East Coast culture and Western convention, and cultivation of thousands of acres of new farm land. [*Correct*]

Occasionally, a verb will masquerade as a gerund, and thus need to be changed. Here is an example:

> Symptoms of a severe allergic reaction to a bee sting may include dizziness, hives or rashes, swelling of the wound, difficulty breathing, intense itching, and losing consciousness. [*Incorrect*]

This sentence has many gerunds ending in *-ing* and one verb pretending to be a gerund. Look at the short list of symptoms of an allergic reaction: *dizziness, hives, swelling, difficulty, itching,* and *losing*. All but the last one are nouns. In order for *losing* to be a noun, it would have to refer to not coming in first, as in *Losing is difficult to swallow*. In the bee sting sentence, *losing* is a verb; it describes an action.

Because the sentence is not parallel, we must change *losing* to a noun:

> Symptoms of a severe allergic reaction to a bee sting may include dizziness, hives or rashes, swelling of the wound, difficulty breathing, intense itching, and *loss of* consciousness.

Remember, gerunds are the only types of noun parallelism tested; if you find a sentence with a verb ending in *–ing*, check to see if that verb is really a noun. If so, immediately check that it is parallel with the other nouns in the sentence.

Parallel Prepositions

The use of prepositions in a series must also be parallel. A preposition must either be used by all members of a series or by only the first member of the series. Both of the following sentences are correct:

> You can succeed on the GMAT *by* reading, *by* studying, and *by* taking a prep class.   [*Correct*]

> You can succeed on the GMAT *by* reading, studying, and taking a prep class.   [*Correct*]

However, this sentence is incorrect:

> You can succeed on the GMAT *by* reading, *by* studying, and taking a prep class.   [*Incorrect*]

Only two of the items in the series use the preposition *by*, making the sentence ungrammatical.

A series using prepositions does not have to repeat the same preposition:

> We have a government *of* the people, *by* the people, and *for* the people.

Just ensure that all of the objects receive a preposition. This sentence is incorrect:

> You can travel to the town *on* a plane, *in* a car, or boat.   [*Incorrect*]

The nouns *plane* and *car* are the objects of the prepositions *on* and *in*. Because the noun *boat* is in the same series, it must also be the object of a preposition:

> You can travel to the town *on* a plane, *in* a car, or *by* a boat.   [*Correct*]

Also check prepositions to ensure that their objects are parallel. Look at an example:

> Critics of the current Bowl Championship Series feel that moving from a computer-ranking format to creating a playoff system will improve the integrity of the competition.   [*Incorrect*]

This sentence employs the common expression *moving from X to Y*. The object of *from* (*X*) should be in the same form as the object of *to* (*Y*). Currently, it looks like *moving from a format to creating*. *From* is followed by a noun, but *to* is followed by a verb. Correct the sentence by giving each preposition a noun object:

> Critics of the current Bowl Championship Series feel that moving *from* a computer-ranking <u>format</u> *to* a playoff <u>system</u> will improve the integrity of the competition.   [*Correct*]

Now the sentence is parallel.

Parallel Conjunctions

The presence of a correlating conjunction should warn you to verify parallel structure.

Like nouns, conjunctions themselves are naturally parallel. The words or phrases that follow a conjunction can cause unparallel sentences, though, so you would be wise to watch for them on the GMAT. Correlative conjunctions, such as *either..or* and *not only..but also*, are the biggest culprits. As we learned in Chapter Three, correlative conjunctions include:

either..or	neither..nor	both..and	not only..but also
	not..but	whether..or	as..as

The words immediately following each conjunction need to be in a similar, parallel format:

either X *or* Y: We accept *either* <u>cash</u> *or* <u>money order</u>.
                                   n.   n.

both X *and* Y: She is *both* <u>artistically gifted</u> *and* <u>academically inclined</u>.
                              adv.   adj.   adv.   adj.

whether X *or* Y: I am deciding *whether* <u>to eat pizza</u> *or* <u>to eat spaghetti</u>.
                           infinitive n.   infinitive   n.

Notice that each word or phrase after the first conjunction matches the format of the word or phrase after the second conjunction. Look at an example of how the GMAT might attempt to trick you with correlative conjunctions:

> Aloe is used not only to soothe burns but also it also heals fungal infections such as ringworm.   [*Incorrect*]

An infinitive verb and a noun (*to soothe burns*) follow *not only*, but a pronoun, simple present verb, and noun (*it heals infections*) follow *but also*. The format, *not only X but also Y*, insists that the X and Y are parallel:

> Aloe is used *not only* <u>to soothe burns</u> *but also* <u>to heal fungal infections</u> such as ringworm.   [*Correct*]

Finally, watch for the use of a conjunction in unparallel clauses. This can occur when one of the clauses is missing a conjunction:

> Behaviorists agree that how a teenage boy dresses and his performance in athletics contribute to his degree of popularity.   [*Incorrect*]

This sentence has two clauses, X and Y, which must be parallel. Currently, X begins with the conjunction *how*: *how a teenage boy dresses*. Y begins with a pronoun: *his performance in athletics*. To make them parallel, they must both begin with a preposition:

> Behaviorists agree that *how* <u>a teenage boy dresses</u> and *how* <u>he performs in athletics</u> contribute to his degree of popularity.

Note that the phrases following the conjunctions are also parallel; they both contain a subject and a present tense verb.

Parallel Comparisons

As discussed in the previous section, comparisons are the source of many errors in the Sentence Correction portion of the GMAT. They cause further problems when they violate parallel structure. Look at the offending sentence below:

> Jim Thorpe, the legendary multi-sport star, enjoyed playing football more than he ran track and field, but it was winning the gold medal at the 1912 Olympic pentathlon that shot him to fame.   [*Incorrect*]

The comparison in this sentence is *enjoyed X more than Y*. Again, the X and the Y must be parallel, but they are not. *Playing football* and *he ran track and field* are not in equivalent format. The first uses a progressive verb followed by a noun. The second adds a subject, past tense verb, and a noun. To correct the sentence, model the second part of the comparison after the first:

Remember to be on the lookout for *more, most, less, least, rather than, like,* and *unlike* to signal a comparison.

> Jim Thorpe, the legendary multi-sport star, enjoyed *playing* <u>football</u> more than *running* <u>track and field</u>, but it was winning the gold medal at the 1912 Olympic pentathlon that shot him to fame.   [*Correct*]

A comparison is a parallel trap, because you must always compare two or more things, setting the stage for an error in one half of the sentence.

Parallel Structure Problem Set

Please complete the problem set and review the answer key and explanations. Answers on page 182-185.

1. By the time Robert Clark Young was fourteen years old, he was reading a second language, authoring a novel, <u>and had published newspaper articles.</u>

   (A) and had published newspaper articles
   (B) and published newspaper articles
   (C) and would publish newspaper articles
   (D) and publishing newspaper articles
   (E) and was publishing newspaper articles

2. A school teacher is no longer responsible for just imparting knowledge; he or she must now take on multiple roles, such as counseling a troubled child, <u>disciplining an unruly student, and to entertain a generation which lacks an attention span.</u>

   (A) disciplining an unruly student, and to entertain a generation which lacks an attention span
   (B) to discipline an unruly student, and to entertain a generation which lacks an attention span
   (C) disciplining an unruly student, and entertaining a generation which lacks an attention span
   (D) disciplining an unruly student, and to entertain a generation lacking an attention span
   (E) as disciplining an unruly student, and to entertaining a generation which lacks an attention span

3. Samoset, the first Native American to make contact with the Pilgrims, assisted the colonists <u>by teaching proper planting techniques, revealing the best fishing locations, and translating</u> native languages.

   (A) by teaching proper planting techniques, revealing the best fishing locations, and translating
   (B) by teaching proper planting techniques, by revealing the best fishing locations, and translating
   (C) by teaching proper planting techniques, revealing the best fishing locations, and to translate
   (D) by teaching proper planting techniques, revealing the best fishing locations, and he translated
   (E) by teaching proper planting techniques, revealing the best fishing locations, and that he translated

4. In order to qualify for the PGA Tour, aspiring golfers are required to place in the top 30 at Qualifying School, <u>win three events on the Nationwide Tour, or to finish in the top 20</u> of the Nationwide Tour's earnings list.

   (A) win three events on the Nationwide Tour, or to finish in the top 20
   (B) win three events on the Nationwide Tour, or finishing in the top 20
   (C) to win three events on the Nationwide Tour, or finishing in the top 20
   (D) to win three events on the Nationwide Tour, finishing in the top 20
   (E) to win three events on the Nationwide Tour, or to finish in the top 20

5. Children at the daycare spend their time either engaging in educational activities, such as math games and reading circles, or <u>they play with their</u> peers in a supervised setting.

   (A) they play with their
   (B) they will play with their
   (C) they are playing with their
   (D) to play with their
   (E) playing with their

6. The human resource department looked at an insurance program that would cover all vision-related procedures, including laser surgery, and <u>if employees paid out-of-pocket expenses they would be reimbursed</u>.

   (A) if employees paid out-of-pocket expenses they would be reimbursed
   (B) paying out-of-pocket expenses would be reimbursed
   (C) reimburse employees who paid out-of-pocket expenses
   (D) reimbursing employees paying out-of-pocket expenses
   (E) employees to be reimbursed for paying out-of-pocket expenses

Parallel Structure Problem Set

Please complete the problem set and review the answer key and explanations. Answers on page 182-185.

7. Doctors Without Borders is a private organization that arranges medical treatment in foreign lands, particularly in nations with an endemic outbreak of disease, <u>states at war, and in poverty-stricken countries</u>.

    (A)   states at war, and in poverty-stricken countries
    (B)   states at war, and in countries that are poverty-stricken
    (C)   by visiting states at war, and helping poverty-stricken countries
    (D)   in states at war, and in poverty-stricken countries
    (E)   states at war, and with poverty-stricken countries

8. Air Force One, the President's main mode of cross-country travel, is not like any ordinary plane; it has rooms for exercising, meeting with staff, <u>operating in case of emergency, and a place to tape interviews</u>.

    (A)   operating in case of medical emergency, and a place to tape interviews
    (B)   operating in case of medical emergency, and taping interviews
    (C)   for operating in case of medical emergency, and for taping interviews
    (D)   to operate in case of medical emergency, and a place to tape interviews
    (E)   to operate in case of medical emergency, and to tape interviews

9. Despite their intimidating size, <u>Great Danes are easy to groom, extremely gentle, and are</u> loyal to their owners.

    (A)   Great Danes are easy to groom, extremely gentle, and are
    (B)   Great Danes are to be easy to groom, extremely gentle, and are
    (C)   Great Danes are easy to groom, extremely gentle, and
    (D)   Great Danes are easy to groom, extremely gentle, and they are
    (E)   Great Danes are easy to groom and extremely gentle, and they are

10. While some dieticians recommend a high protein and low carbohydrate diet in order to lose weight, <u>others advocating</u> a high carbohydrate and low fat diet as the best method to shed pounds.

    (A)   others advocating
    (B)   others advocate
    (C)   others will advocate
    (D)   others have advocated
    (E)   others are advocating

11. William Tecumseh Sherman, the Civil War general who burned Atlanta, was both praised for his military genius <u>and he was criticized for his "scorched earth" policy</u>.

    (A)   and he was criticized for his "scorched earth" policy
    (B)   and he had been criticized for his "scorched earth" policy
    (C)   and he is criticized for his "scorched earth" policy
    (D)   and criticized for his "scorched earth" policy
    (E)   and criticizing that his "scorched earth" policy

12. In an 1893 court case, the Supreme Court ruled that because the tomato is most often served with dinner, it is a vegetable <u>rather than defined as a fruit</u>; the decision ended controversy concerning a tax for vegetables that did not exist for fruit.

    (A)   rather than defined as a fruit
    (B)   rather than as a fruit
    (C)   rather than a fruit
    (D)   instead of defined as a fruit
    (E)   instead of defined as a type of fruit

Parallel Structure Problem Set Answer Key

Correct answers are in bold.

1. By the time Robert Clark Young was fourteen years old, he was reading a second language, authoring a novel, <u>and had published newspaper articles</u>.

   (A) and had published newspaper articles
   (B) and published newspaper articles
   (C) and would publish newspaper articles
   (D) and publishing newspaper articles
   (E) and was publishing newspaper articles

The sentence has a series of two past progressive verbs (*was reading, authoring*) followed by a past perfect verb (*had published*). The third item in the series must use another past progressive verb (*publishing*). Since the first verb uses the helping verb *was* but the second verb does not use it, the third verb should not have a helping verb either. Therefore, Choice (E) is incorrect. Only Choice (D) makes the correction.

2. A school teacher is no longer responsible for just imparting knowledge; he or she must now take on multiple roles, such as counseling a troubled child, <u>disciplining an unruly student, and to entertain a generation which lacks an attention span</u>.

   (A) disciplining an unruly student, and to entertain a generation which lacks an attention span
   (B) to discipline an unruly student, and to entertain a generation which lacks an attention span
   (C) disciplining an unruly student, and entertaining a generation which lacks an attention span
   (D) disciplining an unruly student, and to entertain a generation lacking an attention span
   (E) as disciplining an unruly student, and entertaining a generation which lacks an attention span

The verb phrases should be in the present progressive form to match *counseling*; *counseling, disciplining, and entertaining*. Both (C) and (E) make this correction, but (E) unnecessarily adds *as*. Only (C) is correct.

3. Samoset, the first Native American to make contact with the Pilgrims, assisted the colonists <u>by teaching proper planting techniques, revealing the best fishing locations, and translating</u> native languages.

   (A) by teaching proper planting techniques, revealing the best fishing locations, and translating
   (B) by teaching proper planting techniques, by revealing the best fishing locations, and translating
   (C) by teaching proper planting techniques, revealing the best fishing locations, and to translate
   (D) by teaching proper planting techniques, revealing the best fishing locations, and he translated
   (E) by teaching proper planting techniques, revealing the best fishing locations, and that he translated

This original sentence is parallel making Choice (A) correct. The three verbs are in progressive form; *teaching, revealing*, and *translating* and only the first item uses a preposition.

4. In order to qualify for the PGA Tour, aspiring golfers are required to place in the top 30 at Qualifying School, <u>win three events on the Nationwide Tour, or to finish in the top 20</u> of the Nationwide Tour's earnings list.

    (A) win three events on the Nationwide Tour, or to finish in the top 20
    (B) win three events on the Nationwide Tour, or finishing in the top 20
    (C) to win three events on the Nationwide Tour, or finishing in the top 20
    (D) to win three events on the Nationwide Tour, finishing in the top 20
    (E) to win three events on the Nationwide Tour, or to finish in the top 20

The sentence lists three requirements; *to place, win,* and *to finish.* Two of the verbs are in the infinitive form and one is in simple present. The use of *to* for a list of infinitives must be used with *all* the verbs in the series or with *only the first* verb. So the requirements must be *to place, to win,* and *to finish,* OR *to place, win,* and *finish.* Only Choice (E) makes one of these corrections.

5. Children at the daycare spend their time either engaging in educational activities, such as math games and reading circles, or <u>they play with their</u> peers in a supervised setting.

    (A) they play with their
    (B) they will play with their
    (C) they are playing with their
    (D) to play with their
    (E) playing with their

This sentence uses the coordinating conjunction *either..or.* Phrases following both *either* and *or* must be parallel. *Either* is followed by a present progressive verb and prepositional phrase (*engaging in educational activities*). *Or* is followed by a pronoun, simple present tense verb, and prepositional phrase (*they play with their peers*). It must be changed to a present progressive verb and prepositional phrase to match *either.* Choice (E) is correct.

6. The human resource department looked at an insurance program that would cover all vision-related procedures, including laser surgery, and <u>if employees paid out-of-pocket expenses they would be reimbursed</u>.

    (A) if employees paid out-of-pocket expenses they would be reimbursed
    (B) paying out-of-pocket expenses would be reimbursed
    (C) reimburse employees who paid out-of-pocket expenses
    (D) reimbursing employees paying out-of-pocket expenses
    (E) employees to be reimbursed for paying out-of-pocket expenses

This sentence contains a clause with unparallel verbs. The correct form is *that X and Y.* The X (*would cover*) and Y (*if employees paid out-of-pocket expenses they would be reimbursed*) should be parallel, but the Y goes in a completely different direction. It can be corrected two ways: *would reimburse,* or just *reimburse.* Only (C) makes the correction.

7. Doctors Without Borders is a private organization that arranges medical treatment in foreign lands, particularly in nations with an endemic outbreak of disease, <u>states at war, and in poverty-stricken countries</u>.

(A) states at war, and in poverty-stricken countries
(B) states at war, and in countries that are poverty-stricken
(C) by visiting states at war, and helping poverty-stricken countries
(D) in states at war, and in poverty-stricken countries
(E) states at war, and with poverty-stricken countries

Of the three items in the series, two begin with prepositional phrase *in* (*in nations, states, and in countries*). The rule states that either all of the items must begin with a preposition, or only the first item should receive the preposition. Therefore, the correct answer will either be *in nations, in states, and in countries* or *in nations, states, and countries*. Choice (D) chooses the first option and corrects the sentence. Note that by adding the preposition *in* before *states at war*, we also clear up confusion as to whether *states* is a noun or a verb.

8. Air Force One, the President's main mode of cross-country travel, is not like any ordinary plane; it has rooms for exercising, meeting with staff, <u>operating in case of medical emergency, and a place to tape interviews</u>.

(A) operating in case of medical emergency, and a place to tape interviews
(B) operating in case of medical emergency, and taping interviews
(C) for operating in case of medical emergency, and for taping interviews
(D) to operate in case of medical emergency, and a place to tape interviews
(E) to operate in case of medical emergency, and to tape interviews

The sentence has a list of gerund nouns to describe what the room is used for: *exercising, meeting, operating, and to tape*. The last part of the series is an infinitive verb and does not fit. *Taping* makes the series parallel, which is why (B) is correct.

9. Despite their intimidating size, <u>Great Danes are easy to groom, extremely gentle, and are</u> loyal to their owners.

(A) Great Danes are easy to groom, extremely gentle, and are
(B) Great Danes are to be easy to groom, extremely gentle, and are
(C) Great Danes are easy to groom, extremely gentle, and
(D) Great Danes are easy to groom, extremely gentle, and they are
(E) Great Danes are easy to groom and extremely gentle, and they are

The series consists of adjectives, two of which follow the verb *are*. As discussed, either all of the adjectives must follow a verb, or solely the first one (*are easy, are gentle, and are loyal*, OR *are easy, gentle, and loyal*). (C) makes this correction.

10. While some dieticians recommend a high protein and low carbohydrate diet in order to lose weight, <u>others advocating</u> a high carbohydrate diet and low fat as the best method to shed pounds.

   (A) others advocating
   (B) others advocate
   (C) others will advocate
   (D) others have advocated
   (E) others are advocating

Yet another unparallel comparison. The correct form is *While some dieticians X, others Y*, and the X and Y must be parallel. The X consists of a simple present verb, followed by a noun (*recommend a diet*). The Y consists of a progressive verb and a noun (*advocating a method*). Make the Y parallel by using a simple present verb, followed by a noun (*advocate a method*), as in Choice (B).

11. William Tecumseh Sherman, the Civil War general who burned Atlanta, was both praised for his military genius <u>and he was criticized for his "scorched earth" policy</u>.

   (A) and he was criticized for his "scorched earth" policy
   (B) and he had been criticized for his "scorched earth" policy
   (C) and he is criticized for his "scorched earth" policy
   (D) and criticized for his "scorched earth" policy
   (E) and criticizing that his "scorched earth" policy

The coordinating conjunctions *both..and* set up the format *both X and Y* in which X and Y should be parallel. They are not. The Y portion, following *and*, inserts an unneeded pronoun and helping verb. Choice (D) correctly states *both praised and criticized*.

12. In an 1893 court case, the Supreme Court ruled that because the tomato is most often served with dinner, it is a vegetable <u>rather than defined as a fruit</u>; the decision ended controversy concerning a tax for vegetables that did not exist for fruit.

   (A) rather than defined as a fruit
   (B) rather than as a fruit
   (C) rather than a fruit
   (D) instead of defined as a fruit
   (E) instead of defined as a type of fruit

This is parallel comparison error. The form, *it is X rather than Y*, must have a parallel X and Y. The X is simply *vegetable* so the Y must be simply *fruit*. Only (C) makes the sentence parallel.

A semicolon is used to join two closely-related independent clauses:

> The night before the SAT, Ken stayed up until midnight; he suspected this was the reason he did so poorly on the test.   [*Correct*]

Remember, an independent clause can stand alone as a sentence. Therefore, the clause on either side of the semicolon must be a complete sentence:

> The night before the SAT, Ken stayed up until midnight.
> He suspected this was the reason he did so poorly on the test.

Never use a semicolon with a dependent clause, as in the following:

> The night before the SAT, Ken stayed up until midnight; which is why he did so poorly on the test.   [*Incorrect*]

Semicolons are the only punctuation tested on the GMAT.

If the clause on either side of the semicolon cannot stand alone as a sentence, you cannot use a semicolon. *Which is why he did so poorly on the test* is a dependent clause, so the sentence is structurally flawed.

Semicolon errors on the GMAT occur when the one side of the semicolon is a dependent clause. To correct the error, you may be required to change the dependent clause into an independent clause, or you may remove the semicolon and use a subordinating conjunction instead.

> The worst pandemic in history, the bubonic plague swept through Eurasia during the 1300s and killed over 200 million; nearly one in three people.   [*Incorrect*]

The portion after the semicolon (*nearly one in three people*) is not an independent clause and cannot stand alone as a sentence, as it is completely missing a verb. To correct the sentence, create an independent clause:

> The worst pandemic in history, the bubonic plague swept through Eurasia during the 1300s and killed over 200 million; *nearly one in three people died*.   [*Correct*]

Or, remove the semicolon by using a relative clause:

> The worst pandemic in history, the bubonic plague swept through Eurasia during the 1300s and killed over 200 million, *which was nearly one in three people*.   [*Correct*]

These errors are easy to spot; if you see a semicolon in a question on the GMAT, immediately check that the clauses on both sides of the semicolon are independent clauses.

Semicolon Problem Set

Please complete the problem set and review the answer key and explanations. Answers on page 188.

1. Despite the fact that it has a duck-shaped bill and lays eggs, the platypus is not a <u>bird; rather</u> the most unique mammal in Australia and quite possibly the world.

   (A) bird; rather
   (B) bird, but rather
   (C) bird; rather that of
   (D) bird; it is that of
   (E) bird, but that of

2. Barbra Steisand, whose career spans four decades, has received ten Grammy awards, including three for Best Female <u>Vocal; in 1964, 1965, and 1966</u>.

   (A) Vocal; in 1964, 1965, and 1966
   (B) Vocal, winning in 1964, 1965, and 1966
   (C) Vocal; occurring in 1964, 1965, and 1966
   (D) Vocal; a win in 1964, 1965, and 1966
   (E) Vocal; having won in 1964, 1965, and 1966

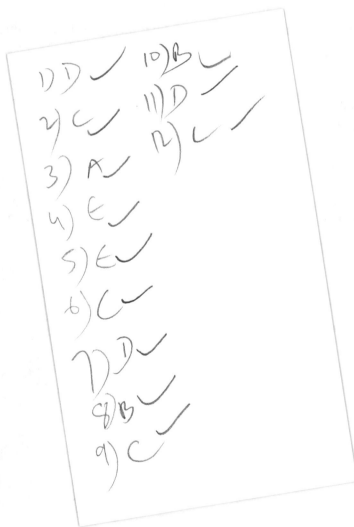

Semicolon Problem Set Answer Key

Correct answers are in bold.

1. Despite the fact that it has a duck-shaped bill and lays eggs, the platypus is not a <u>bird; rather</u> the most unique mammal in Australia and quite possibly the world.

    (A) bird; rather
    (B) bird, but rather
    (C) bird; rather that of
    (D) bird; it is that of
    (E) bird, but that of

The portion behind the semicolon is a dependent clause; it is completely lacking a verb (*rather the most unique mammal in Australia and quite possibly the world*). Only Choice (B) correctly joins the two clauses by subordinating the dependent clause with the subordinating conjunction *but*.

2. Barbra Steisand, whose career spans four decades, has received ten Grammy awards, including three for Best Female <u>Vocal; in 1964, 1965, and 1966</u>.

    (A) Vocal; in 1964, 1965, and 1966
    (B) Vocal, winning in 1964, 1965, and 1966
    (C) Vocal; occurring in 1964, 1965, and 1966
    (D) Vocal; a win in 1964, 1965, and 1966
    (E) Vocal; having won in 1964, 1965, and 1966

The portion behind the semicolon (*in 1964, 1965, and 1966*) is a prepositional phrase and cannot stand alone as a sentence. Choices (C), (D), and (E) all place a dependent clause after the semicolon. Only (B) creates a verb phrase that correctly modifies the subject.

Idioms

Traditionally, an idiom is an expression that does not make literal sense. To native speakers of American English, idioms are as natural as baseball and apple pie. To non-native speakers, however, idioms can sometimes pose problems. Look at the following idiom as an example.

Make up your mind!

Most people know that this means "*Decide!*," but for many foreign-born speakers of English, the expression can mean one of two things:

1. Put together your brain!
2. Apply cosmetics to your brain!

Idioms are everywhere:

Hold your horses; I'll be ready in a minute!
That comment was *below the belt* and you should apologize.
The toddler screamed *at the top of her lungs*.
The news of their engagement *came out of left field*.

Imagine what a person might picture when hearing the idioms above if he or she is unfamiliar with American idiom! Of course, America is not the only English-speaking country to create idioms. In New Zealand, you can be *off your oats* (meaning you've lost your appetite); in Australia, you can be *up a gum-tree* (meaning you're puzzled); and in Great Britain, you can be *in bulk* (meaning you're laughing).

Our language has all kind of quirks. *Slim* and *fat* are opposites, but *slim chance* and *fat chance* mean the same thing. You can fill *in* the blank while you fill *out* a form. Barns burn *down*, newspaper burns *up*, fog burns *off*, fires burn *out*, and meatloaf just burns. These idioms, however silly when broken down and analyzed, are Standard American English.

If *true* idioms such as these were used on the GMAT, the test might be a bit easier. But the term "idiom" has become a catch-all on standardized tests, used to refer to any expression or word combination that is accepted as Standard American English. So it should be no surprise, then, that a quarter of the sentences in *The Official Guide to GMAT Review* are guilty of idiom violations.

On the GMAT, faulty idiom can occur in all parts of speech. Smaller words, such as prepositions and conjunctions, are more prone to fall victim to faulty idiom, because the makers of the test are hoping you won't notice such a small mistake, especially when they put more difficult words in between.

One of the biggest Sentence Correction culprits—the erroneous idiom—often occurs because of the smallest words.

Look at an example:

> During the Civil War, a fierce disagreement in Kentucky took place among those residents who supported the election of Abraham Lincoln with those who wanted to secede with Jefferson Davis.   [*Incorrect*]

The choice of *among* or *between* is often tested on the GMAT.

This sentence contains two idiom errors. The first is the use of *among*. *Among* is a preposition used to refer to relationships with three or more objects. The correct preposition is *between*, which cites a relationship between two objects. There are two groups of residents in the sentence, so *between* is a better preposition:

> During the Civil War, a fierce disagreement in Kentucky took place *between* those residents who supported the election of Abraham Lincoln with those who wanted to secede with Jefferson Davis.   [*Incorrect*]

One little preposition still causes this entire sentence to be ungrammatical, but you might not notice the error due to the words surrounding the idiom. When the modifiers are removed, the correct idiom is:

> *a disagreement between X <u>and</u> Y*

The conjunction *and* should be used to link the two nouns in disagreement. However, the current sentence uses the preposition *with* in the idiom: *a disagreement between X <u>with</u> Y*. To correct the sentence, substitute *and* for *with*:

> During the Civil War, a fierce disagreement in Kentucky took place *between* those residents who supported the election of Abraham Lincoln *<u>and</u>* those who wanted to secede with Jefferson Davis.   [*Correct*]

The faulty idiom might also occur in phrases:

> The number of volunteers at the Relay for Life increased by more than twice from 2002 to 2005.   [*Incorrect*]

The error should be easier to spot in this sentence. The idiom violation, *increased by more than twice*, should be replaced by *more than doubled*:

> The number of volunteers at the Relay for Life *<u>more than doubled</u>* from 2002 to 2005.   [*Correct*]

PowerScore has compiled a list of the most common idiom errors found in *The Official Guide to GMAT Review*. These errors and their corrections are presented in the chart on the following two pages.

Unidiomatic Expression:	Correction:	Correct Idiom Form:
The problem developed *after when* the meeting was over.	The problem developed *after* the meeting was over.	verb + *after*
The teachers want a discipline plan *as strong or stronger than* the present policy.	The teachers want a discipline plan *as strong as* the present policy.	*X as strong as Y*
The students are *better served by* discipline *instead of by* leniency.	The students are *better served by* discipline *than by* leniency.	*better served by X than by Y*
There is an argument *between* those who want red *with* those who want blue.	There is an argument *between* those who want red *and* those who want blue.	*between X and Y*
It is best to train a dog *by* reward, *but not* punishment.	It is best to train a dog *by* reward, *rather than* punishment.	*by X rather than Y*
The *connection of* height *and* weight influences weight loss.	The *connection between* height *and* weight influences weight loss.	*connection between X and Y*
Adam *considers* education *to be* a part of the problem.	Adam *considers* education a part of the problem.	*considers X Y* (when considers means "regard as")
The doctor is *credited as* having cured polio.	The doctor is *credited with* having cured polio.	*credited with*
The newly-hatched butterfly's survival *depends on if* it can dry its wings by nightfall.	The newly-hatched butterfly's survival *depends on whether* it can dry its wings by nightfall.	*depends on whether*
The teams were *determined from* a random drawing.	The teams were *determined by* a random drawing.	*determined by* (when expressing cause)
Brett has *double as many* candy bars as Rob.	Brett has *twice as many* candy bars as Rob.	*twice as many*
I fell asleep *due to the fact that* I was tired.	I fell asleep *because* I was tired.	*because* (due to means attributable to)
Internal Affairs was created *for monitoring* conduct.	Internal Affairs was created *to monitor* conduct.	*to monitor* + noun
The number of volunteers *increased by more than twice*.	The number of volunteers *more than doubled*.	*more than doubled*
Heidi decided to eat *instead of* starving.	Heidi decided to eat *rather than* starve.	*rather than* (more formal)
The fight was caused by the *interaction where* two personalities collide.	The fight was caused by the *interaction of* two colliding personalities.	*interaction of*
The flower will continue <u>its growth</u> *into the coming* months.	The flower will continue <u>to grow</u> *in the coming* months.	*in the coming* + noun.
The final decision *is if* Jud deserves a raise.	The final decision *is whether* Jud deserves a raise.	*is whether*
School supplies, *like* paper and pencils, are provided.	School supplies, *such as* paper and pencils, are provided.	*such as* (to list examples)
Tasha is *maybe* the tallest person in our office.	Tasha is *probably* the tallest person in our office.	verb + *probably*
He *mistook* the Honda *as* a Toyota.	He *mistook* the Honda *for* a Toyota.	*mistook X for Y*
Hip problems are much *more common among* large dogs *than* smaller breeds.	Hip problems are *much more common among* large dogs *than among* smaller breeds.	*more common among X than among y*
Miranda spoke *more* openly *than never before*.	Miranda spoke *more* openly *than ever before*.	*more X than ever before*
The sweater is *not* made of wool; *rather* cotton.	The sweater is made *not* of wool, *but rather* of cotton.	*not X but rather Y*
Her guess *of there being* 112 marbles in the jar was wrong.	Her guess *that* 112 marbles were in the jar was wrong.	*that* (to begin relative clause)
Jupiter cannot be explored by man *on account of* it being made of gas.	Jupiter cannot be explored by man *because* it is made of gas.	*because X is Y*
Jupiter cannot be explored by man *because of* it being made of gas.	Jupiter cannot be explored by man *because* it is made of gas.	*because X is Y*
I *question if* Chris is telling the truth.	I *question whether* Chris is telling the truth.	*question whether*
The *raising of costs* of automobile ownership has convinced me to continue riding my bike.	The *rising cost* of automobile ownership has convinced me to continue riding my bike.	*rising cost*
Dave's music ranges from classical sounds that belong to another era *and* modern beats heard in nightclubs.	Dave's music ranges from classical sounds that belong to another era *to* modern beats heard in nightclubs.	*ranges from X to Y*

Unidiomatic Expression:	Correction:	Correct Idiom Form:
The camp has passed a rule *requiring* the uncertified counselors *should* complete CPR training.	The camp has passed a rule *requiring* the uncertified counselors *to* complete CPR training.	*requiring X to Y* OR *requiring that X Y*
The *rivalry between* the Boston Red Sox *with* the New York Yankees is most prominent in October.	The *rivalry between* the Boston Red Sox *and* the New York Yankees is most prominent in October.	*rivalry between X and Y*
The power is *shifting from* the employer *with* the employee.	The power is *shifting from* the employer *to* the employee.	*shifting from X to Y*
The more you practice typing, your skill becomes *greater*.	*The more* you practice typing, *the greater* your skill becomes.	*the more X, the greater Y*
I do not *think of* the tomato *to be* a fruit.	I do not *think of* the tomato *as* a fruit.	*think of X as Y*
The teacher *was influential on* James.	The teacher *was an influence on* James.	*was an influence on*
While being a medical student, she performed her first surgery.	As a medical student, she performed her first surgery.	*as* (to introduce a phrase)
The bar *requires that* patrons *are* over eighteen years of age.	The bar *requires that* patrons *be* over eighteen years of age.	*requires that X be Y*
Dr. Watts is *worried over* the cat's recovery.	Dr. Watts is *worried about* the cat's recovery.	*worried about*
The object floated when we *expected for* it *to* sink.	The object floated when we *expected* it *to* sink.	*X is expected to Y*
The company *prohibits* sales representatives *to* make unsolicited calls.	The company *prohibits* sales representatives *from* making unsolicited calls.	*X prohibits Y from doing Z*

This chart represents the idiom errors that occur most frequently in *The Official Guide to GMAT Review*. Please see the appendix for an additional list of other idiomatic expressions.

Remember, idiom errors are in a quarter of the questions from the book. It is imperative to memorize the correct idiom formats from the previous chart, as well as look for additional idiom error in each question on the GMAT.

Idiom Problem Set

Please complete the problem set and review the answer key and explanations. Answers on page 196-200.

1. <u>Perched atop</u> a high mountain ridge in the Andes, the Incan city of Machu Picchu is believed to have served as a country retreat for Incan nobility.

   (A) Perched atop
   (B) Perched high atop
   (C) Perched on top
   (D) Perched on
   (E) Perched above

2. Jacobs Field, completed in Cleveland in 1994, did much <u>to raise the energy and revive</u> a worn-down city formally referred to as "the mistake by the lake."

   (A) to raise the energy and revive
   (B) to raise the energy of a worn down city and revive
   (C) to raise the energy and to revive
   (D) in reviving and raising the energy of
   (E) to revive and raise the energy of

3. During a divorce, children are often <u>viewed like bargaining chips; it is important</u> for parents to remember that a child's well-being must be considered separately from the division of property.

   (A) viewed like bargaining chips; it is important
   (B) viewed as bargaining chips; it is important
   (C) viewed to be bargaining chips; it is important
   (D) viewed like bargaining chips, and it is important
   (E) viewed like bargaining chips, so it is important

4. Upon his death, it was discovered that Secretariat's heart <u>was bigger by three times the size of an average horse</u>, which many believe to be the reason for the stallion's stunning speed.

   (A) was bigger by three times the size of an average horse
   (B) was three times the size bigger of an average horse
   (C) was three times the size larger of an average horse's heart
   (D) was three times the size of an average horse's heart
   (E) was three times as large as an average horse

5. A recent study indicates that more and more college graduates are opting <u>to rent a home or apartment instead of</u> to buy real estate—a trend fueled by rising market costs and new spending habits.

   (A) to rent a home or apartment instead of
   (B) to rent a home or apartment rather than
   (C) to rent a home or apartment opposed to
   (D) renting a home or apartment instead of
   (E) renting a home or apartment instead of choosing

6. Spam, the unsolicited e-mails that litter inboxes across the world, <u>is estimated at 90% of all internet traffic</u> in the United States today.

   (A) is estimated at 90% of all internet traffic
   (B) is estimated for 90% of all internet traffic
   (C) is estimated to be 90% of all internet traffic
   (D) is estimated at 90% in all internet traffic
   (E) is estimated as 90% of all internet traffic

7. Here at PowerScore, we <u>arrange with our customers access to</u> the Online Student Area prior to the start of the course; this enables the students to read pre-course material and take a practice test.

   (A) arrange with our customers access to
   (B) arrange between our customers access to
   (C) arrange for our customers to access
   (D) arrange with our customers to access
   (E) arrange for our customers to access to

8. Of the 112 potential jurors, twenty-six <u>were excused in serving in the jury</u> because they had read about the case in the newspaper.

   (A) were excused in serving in the jury
   (B) were excused in serving on the jury
   (C) were excused on serving in the jury
   (D) were excused from serving in the jury
   (E) were excused from serving on the jury

9. <u>Critics question if</u> the new Food Guide Pyramid is too heavily loaded with dairy products and grains, commodities supported by the USDA—the makers of the Pyramid.

   (A) Critics question if
   (B) Critics question whether
   (C) Critics question why
   (D) Critics question how
   (E) Critics of the USDA question if

10. Professionals who work with children, including doctors, teachers, and social workers, have an obligation <u>of reporting suspected abuse to</u> authorities.

    (A) of reporting suspected abuse to
    (B) of reporting suspected abuse with
    (C) for reporting suspected abuse to
    (D) to report suspected abuse to
    (E) with reporting abuse suspected of

11. With the release <u>of his fourth book of research, the associate professor had met the university's criteria for consideration of</u> promotion and tenure.

    (A) of his fourth book of research, the associate professor had met the university's criteria for consideration of
    (B) of his fourth book in research, the associate professor had met the university's criteria for consideration of
    (C) of his fourth book of research, the associate professor had met the university's criteria of consideration of
    (D) of his fourth book of research, the associate professor had met the university's criteria for consideration for
    (E) by his fourth book of research, the associate professor had met the university's criteria for consideration of

12. Homing pigeons have <u>a sort of magnetic attraction for home</u>, which is why so many of the birds were used to deliver secret messages during World War II.

(A) a sort of magnetic attraction for home
(B) a magnetic attraction for home
(C) a sort of magnetic attraction to home
(D) a type of magnetic attraction for home
(E) a sort of magnetic attraction with home

13. In the 2000 controversy that captured the attention of the world, the relatives of six-year old Elian Gonzalez <u>appealed with the United States for his asylum from Cuba, but were forced to return him to his father and his homeland</u>.

(A) appealed with the United States for his asylum from Cuba, but were forced to return him to his father and his homeland
(B) appealed to the United States for his asylum from Cuba, but were forced to return him to his father and his homeland
(C) appealed with the United States concerning his asylum from Cuba, but were forced to return him to his father and his homeland
(D) appealed with the United States for his asylum from Cuba, but were forced to return him with his father and his homeland
(E) appealed with the United States for his asylum from Cuba, but were forced into returning him to his father and his homeland

14. Lawyers in Massachusetts are working to abolish a long list of antiquated laws, some of which can send a citizen <u>to jail for silly offenses like buying a rabbit</u> or spitting on a steamboat.

(A) to jail for silly offenses like buying a rabbit
(B) to jail for silly offenses as buying a rabbit
(C) to jail for silly offenses such as buying a rabbit
(D) to jail over silly offenses like buying a rabbit
(E) to jail for such silly offenses like buying a rabbit

15. <u>Because of it being damaged</u>, the space shuttle could not reenter the Earth's atmosphere; the crew had to make a daring attempt to repair the vessel before they could come home.

(A) Because of it being damaged
(B) The reason it was damaged
(C) Having it been damaged
(D) Because of it having been damaged
(E) Because it was damaged

16. Many people are surprised to learn <u>that the internet is different from the</u> World Wide Web; the net is a giant infrastructure that contains the web, along with many other subnetworks.

(A) that the internet is different from the
(B) that the internet is different than the
(C) that the internet is different with the
(D) the internet is different from the
(E) how the internet is different than the

Idiom Problem Set Answer Key

Correct answers are in bold.

1. <u>Perched atop</u> a high mountain ridge in the Andes, the Incan city of Machu Picchu is believed to have served as a country retreat for Incan nobility.

   (A) Perched atop
   (B) Perched high atop
   (C) Perched on top
   (D) Perched on
   (E) Perched above

Perched atop is correct idiom. Choice (A) is correct. While Choice (B) also uses *atop*, it adds a second *high* to the introductory phrase which changes the meaning of the original sentence.

2. Jacobs Field, completed in Cleveland in 1994, did much <u>to raise the energy and revive</u> a worn-down city formally referred to as "the mistake by the lake."

   (A) to raise the energy and revive
   (B) to raise the energy of a word down city and revive
   (C) to raise the energy and to revive
   (D) in reviving and raising the energy of
   (E) to revive and raise the energy of

The correct idiom is *to raise the X of Y*. Without the preposition *of*, the idiom no longer makes sense. Choice (E) correctly states *to raise the energy of*, and puts the phrase closer to the object of the preposition so that it does not get lost in a lengthy sentence.

3. During a divorce, children are often <u>viewed like bargaining chips; it is important</u> for parents to remember that a child's well-being must be considered separately from the division of property.

   (A) viewed like bargaining chips; it is important
   (B) viewed as bargaining chips; it is important
   (C) viewed to be bargaining chips; it is important
   (D) viewed like bargaining chips, and it is important
   (E) viewed like bargaining chips, so it is important

The correct idiom is *viewed as*. The current sentence incorrectly uses *viewed like*. Choice (B) uses the correct idiom. The semicolon is correctly used in the sentence, so Choices (D) and (E) are incorrect.

4. Upon his death, it was discovered that Secretariat's heart <u>was bigger by three times the size of an average horse</u>, which many believe to be the reason for the stallion's stunning speed.

   (A) was bigger by three times the size of an average horse
   (B) was three times the size bigger of an average horse
   (C) was three times the size larger of an average horse's heart
   (D) was three times the size of an average horse's heart
   (E) was three times as large as an average horse

The correct idiom is *X is three times the size of Y* or *X is three times as large as Y*. Both (B) and (C) can be eliminated as they do not follow this format. Choice (E) is incorrect due to an illogical comparison; it compares Secretariat's heart to the average horse, rather than to the average horse's heart. Choice (D) is correct.

5. A recent study indicates that more and more college graduates are opting <u>to rent a home or apartment instead of</u> to buy real estate—a trend fueled by rising market costs and new spending habits.

   (A) to rent a home or apartment instead of
   (B) to rent a home or apartment rather than
   (C) to rent a home or apartment opposed to
   (D) renting a home or apartment instead of
   (E) renting a home or apartment instead of choosing

The preferred idiom when discussing choice is *to X rather than to Y*. The current sentence incorrectly uses *instead of: to X instead of to Y*. Choices (D) and (E) incorrectly change verb forms, and Choice (C) uses the faulty idiom *to X opposed to Y*.

6. Spam, the unsolicited e-mails that litter inboxes across the world, <u>is estimated at 90% of all internet traffic</u> in the United States today.

   (A) is estimated at 90% of all internet traffic
   (B) is estimated for 90% of all internet traffic
   (C) is estimated to be 90% of all internet traffic
   (D) is estimated at 90% in all internet traffic
   (E) is estimated as 90% of all internet traffic

The correct idiom is *estimated to be*. Only (C) makes this correction. All other answer choices contain incorrect idiom.

7. Here at PowerScore, we <u>arrange with our customers access to</u> the Online Student Area prior to the start of the course; this enables the students to read pre-course material and take a practice test.

    (A) arrange with our customers access to
    (B) arrange between our customers access to
    (C) arrange for our customers to access
    (D) arrange with our customers to access
    (E) arrange for our customers to access to

The correct idiom is *arrange <u>for</u> X to Y*. Choices (A), (B), (D), and (E) all contain incorrect idiom. (C) is correct.

8. Of the 112 potential jurors, twenty-six <u>were excused in serving in the jury</u> because they had read about the case in the newspaper.

    (A) were excused in serving in the jury
    (B) were excused in serving on the jury
    (C) were excused on serving in the jury
    (D) were excused from serving in the jury
    (E) were excused from serving on the jury

This sentence has two faulty idiom phrases. The correct expressions are *X was excused from Y* and *on the jury*. Choice (E) makes both corrections.

9. <u>Critics question if</u> the new Food Guide Pyramid is too heavily loaded with dairy products and grains, commodities supported by the USDA—the makers of the Pyramid.

    (A) Critics question if
    (B) Critics question whether
    (C) Critics question why
    (D) Critics question how
    (E) Critics of the USDA question if

The correction idiom is *question <u>whether</u>*. Only (B) uses an idiomatic expression.

10. Professionals who work with children, including doctors, teachers, and social workers, have an obligation <u>of reporting suspected abuse to</u> authorities.

    (A) of reporting suspected abuse to
    (B) of reporting suspected abuse with
    (C) for reporting suspected abuse to
    (D) to report suspected abuse to
    (E) with reporting abuse suspected of

The idiom is *obligation <u>to</u> X*. Choice (D) is the only choice with correct idiom.

11. With the release <u>of his fourth book of research, the associate professor had met the university's criteria for consideration of</u> promotion and tenure.

    (A) of his fourth book of research, the associate professor had met the university's criteria for consideration of
    (B) of his fourth book in research, the associate professor had met the university's criteria for consideration of
    (C) of his fourth book of research, the associate professor had met the university's criteria of consideration of
    (D) of his fourth book of research, the associate professor had met the university's criteria for consideration for
    (E) by his fourth book of research, the associate professor had met the university's criteria for consideration of

The correct idiom is *consideration for*. This sentence becomes confusing because so much of it is underlined. Check the expressions in the underlined portion one at a time; *release of, book of research, criteria for,* and *consideration of.* All are correct idiom except for the last one. It should be *consideration for*.

12. Homing pigeons have <u>a sort of magnetic attraction for home</u>, which is why so many of the birds were used to deliver secret messages during World War II.

    (A) a sort of magnetic attraction for home
    (B) a magnetic attraction for home
    (C) a sort of magnetic attraction to home
    (D) a type of magnetic attraction for home
    (E) a sort of magnetic attraction with home

The idiom in question is *attraction to X.* Choice (C) is correct.

13. In the 2000 controversy that captured the attention of the world, the relatives of six-year old Elian Gonzalez <u>appealed with the United States for his asylum from Cuba, but were forced to return him to his father and his homeland.</u>

    (A) appealed with the United States for his asylum from Cuba, but were forced to return him to his father and his homeland
    (B) appealed to the United States for his asylum from Cuba, but were forced to return him to his father and his homeland
    (C) appealed with the United States concerning his asylum from Cuba, but were forced to return him to his father and his homeland
    (D) appealed with the United States for his asylum from Cuba, but were forced to return him with his father and his homeland
    (E) appealed with the United States for his asylum from Cuba, but were forced into returning him to his father and his homeland

The idiom in question is *appealed to X for Y.* Only Choice (B) is right. The other expressions in the underlined portion are all idiomatic.

14. Lawyers in Massachusetts are working to abolish a long list of antiquated laws, some of which can send a citizen <u>to jail for silly offenses like buying a rabbit</u> or spitting on a steamboat.

   (A) to jail for silly offenses like buying a rabbit
   (B) to jail for silly offenses as buying a rabbit
   (C) to jail for silly offenses such as buying a rabbit
   (D) to jail over silly offenses like buying a rabbit
   (E) to jail for such silly offenses like buying a rabbit

When introducing a list of examples, *such as* should be used. *Like* is a preposition used to compare two things. Choice (C) is correct.

15. <u>Because of it being damaged</u>, the space shuttle could not reenter the Earth's atmosphere; the crew had to make a daring attempt to repair the vessel before they could come home.

   (A) Because of it being damaged
   (B) The reason it was damaged
   (C) Having it been damaged
   (D) Because of it having been damaged
   (E) Because it was damaged

The correct idiomatic expression is *because X was Y*, as in Choice (E). The remaining choices are all wordy or unidiomatic.

16. Many people are surprised to learn <u>that the internet is different from the</u> World Wide Web; the net is a giant infrastructure that contains the web, along with many other subnetworks.

   (A) that the internet is different from the
   (B) that the internet is different than the
   (C) that the internet is different with the
   (D) the internet is different than the
   (E) how the internet is different than the

The sentence is correct. *Different from* is correct idiom. Both (B), (D), and (E) contain the incorrect *different than*. (C) is incorrect with *different with*.

CHAPTER NINE: ERRORS INVOLVING STYLE

Wordy Language

There is a common misconception among many students and even some professionals that a longer, more verbose sentence creates a more formal, eloquent essay. But long-winded sentences lead to overworked readers, who often lose the meaning of the sentence in the sea of meaningless words. Sentences such as these are dismissed by English teachers as "wordy." Concise sentences are preferred, meaning that much is expressed in few words. On the GMAT, you will encounter wordy sentences in which you must choose a concise correction.

Your analytical writing assignment must also avoid wordiness and redundancy.

There are two types of wordiness to avoid on the GMAT. The first type is wordy expressions, which are common in everyday speech. Look at an example:

> Regardless of the fact that Jay Gatsby had become a millionaire, it is obvious that his sense of accomplishment was not fulfilled until the day that he was able to win Daisy's heart.   [*Incorrect*]

There are three very wordy expressions in this sentence; *regardless of the fact, it is obvious that,* and *until the day he was able to win.* These phrases can be removed or shortened in order to create a more concise sentence:

> <u>Although</u> Jay Gatsby had become a millionaire, his sense of accomplishment was not fulfilled <u>until</u> he <u>won</u> Daisy's heart.   [*Correct*]

Although shorter, this sentence is stronger, more vivid, and more direct than its wordy predecessor.

Examine some examples of common wordy expressions and their concise corrections. A much more detailed list of wordy expressions is available in the appendix.

Wordy Expression	*Concise Correction*
after the conclusion of	after
at this point in time	now
despite the fact that	although, even though, despite
due to the fact that	because, because of, since, for, as
excessive number of	too many
in order to	to
in the event that	if
is in a position to	can
regardless of the fact that	although, despite

While the wordy expressions in the chart are common errors in everyday speech, some wordiness is created by the context of the sentence. The author may use a pronoun and a second verb when a compound verb would have sufficed. Or there may be a prepositional phrase modifying a noun, when a one-word adjective might have accomplished the same feat. Try an example:

> Many border collies, intelligent working dogs used on ranches, have been known to herd cattle without their being trained.   [*Incorrect*]

This sentence adds an unnecessary pronoun: *their*. In fact, the pronoun adds ambiguity and awkwardness, causing the reader to briefly wonder if the *cattle* were untrained. But upon a second reading, it is evident that the prepositional phrases at the end of the sentence refer to border collies. Remove the wordy *their* and the sentence is less awkward and more concise:

> Many border collies, intelligent working dogs used on ranches, have been known to herd cattle without being trained.   [*Correct*]

Look at another:

> The proceeds from the charity auction were used in the funding of the new playground equipment at the town park.   [*Incorrect*]

The sentence is awkward because of the prepositional phrase *in the funding of*. The verb *used* needs an object of the verb in an infinitive form:

> The proceeds from the charity auction were used *to fund* the new playground equipment at the town park.   [*Correct*]

Be wary of an unnecessary repeated subject on a Sentence Correction question. A subject need only appear one time in a clause:

> Upon reaching the crocodile-filled river, the gazelles, which are a type of antelope, they swim across in a large herd to increase their group survival rate.   [*Incorrect*]

The subject of this sentence is *gazelles*, which is stated just after the introductory phrase (*upon reaching the crocodile-filled river*). A relative clause (*which are a type of antelope*) follows the subject. Remember, relative clauses add modifying information, but can be removed without ruining the sentence. If we take this relative clause away, the error is much more obvious:

> Upon reaching the crocodile-filled river, the *gazelles they* swim across in a large herd to increase their group survival rate.

This sentence has unnecessarily repeated the subject after a relative clause.

To correct the sentence, simply remove the second subject, *they*:

> Upon reaching the crocodile-filled river, the gazelles, which are a type of antelope, swim across in a large herd to increase their group survival rate. [*Correct*]

Because wordiness is often more of an offense in style rather than an outright error in grammar, it is commonly a secondary correction on the GMAT. A sentence will likely contain a blatant error in grammar, such as in subject verb agreement or verb tense, with two answer choices that correct the major error. However, only one of those answer choices will present a concise correction for the bout of wordiness. Look at an example:

> Researchers have proven that eating broccoli helps <u>in the prevention of cancer due to the fact that they contain</u> multiple cancer-fighting chemicals.
>
> (A) in the prevention of cancer due to the fact that they contain
> (B) in the prevention of cancer since they contain
> (C) prevent cancer due to the fact that they are containing
> (D) in the prevention of cancer due to the fact that it contains
> (E) prevent cancer because it contains

The main error in this sentence is that the pronoun <u>*they*</u> does not agree with its antecedent *broccoli*. Choices (D) and (E) change *they* to *it*, correcting the most prominent error. However, the sentence contains two secondary errors involving wordiness; *in the prevention of* can be economically written as *prevent*, and *due to the fact that* is a wordy expression that can be replaced with *because*. Only choice (E) corrects the main pronoun antecedent agreement error while also correcting the wordy language.

Expect to see wordiness errors in a large number of the questions in *The Official Guide to GMAT Review*.

Redundant Expressions

A subcategory of wordiness is redundancy, in which unnecessary repetition detracts from a sentence. One type of redundant phrase occurs when a word is used to modify another word that is defined by the first word. Study an example:

terrible disaster

Isn't a disaster by definition *terrible*? You don't hear of fantastic disasters, or pretty good disasters, or even mediocre disasters. They are all terrible! So it would be a terrible mistake to allow this redundant expression to go uncorrected on the GMAT.

Beware of these other redundant expressions:

advance planning	meet together
all year round	necessary requirement
annually each year	new breakthrough
biography of his life	past history
close proximity	postpone until later
customary habit	protest against
end result	reduced down
essential requirement	repeat again
exactly identical	reverse back
forward progress	rising increase
free gift	sharing the same
group together	temporary loan
honest truth	usual habit
joint cooperation	wealthy millionaire

Unfortunately, redundant expressions will not always be situated next to each other in a GMAT sentence:

The plummeting attendance figures have fallen so low that the owner closed the speedway.　　[*Incorrect*]

In this sentence, the word *plummeting* has already established that the figures have *fallen* and are *low*, so it is redundant to mention this again. The sentence must be edited:

The plummeting attendance figures caused the owner to close the speedway.　　[*Correct*]

Finally, beware of conjunctions becoming redundant. Certain conjunctions correlate and are meant to work together, like *not only..but also* and *both..and*. However, when these are not correctly matched and they are used with another conjunction, such as *and*, *as well as*, and *and also*, it creates a redundant expression:

> Studies of several successful entrepreneurs have shown that they all share two common characteristics; they are both motivated by an overwhelming need for achievement as well as driven by desire for independence. [*Incorrect*]

As a coordinating conjunction, *both* should always be accompanied by *and*. However, in this sentence, *as well as* takes the place of *and*, and the conjunctions become redundant. A sentence does not need *both* and *as well as* to express the presence of two items. Correct the sentence with *and*:

> Studies of several successful entrepreneurs have shown that they all share two common characteristics; they are *both* motivated by an overwhelming need for achievement *and* driven by desire for independence.   [*Correct*]

Redundancy occurs a small portion of the sentences in *The Official Guide to GMAT Review*.

Wordy Language and Redundant Expressions Problem Set

Please complete the problem set and review the answer key and explanations. Answers on page 208-209.

1. A new appliance's energy guide label, which is the yellow tag required by the federal government, <u>displays the yearly cost of operating that appliance on an annual basis</u>.

   (A) displays the yearly cost of operating that appliance on an annual basis
   (B) displays the yearly operating cost of that appliance on an annual basis
   (C) displays the yearly operating cost of that appliance
   (D) displays the annual cost of operating that appliance each year
   (E) displays the per year cost of operating that appliance

2. The senator, <u>who had previously been in opposition of government funding of stem-cell research,</u> reconsidered her position when her party's presidential candidate promised to support its expansion.

   (A) who had previously been in opposition of government funding of stem-cell research
   (B) who had been in prior opposition to government funding of stem-cell research
   (C) who had previously been in opposition of government funded stem-cell research
   (D) who had previously been in opposition of government stem-cell research funding
   (E) who had previously opposed government funding of stem-cell research

3. <u>Because Jupiter's gravity disrupts Mars' orbit, astronomers cannot precisely determine</u> the last time that Mars was this close to Earth, nor can they predict when it will be this close again.

   (A) Because Jupiter's gravity disrupts Mars' orbit, astronomers cannot precisely determine
   (B) Due to the fact that Jupiter's gravity disrupts Mars' orbit, astronomers cannot precisely determine
   (C) Since Jupiter's gravity disrupts Mars' orbit, astronomers cannot precisely determine
   (D) Because Jupiter's gravity disrupts Mars' orbit, astronomers cannot determine with precision
   (E) Because Jupiter's gravity disrupts the orbit of Mars, astronomers cannot precisely determine

Wordy Language and Redundant Expressions Problem Set

Please complete the problem set and review the answer key and explanations. Answers on page 208-209.

4. With the advent of MP3 players, researchers believe that the Compact Disc <u>may in the very near future face the same fate as the long-playing record</u>.

   (A) may in the very near future face the same fate as the long-playing record
   (B) might face in the very near future the same fate as the long-playing record
   (C) might in the very near future face the same fate as the long-playing record
   (D) may soon face the same fate as the long-playing record
   (E) in near future may face the same fate as the long-playing record

5. <u>As history has revealed, a sudden irrational panic among stockholders has caused the Dow Jones Industrial Average to plummet in the past</u>.

   (A) As history has revealed, a sudden irrational panic among stockholders has caused the Dow Jones Industrial Average to plummet in the past
   (B) A sudden irrational panic among stockholders has caused the Dow Jones Industrial Average to plummet in the past, as revealed by history
   (C) A sudden irrational panic among stockholders can cause the Dow Jones Industrial Average to plummet in the past
   (D) As history has revealed, a sudden irrational panic can cause the Dow Jones Industrial Average stockholders to plummet in the past
   (E) As history has revealed, a sudden irrational panic among stockholders can cause the Dow Jones Industrial Average to plummet

6. The Coast Guard believes that the crew of the Edmund Fitzgerald was unaware that the boat was taking on water, not only because of their last radio transmission, but also <u>because of the lack of a distress signal, too</u>.

   (A) because of the lack of a distress signal, too
   (B) because of the lack of a distress signal
   (C) because the distress signal was lacking, too
   (D) the lack of a distress signal, too
   (E) due to the lack of a distress signal, too

Wordy Language and Redundant Expressions Problem Set Answer Key

Correct answers are in bold.

1. A new appliance's energy guide label, which is the yellow tag required by the federal government, <u>displays the yearly cost of operating that appliance on an annual basis.</u>

    (A) displays the yearly cost of operating that appliance on an annual basis
    (B) displays the yearly operating cost of that appliance on an annual basis
    (C) displays the yearly operating cost of that appliance
    (D) displays the annual cost of operating that appliance each year
    (E) displays the per year cost of operating that appliance

The underlined portion of the sentence contains a redundant expression and is wordy. First of all, *yearly* and *annual* mean the same thing, so only one is needed. Choices (C) and (E) make this correction. Second, *cost of operating* can be shortened to *operating cost*. Choice (C) is correct.

2. The senator, <u>who had previously been in opposition of government funding of stem-cell research,</u> reconsidered her position when her party's presidential candidate promised to support its expansion.

    (A) who had previously been in opposition of government funding of stem-cell research
    (B) who had been in prior opposition to government funding of stem-cell research
    (C) who had previously been in opposition of government funded stem-cell research
    (D) who had previously been in opposition of government stem-cell research funding
    (E) who had previously opposed government funding of stem-cell research

The expression *been in opposition of* is wordy and unidiomatic. The only correction is *opposed*, as in Choice (E).

3. <u>Because Jupiter's gravity disrupts Mars' orbit, astronomers cannot precisely determine</u> the last time that Mars was this close to Earth, nor can they predict when it will be this close again.

    (A) Because Jupiter's gravity disrupts Mars' orbit, astronomers cannot precisely determine
    (B) Due to the fact that Jupiter's gravity disrupts Mars' orbit, astronomers cannot precisely determine
    (C) Since Jupiter's gravity disrupts Mars' orbit, astronomers cannot precisely determine
    (D) Because Jupiter's gravity disrupts Mars' orbit, astronomers cannot determine with precision
    (E) Because Jupiter's gravity disrupts the orbit of Mars, astronomers cannot precisely determine

The current sentence is better than any of the answer choices, so Choice (A) is correct. Choice (B) creates wordiness by removing *because*. Choice (C) uses a synonym for *because*, and *because* is better to begin an introductory clause. Choice (D) creates a wordy phrase with *determine with precision*. Choice (E) creates the wordy *orbit of Mars*.

4. With the advent of MP3 players, researchers believe that the Compact Disc <u>may in the very near future face the same fate as the long playing record</u>.

    (A) may in the very near future face the same fate as the long-playing record
    (B) might face in the very near future the same fate as the long-playing record
    (C) might in the very near future face the same fate as the long-playing record
    (D) may soon face the same fate as the long-playing record
    (E) in near future may face the same fate as the long-playing record

The wordy expression in this sentence is *in the very near future*. The most economical version of this phrase is *soon*, as seen in Choice (D).

5. <u>As history has revealed, a sudden irrational panic among stockholders has caused the Dow Jones Industrial Average to plummet in the past</u>.

    (A) As history has revealed, a sudden irrational panic among stockholders has caused the Dow Jones Industrial Average to plummet in the past
    (B) A sudden irrational panic among stockholders has caused the Dow Jones Industrial Average to plummet in the past, as revealed by history
    (C) A sudden irrational panic among stockholders can cause the Dow Jones Industrial Average to plummet in the past
    (D) As history has revealed, a sudden irrational panic can cause the Dow Jones Industrial Average stockholders to plummet in the past
    (E) As history has revealed, a sudden irrational panic among stockholders can cause the Dow Jones Industrial Average to plummet

The sentence has a redundancy issue. The introductory clause, *as history has revealed*, shows that the event took place in the past. Therefore, *in the past* is redundant anywhere else in the sentence. This eliminates Choices (A), (B), and (D). Choice (C) has a verb tense problem. *Can cause* does not agree with *in the past*. However, the same verb in the correct answer choice, (E) shows that the panic has happened in the past and can happen again in the future.

6. The Coast Guard believes that the crew of the Edmund Fitzgerald was unaware that the boat was taking on water, not only because of their last radio transmission, but also <u>because of the lack of a distress signal, too</u>.

    (A) because of the lack of a distress signal, too
    (B) because of the lack of a distress signal
    (C) because the distress signal was lacking, too
    (D) the lack of a distress signal, too
    (E) due to the lack of a distress signal, too

This sentence also has a redundant expression. Because it is already using *also*, *too* is redundant. Only Choice (B) removes *too*, making it the correct answer choice. Choice (C) is awkward and unparallel. Choice (D) is unparallel without *because*. Choice (E) is wordy.

THE POWERSCORE GMAT SENTENCE CORRECTION BIBLE

CHAPTER TEN: MULTIPLE ERRORS

Double and Triple Errors

There are often multiple errors in a sentence on the GMAT. Sentences with two errors occur in nearly one-third of the questions in *The Official Guide to GMAT Review*. Triple error sentences occur less frequently, but you are still likely to encounter one or two on your test.

As we saw in the sections on passive voice and wordiness, sentences with multiple errors often have a blatant main error that is easily identified and a secondary error that might be much harder to spot. It is extremely important to read all of the answer choices; Choice (B) or (C) might correct the main error, but fail to address the secondary issue. You might not even realize that there is a second error until you read Choices (D) and (E). Let's look at an example:

> During the charity walk-a-thon, the number of miles walked by the fifteen volunteers <u>were combined to total 110 miles, a distance that is about Long Island's length</u>.
>
> (A) were combined to total 110 miles, a distance that is about Long Island's length
> (B) were combined to total 110 miles, a distance about the length of Long Island
> (C) was combined to total 110 miles, a distance that is about Long Island's length
> (D) was combined to total 110 miles, about Long Island's length
> (E) was combined to total 110 miles, a distance about the length of Long Island

The major error in this sentence involves subject verb agreement. The subject, *number*, is singular, but the verb, *were*, is plural. We can eliminate Choices (A) and (B) because they do not correct this major error. Choice (C) changes the plural *were* to the singular *was*, and leaves the rest of the sentence as is. Many hasty test takers would choose (C) and move on to the next sentence. You must approach the GMAT much more cautiously! Choice (D) and (E) also change *were* to *was*, so you should examine each of these answers to see if any other corrections are made to the sentence. Choice (D) removed *a distance*, causing the sentence to become less clear and leaving *about* without a definite noun to modify. You can eliminate (D). Choice (E) has removed the wordy relative clause *that is* without ruining the meaning of the sentence. Choice (C) failed to do this. Choice (E) also uses a noun and prepositional phrase to discuss the length of Long Island, and this removes the bit of awkwardness that existed with the possessive formation *Long Island's length*. Choice (E) is best.

Although we eliminated choice (B) immediately, notice that it removed the wordy *that is* and reworded the awkward possessive. It corrected the minor errors, but ignored the main error. Choice (C) corrected the blatant error, but did not fix the flaw in style. Again, it is imperative to read each answer choice before making your selection!

Sentences with two or more errors appear in nearly one-third of Sentence Completion questions.

After Choice (A), be sure to read all of the remaining answer choices! In sentences with multiple errors, some choices will trick test takers by only correcting one of the errors.

Other sentences will have double or triple errors that are equally destructive in their grammatical downfalls. For example, a sentence might have an obvious error in pronoun agreement coupled with an equally blatant error in parallel structure. Whether a sentence has multiple secondary mistakes or multiple obvious errors, it will likely have misleading answer choices that only correct one of the errors rather than both. This is why it is imperative to read each answer choice before moving on; you may find one selection further down the list that has the same correction you just chose for one error, but goes one step further to correct another problem with the sentence.

The following practice set will not only test your ability to find multiple errors, but also your knowledge of all of the grammatical errors and usage flaws discussed in this book. Good luck!

Double and Triple Errors Problem Set

Please complete the problem set and review the answer key and explanations. Answers on page 217-224.

1. After the announcement that London would host the 2012 Olympics, the Olympic Committee revealed that Paris had <u>been in competition with London much longer than Madrid</u>.

   (A) been in competition with London much longer than Madrid
   (B) competed with London much longer than Madrid
   (C) been in competition with London much longer than had Madrid
   (D) competed with London much longer than had Madrid
   (E) been in competition much longer with London than Madrid

2. The manager believed that the sales contest was responsible for a reduction in absenteeism, <u>increase in customer satisfaction as well as an increase in employee morale</u>, and a boost in profits.

   (A) increase in customer satisfaction as well as an increase in employee morale
   (B) an increase in customer satisfaction and in employee morale
   (C) an increase in customer satisfaction along with employee morale
   (D) customer satisfaction increasing, along with employee morale
   (E) customer satisfaction and employee morale being increased

3. In ancient Greece, a male member of the Spartan society did not become a full citizen <u>until when the age of thirty was reached</u>, at which point he had already given ten years of military service.

   (A) until when the age of thirty was reached
   (B) until the age of thirty was reached
   (C) until he reached the age of thirty
   (D) when the age of thirty was reached
   (E) until when he reached the age of thirty

4. In Aztec society, childbirth was compared to warfare, and women <u>who died in labor were honored in the same way as men who died in battle</u>.

   (A) who died in labor were honored in the same way as men who died in battle
   (B) whom died in labor were honored just as men whom died in battle
   (C) whom died in labor were honored in the same way as men whom died in battle
   (D) who died in labor were honored just as men who died in battle
   (E) in labor who died were honored in the same way as men in battle who died

5. Of all the musicians who attended Juilliard School, Yo-Yo Ma <u>is maybe the more prolific and definitely the most celebrated cellist, in large part due to his wide-ranging</u> repertoire.

   (A) is maybe the more prolific and definitely the most celebrated cellist, in large part due to his wide-ranging
   (B) is maybe the most prolific and definitely the most celebrated cellist, in large part due to his wide-ranging
   (C) is probably the most prolific and definitely the most celebrated cellist, in large part due to his wide-ranging
   (D) is probably the more prolific and definitely the most celebrated cellist, in large part because of his wide-ranging
   (E) is maybe the most prolific and definitely the most celebrated cellist, in large part because of his wide-ranging

6. Unlike most other crustaceans, such as lobsters, crabs, and barnacles, <u>dry land provides a terrestrial habitat for the woodlouse</u>.

   (A) dry land provides a terrestrial habitat for the woodlouse
   (B) a terrestrial habitat is the home of a woodlouse
   (C) woodlice live in a terrestrial habitat
   (D) dry land provides a terrestrial habitat for woodlice
   (E) the woodlouse lives in a dry, terrestrial habitat

Double and Triple Errors Problem Set

Please complete the problem set and review the answer key and explanations. Answers on page 217-224.

7. Many South Carolina residents who have <u>displayed or flew its state flag believe that</u> the crescent above the palmetto tree is a moon; further research reveals that it is actually a symbol from the Confederate uniform.

   (A) displayed or flew its state flag believe that
   (B) displayed or flown their state flag believe that
   (C) displayed or flown its state flag believe that
   (D) displayed or flew their state flag believe
   (E) displayed or flown its state flag believe

8. Several of the former school teachers said they left teaching because they felt more like they were babysitting <u>than as if young minds were educated</u>; one even figured out that he made 69¢ per hour per child.

   (A) than as if young minds were educated
   (B) than like young minds were educated
   (C) than like they educated young minds
   (D) than as if they educated young minds
   (E) than educating young minds

9. The defendant adamantly reassured his supporters that his guilty plea was neither an admission of guilt <u>or that he was indicating he was surrendering</u>.

   (A) or that he was indicating he was surrendering
   (B) or surrender
   (C) nor was it a surrender
   (D) nor was he indicating he was surrendering
   (E) nor an indication of surrender

10. In order for the institute to release a report on workplace diversity, researchers are studying <u>the amount of progress and changes that had occurred</u> since 1950.

    (A) the amount of progress and changes that had occurred
    (B) the amount of progress and changes which have occurred
    (C) the amount of progress and the amount of changes that have occurred
    (D) the amount of progress and the number of changes that have occurred
    (E) the progress and changes that had occurred

11. Mozambique contains Africa's largest coastal plain, <u>much of which is below sea level</u>, making the country highly susceptible to cyclone devastation.

    (A) much of which is below sea level
    (B) many of which are below sea level
    (C) much of which are below sea level
    (D) many of which are below sea level
    (E) much below sea level

12. Tropical cyclones <u>are referred to as hurricanes in the North Atlantic and North Pacific Oceans, typhoons in the Northwest Pacific Ocean, and in the Indian Ocean they are called cyclones.</u>

    (A) are referred to as hurricanes in the North Atlantic and North Pacific Oceans, typhoons in the Northwest Pacific Ocean, and in the Indian Ocean they are called cyclones
    (B) are referred to as hurricanes in the North Atlantic and North Pacific Oceans, as typhoons in the Northwest Pacific Ocean, and cyclones in the Indian Ocean
    (C) are called hurricanes in the North Atlantic and North Pacific Oceans, called typhoons in the Northwest Pacific Ocean, and in the Indian Ocean they are called cyclones
    (D) are referred to as hurricanes in the North Atlantic and North Pacific Oceans, typhoons in the Northwest Pacific Ocean, and cyclones in the Indian Ocean
    (E) are in reference to hurricanes in the North Atlantic and North Pacific Oceans, typhoons in the Northwest Pacific Ocean, and cyclones in the Indian Ocean

13. Researchers fear that the medicine may not work the same for a child <u>that has leukemia as an adult with the disease</u>.

    (A) that has leukemia as an adult with the disease
    (B) that has leukemia as for an adult with the disease
    (C) who has leukemia as for an adult with the disease
    (D) who has leukemia as for the disease in an adult
    (E) which has leukemia as an adult with the disease

Double and Triple Errors Problem Set

Please complete the problem set and review the answer key and explanations. Answers on page 217-224.

14. Since 2000, the number of registered lobbyists in Washington, D.C. <u>have grown by more than twice, due to the government growing rapidly</u> and the single party control of the executive and legislative branches.

   (A) have grown by more than twice, due to the government growing rapidly
   (B) has more than doubled, due to the government growing rapidly
   (C) has grown by more than twice, due to the rapid growth of government
   (D) have increased by twice as much, due to the government rapidly growing
   (E) has more than doubled, due to the rapidly growing government

15. Published in 1892, <u>Charlotte Gilman Perkins tells the story of a woman's descent in madness when she is confined to a room by her dictatorial husband in *The Yellow Wallpaper*</u>.

   (A) Charlotte Gilman Perkins tells the story of a woman's descent in madness when she is confined to a room by her dictatorial husband in *The Yellow Wallpaper*
   (B) *The Yellow Wallpaper*, by Charlotte Gilman Perkins, describes a woman's descent into madness when she is confined to a room by her dictatorial husband
   (C) Charlotte Gilman Perkins' *The Yellow Wallpaper* tells the story of a woman's descent in madness when she is confined to a room by her dictatorial husband
   (D) a woman's descent in madness when she is confined to a room by her dictatorial husband is told by Charlotte Gilman Perkins in *The Yellow Wallpaper*
   (E) *The Yellow Wallpaper* tells of a woman's descent into madness when she is confined to a room by her dictatorial husband, a story by Charlotte Gilman Perkins.

16. By a vote of 98 to 1, the United States Senate enacted the USA Patriot Act, <u>which grants law enforcement officials greater authority in investigating suspected terrorists</u>.

   (A) which grants law enforcement officials greater authority in investigating suspected terrorists
   (B) that grants law enforcement officials greater authority to investigate suspected terrorists
   (C) granting law enforcement officials greater authority with investigating suspected terrorists
   (D) which will grant law enforcement officials greater authority for suspected terrorists investigations
   (E) having granted law enforcement officials greater authority for investigating suspected terrorists

17. Of the dozen hybrid automobiles tested, three of the models that used battery power <u>for the conservation of gasoline went over 250 miles per gallon.</u>

   (A) for the conservation of gasoline went over 250 miles per gallon
   (B) for the conservation of gasoline had 250 miles per gallon
   (C) to conserve gasoline got over 250 miles per gallon
   (D) to conserve gasoline went at 250 miles per gallon
   (E) for conserving gasoline went over 250 miles per gallon

Double and Triple Errors Problem Set

Please complete the problem set and review the answer key and explanations. Answers on page 217-224.

18. While the Fair Labor Standards Act requires youth to be 14 year of age or older to work in non-agriculture jobs, children <u>will have been allowed to baby-sit, deliver newspapers, and to perform in theatrical productions at any age.</u>

    (A) will have been allowed to baby-sit, deliver newspapers, and to perform in theatrical productions at any age
    (B) have been allowed to baby-sit, to deliver newspapers, and to perform in theatrical productions at any age
    (C) will have been allowed to baby-sit, deliver newspapers, and they are able to perform in theatrical productions at any age
    (D) are allowed to baby-sit, deliver newspapers, and perform in theatrical productions at any age
    (E) are allowed to baby-sit, deliver newspapers, and they are able to perform in theatrical productions at any age

19. The members of the hiring committee agreed that if the applicant had been honest <u>about his lacking a college degree, they would hire him</u>; unfortunately, the lie cost him the job.

    (A) about his lacking a college degree, they would hire him
    (B) concerning his lacking of a college degree, they would hire him
    (C) about the lack of a college degree, they would still hire him
    (D) about his lack of a college degree, they would have hired him
    (E) as to his lacking a college degree, they were hiring him

20. Hunters and warriors, <u>bison were hunted by the native Navajo, and they used the hides for shelters and meat for food.</u>

    (A) bison were hunted by the native Navajo, and they used the hides for shelters and meat for food
    (B) the native Navajo hunted bison, using the hides for shelters and meat for food
    (C) bison were hunted by the native Navajo, and used shelters and for food
    (D) the native Navajo had hunted bison, and they used the hides for shelters and meat for food
    (E) hunting by the native Navajo included bison, which they used for shelters and food

Double and Triple Errors Problem Set Answer Key

Correct answers are in bold.

1. After the announcement that London would host the 2012 Olympics, the Olympic Committee revealed that Paris had <u>been in competition with London much longer than Madrid</u>.

    (A) been in competition with London much longer than Madrid
    (B) competed with London much longer than Madrid
    (C) been in competition with London much longer than had Madrid
    (D) competed with London much longer than had Madrid
    (E) been in competition much longer with London than Madrid

The comparison in the sentence is incomplete. Right now, both *with* and *had* can follow *longer than*, so the comparison is incomplete. You do not know whether Paris had competed with London much longer than Paris had competed with Madrid, or whether Paris had competed with London longer than Madrid had completed with London. Choices (A), (B), and (E) are therefore wrong. Choices (C) and (D) let us know that it is the latter (Paris had competed with London longer than Madrid had competed with London), but Choice (D) corrects the wordy phrase *been in competition with*. Choice (D) is correct.

2. The manager believed that the sales contest was responsible for a reduction in absenteeism, <u>increase in customer satisfaction as well as an increase in employee morale</u>, and a boost in profits.

    (A) increase in customer satisfaction as well as an increase in employee morale
    (B) an increase in customer satisfaction and in employee morale
    (C) an increase in customer satisfaction along with employee morale
    (D) customer satisfaction increasing, along with employee morale
    (E) customer satisfaction and employee morale being increased

The main error is a lack of parallelism between three noun phrases in a series *(a reduction in, increase in, and a boost in)*. *An* must be added before the second noun phrase *(increase in)* not only to make the series parallel, but also to signify that *increase* is a noun rather than a verb. We can eliminate choices (A), (D), and (E) based on this analysis. The secondary error is one of wordiness and redundancy. *As well as* is wordy, and the use of *increase* twice is redundant. Choice (C) uses *along with*, which is wordy and unidiomatic. Choice (B) is best.

3. In ancient Greece, a male member of the Spartan society did not become a full citizen <u>until when the age of thirty was reached</u>, at which point he had already given ten years of military service.

    (A) until when the age of thirty was reached
    (B) until the age of thirty was reached
    (C) until he reached the age of thirty
    (D) when the age of thirty was reached
    (E) until when he reached the age of thirty

The most blatant error in the sentence is the unidiomatic phrase *until when*. It should strictly be *until*, eliminating (D) and (E). The other error in the sentence is the use of the passive voice—*the age of thirty was reached [by him]*. The active voice—*he reached the age of thirty*—must be used to match the active voice in the final clause (*he had already given*). Choice (C) makes this second correction.

4. In Aztec society, childbirth was compared to warfare, and women who died in labor were honored in the same way as men who died in battle.

   (A) **who died in labor were honored in the same way as men who died in battle**
   (B) whom died in labor were honored just as men whom died in battle
   (C) whom died in labor were honored in the same way as men whom died in battle
   (D) who died in labor were honored just as men who died in battle
   (E) in labor who died were honored in the same way as men in battle who died

The sentence is grammatically correct. Choices (B) and (C) incorrectly use *whom*. Choices (B) and (D) incorrectly use *just*—an incomplete comparison is created without *in the same way as*. And Choice (E) is an awkward nightmare.

5. Of all the musicians who attended Juilliard School, Yo-Yo Ma is maybe the more prolific and definitely the most celebrated cellist, in large part due to his wide-ranging repertoire.

   (A) is maybe the more prolific and definitely the most celebrated cellist, in large part due to his wide-ranging
   (B) is maybe the most prolific and definitely the most celebrated cellist, in large part due to his wide-ranging
   (C) **is probably the most prolific and definitely the most celebrated cellist, in large part due to his wide-ranging**
   (D) is probably the more prolific and definitely the most celebrated cellist, in large part because of his wide-ranging
   (E) is maybe the most prolific and definitely the most celebrated cellist, in large part because of his wide-ranging

The most flagrant error is the incorrect use of comparative degree. Yo-Yo Ma is being compared to all of the musicians who attended Juilliard, and the use of the word *all* indicates that more than two attended. This is verified by the use of *most* in the second part of the phrase. Therefore, *more prolific* must be *most prolific*. Choices (A) and (D) are eliminated. The other error is the unidiomatic use of *maybe*. The correct word is *probably*. This eliminates (B) and (E), leaving (C) as the best choice.

6. Unlike most other crustaceans, such as lobsters, crabs, and barnacles, dry land provides a terrestrial habitat for the woodlouse.

   (A) dry land provides a terrestrial habitat for the woodlouse
   (B) a terrestrial habitat is the home of a woodlouse
   (C) **woodlice live in a terrestrial habitat**
   (D) dry land provides a terrestrial habitat for woodlice
   (E) the woodlouse lives in a dry, terrestrial habitat

This sentence contains three errors. The most prominent error is the misplaced modifier in the introductory clause. Currently, *crustaceans* are compared to *dry land*. In order for the woodlouse to be compared to crustaceans, it must appear after the clause. Choices (A), (B), and (D) can be removed. The sentence also has a noun agreement error. *Crustaceans* is plural, but *woodlouse* is singular. The correct noun is *woodlice*. Finally, *dry land* and *terrestrial habitat* are redundant. Only one is needed. Choice (C) makes all three corrections.

7. Many South Carolina residents who have <u>displayed or flew its state flag believe that</u> the crescent above the palmetto tree is a moon; further research reveals that it is actually a symbol from the Confederate uniform.

   (A) displayed or flew its state flag believe that
   (B) displayed or flown their state flag believe that
   (C) displayed or flown its state flag believe that
   (D) displayed or flew their state flag believe
   (E) displayed or flown its state flag believe

The sentence has two main errors. One is the implied pronoun *its*. *South Carolina* is acting as an adjective in the sentence (modifying *residents*), so it cannot be the antecedent for *its*. The actual antecedent is *residents*, so the correct pronoun is *their*. This eliminates choice (A), (C), and (E). The second error is the incorrect form of the past participle of *to fly*. *Flew* is simple past tense, but *flown* must be used with *has*, *have*, or *had*. The verb is a compound verb, so *have* applies to both *to display* and *to fly*. Choice (B) makes both corrections.

8. Several of the former school teachers said they left teaching because they felt more like they were babysitting <u>than as if young minds were educated</u>; one even figured out that he made 69¢ per hour per child.

   (A) than as if young minds were educated
   (B) than like young minds were educated
   (C) than like they educated young minds
   (D) than as if they educated young minds
   (E) than educating young minds

The form of the comparison should be *more like X than Y*, in which the X and Y are parallel in structure. Since *babysitting* is not underlined, we cannot change it; therefore, the Y portion of the comparison must be parallel to the progressive verb *babysitting*. The other error is the unidiomatic *as if*. Choice (E) is the only one that uses a progressive verb form and removes the *as if*.

9. The defendant adamantly reassured his supporters that his guilty plea was neither an admission of guilt <u>or that he was indicating he was surrendering</u>.

   (A) or that he was indicating he was surrendering
   (B) or surrender
   (C) nor was it a surrender
   (D) nor was he indicating he was surrendering
   (E) nor an indication of surrender

The first error is in the correlative conjunction. *Neither* must always be with *nor* and never with *or*. This removes Choices (A) and (B). In a *neither..nor* statement, the format is *neither X nor Y* and the X and Y must be parallel. The X (*admission of guilt*) is a noun followed by a preposition and its object. While Choice (C) may be attractive to many test takers, Choice (E) has proper parallelism with a noun followed by a preposition and its object.

10. In order for the institute to release a report on workplace diversity, researchers are studying <u>the amount of progress and changes that had occurred</u> since 1950.

    (A) the amount of progress and changes that had occurred
    (B) the amount of progress and changes which have occurred
    (C) the amount of progress and the amount of changes that have occurred
    (D) the amount of progress and the number of changes that have occurred
    (E) the progress and changes that had occurred

There are two significant errors in the sentence. The first is the verb tense of *had occurred*. Currently, the phrase is in past perfect tense, which indicates that the action was started and completed in the past. Based on the verb *are studying*, which is not underlined, we know at the changes may continue to happen. The present perfect *have occurred* is the correct verb tense. This eliminates (A) and (E). The second error is the quantifier *the amount of*. This quantifier is used to modify non-count nouns, such as *progress*, but is also incorrectly modifying the count noun *changes* because it is part of the compound subject. *The number of* is used with count nouns, as in choice (D).

11. Mozambique contains Africa's largest coastal plain, <u>much of which is below sea level</u>, making the country highly susceptible to cyclone devastation.

    (A) much of which is below sea level
    (B) many of which are below sea level
    (C) much of which are below sea level
    (D) many of which are below sea level
    (E) much below sea level

This sentence is grammatically sound as it stands. Choice (B) and Choice (D) use the incorrect determiner (*many*). Choices (B), (C), and (D) use the incorrect verb (*are*), and Choice (E) creates ambiguity; is Mozambique far below sea level, or is much of the plain below sea level? Choice (A) is correct.

12. Tropical cyclones <u>are referred to as hurricanes in the North Atlantic and North Pacific Oceans, typhoons in the Northwest Pacific Ocean, and in the Indian Ocean they are called cyclones.</u>

    (A) are referred to as hurricanes in the North Atlantic and North Pacific Oceans, typhoons in the Northwest Pacific Ocean, and in the Indian Ocean they are called cyclones
    (B) are referred to as hurricanes in the North Atlantic and North Pacific Oceans, as typhoons in the Northwest Pacific Ocean, and cyclones in the Indian Ocean
    (C) are called hurricanes in the North Atlantic and North Pacific Oceans, called typhoons in the Northwest Pacific Ocean, and in the Indian Ocean they are called cyclones
    (D) are referred to as hurricanes in the North Atlantic and North Pacific Oceans, typhoons in the Northwest Pacific Ocean, and cyclones in the Indian Ocean
    (E) are in reference to hurricanes in the North Atlantic and North Pacific Oceans, typhoons in the Northwest Pacific Ocean, and cyclones in the Indian Ocean

Surprise! This sentence only contains one error. In a noun series, all three elements must be parallel: *cyclones are called X, Y, and Z*. Choice (D) makes the three phrases parallel. Choice (B) puts an *as* in the second element, but the rule states that the conjunction can appear solely in the first element or in all three elements, but not in only two of the elements. Choice (C) does not correct the parallel error, and uses the verb *called* in only two of the elements. Choice (E) creates a wordy version of the verb.

13. Researchers fear that the medicine may not work the same for a child <u>that has leukemia as an adult with the disease</u>.

    (A) that has leukemia as an adult with the disease
    (B) that has leukemia as for an adult with the disease
    (C) who has leukemia as for an adult with the disease
    (D) who has leukemia as for the disease in an adult
    (E) which has leukemia as an adult with the disease

The sentence has two errors. First, the comparison must be parallel. The correct parallel form is *the same for X as for Y*. We can eliminate Choices (A) and (E) because they do not use *for* for the second part of the comparison. We can also eliminate (D) because it compares a child to a disease, rather than a child to an adult. The second error is the relative pronoun *that*. A child is a person, so the correct pronoun is *who*. Choice (C) is correct.

14. Since 2000, the number of registered lobbyists in Washington, D.C. <u>have grown by more than twice, due to the government growing rapidly</u> and the single party control of the executive and legislative branches.

    (A) have grown by more than twice, due to the government growing rapidly
    (B) has more than doubled, due to the government growing rapidly
    (C) has grown by more than twice, due to the rapid growth of government
    (D) have increased by twice as much, due to the government rapidly growing
    (E) has more than doubled, due to the rapidly growing government

This sentence has three errors. The first is an error of subject verb agreement. The subject is *number* (not *lobbyists*), so the verb *have* does not agree. The correct verb is *has*, eliminating Choices (A) and (D). The second error is an unidiomatic expression. *Grown by more that twice* is incorrect idiom. The correct phrase is *more than doubled*. This eliminates Choice (C). The final error is in parallel structure. The correct format is *due to X and Y*, where X and Y are parallel. In the current sentence, the X consists of a noun and verb, while the Y consists of just a noun. Only Choice (E) takes care of the prior issues and makes X and Y parallel with two nouns (*government* and *control*).

15. Published in 1892, <u>Charlotte Gilman Perkins tells the story of a woman's descent in madness when she is confined to a room by her dictatorial husband in *The Yellow Wallpaper*</u>.

   (A) Charlotte Gilman Perkins tells the story of a woman's descent in madness when she is confined to a room by her dictatorial husband in *The Yellow Wallpaper*

   (B) *The Yellow Wallpaper*, by Charlotte Gilman Perkins, describes a woman's descent into madness when she is confined to a room by her dictatorial husband

   (C) Charlotte Gilman Perkins' *The Yellow Wallpaper* tells the story of a woman's descent in madness when she is confined to a room by her dictatorial husband

   (D) a woman's descent in madness when she is confined to a room by her dictatorial husband is told by Charlotte Gilman Perkins in *The Yellow Wallpaper*

   (E) *The Yellow Wallpaper* tells of a woman's descent into madness when she is confined to a room by her dictatorial husband, a story by Charlotte Gilman Perkins.

As the sentence is written now, *published in 1892* incorrectly modifies *Charlotte Gilman Perkins*, and people are not published! Choices (B), (C), and (E) make a correction that modifies the story, rather than the person, thus eliminating (A) and (D). Also, there is an idiom error with *descent*; the correct form is *descent into X*. Choices (B) and (E) make this correction. However, Choice (E) is awkward and has misplaced the modifying phrase *a story by Charlotte Gilman Perkins*. Choice (B) is best.

16. By a vote of 98 to 1, the United States Senate enacted the USA Patriot Act, <u>which grants law enforcement officials greater authority in investigating suspected terrorists</u>.

   (A) which grants law enforcement officials greater authority in investigating suspected terrorists

   (B) that grants law enforcement officials greater authority to investigate suspected terrorists

   (C) granting law enforcement officials greater authority with investigating suspected terrorists

   (D) which will grant law enforcement officials greater authority for suspected terrorists investigations

   (E) having granted law enforcement officials greater authority for investigating suspected terrorists

The sentence is correct. Choice (B) incorrectly uses *that* to introduce a clause. Choice (C) used the unidiomatic *authority with*. Choice (D) is awkward and unidiomatic, and uses a future tense verb for something that is occurring in the present. Choice (E) improperly uses a progressive form of *to grant* and is unidiomatic.

17. Of the dozen hybrid automobiles tested, three of the models that used battery power <u>for the conservation of gasoline went over 250 miles per gallon.</u>

    (A) for the conservation of gasoline went over 250 miles per gallon
    (B) for the conservation of gasoline had 250 miles per gallon
    (C) to conserve gasoline got over 250 miles per gallon
    (D) to conserve gasoline went at 250 miles per gallon
    (E) for conserving gasoline went over 250 miles per gallon

The sentence is wordy and unidiomatic. The infinitive form of the verb *to conserve* is much more concise and less awkward than the wordy *for the conservation of gasoline. Went over* would be correct idiom if we were measuring how far the cars traveled (*went over 250 miles*), but is incorrect when used with gas mileage. The correct idiom is *got over 250 miles per gallon*. Only Choice (C) makes these two corrections.

18. While the Fair Labor Standards Act requires youth to be 14 year of age or older to work in non-agriculture jobs, children <u>will have been allowed to baby-sit, deliver newspapers, and to perform in theatrical productions at any age.</u>

    (A) will have been allowed to baby-sit, deliver newspapers, and to perform in theatrical productions at any age
    (B) have been allowed to baby-sit, to deliver newspapers, and to perform in theatrical productions at any age
    (C) will have been allowed to baby-sit, deliver newspapers, and they are able to perform in theatrical productions at any age
    (D) are allowed to baby-sit, deliver newspapers, and perform in theatrical productions at any age
    (E) are allowed to baby-sit, deliver newspapers, and they are able to perform in theatrical productions at any age

The sentence contains a parallel structure error and a verb tense error. The parallel structure in question is the use of *to* with only two of the items in the list: *to baby-sit, deliver newspapers, and to perform.* The correct form is *to X, to Y, and to Z*, or *to X, Y, and Z*. Either all of the items in the list must have the preposition, or only the first item. Choices (B) and (D) present one of these solutions. The other error is a verb tense error. The verb *requires* is in the present tense, while *will have been allowed* is in the future perfect tense. The children have been allowed and are currently allowed, so *are allowed* conveys this best. Choice (D) is correct.

19. The members of the hiring committee agreed that if the applicant had been honest <u>about his lacking a college degree, they would hire him</u>; unfortunately, the lie cost him the job.

    (A) about his lacking a college degree, they would hire him
    (B) concerning his lacking of a college degree, they would hire him
    (C) about the lack of a college degree, they would still hire him
    (D) about his lack of a college degree, they would have hired him
    (E) as to his lacking a college degree, they were hiring him

The errors in this sentence are awkward word choice and conditional verb tense. The phrase *his lacking a college degree* is awkward, and *lacking* can be mistaken for a verb rather than the noun object of the preposition *about*. *About his lack of* is much more clear. The second error is the verb tense of a conditional statement. The conditional statement is hypothetical and in the past tense. Therefore the verb in the conditional clause (*if the applicant <u>had been</u> honest*) must be one step behind the tense of the verb in the independent clause, which receives a form of *will, can, shall,* or *might* (*they would have hired him*). Choice (D) makes both of these corrections.

20. Hunters and warriors, <u>bison were hunted by the native Navajo, and they used the hides for shelters and meat for food</u>.

    (A) bison were hunted by the native Navajo, and they used the hides for shelters and meat for food
    (B) the native Navajo hunted bison, using the hides for shelters and meat for food
    (C) bison were hunted by the native Navajo, and used shelters and for food
    (D) the native Navajo had hunted bison, and they used the hides for shelters and meat for food
    (E) hunting by the native Navajo included bison, which they used for shelters and food

The introductory phrase, *hunters and warriors*, is incorrectly modifying *bison*. The bison were not hunters and warriors! Only Choices (B) and (D) correctly place *the Navajo* next to *hunters and warriors*. Choice (D) uses the past perfect *had hunted*, which is incorrect, since there are not two events occurring at two different times. Choice (B) is best.

CHAPTER ELEVEN: SENTENCE CORRECTION STRATEGIES

Now that you are armed with the grammatical concepts covered on the GMAT, it is time to learn some strategies for attacking Sentence Correction questions. Your new knowledge of grammar may help you quickly locate sentence errors, but the following strategies can add to your problem-solving ability, as well as assist you with errors that are not immediately evident.

Look for Error Indicators

Throughout this book, PowerScore has featured certain words, phrases, or grammatical patterns that are prevalent on the GMAT. These words and patterns are indicators of specific errors, and should act as "warning signs" when you encounter them on the test. If your Sentence Completion question has an error indicator, you should check that word, phrase, or pattern for the specific error that often accompanies it. For example, if the smart test taker found the word *like* in a sentence, he would immediately verify that *like* is being correctly used to make a comparison, rather than incorrectly used in the place of *as*.

In the following list, you'll find all of the indicators and the characteristic errors that often occur with the word or phrase. We've also listed the chapter in which the error was discussed.

Error Indicator: **Long phrase between the subject and the verb**
Common Error(s): Faulty subject verb agreement
Reviewed in: Chapter Four

Error Indicator: **The subject comes after the verb (inverted sentence)**
Common Error(s): Faulty subject verb agreement
Reviewed in: Chapter Four

Error Indicator: ***The number of***
Common Error(s): Faulty subject verb agreement
Reviewed in: Chapter Four
Notes: Remember that *number* is a singular subject. However, the object of the preposition *of* will often be plural, such as *the number of applicants*. This will lead many test takers to use a plural verb, when a singular verb is required.

Error Indicator:	***Each* or *every***
Common Error(s):	Faulty subject verb agreement
	Faulty pronoun antecedent agreement
Reviewed in:	Chapter Four and Chapter Five
Notes:	*Each* and *every* are always singular, but are often assigned plural verbs or pronouns on the GMAT

Error Indicator:	**The use of *had* with a main verb**
Common Error(s):	Incorrect verb tense
Reviewed in:	Chapter Four

Error Indicator:	**Dates or time periods mentioned in the sentence**
Common Error(s):	Incorrect verb tense
Reviewed in:	Chapter Four
Notes:	Dates and time periods are often the contextual clues for the placement of the verb in the past, present, or future tense.

Error Indicator:	***If***
Common Error(s):	Incorrect verb tense in a conditional clause
Reviewed in:	Chapter Four
Notes:	The word *if* may signify a conditional clause, which is often involved in illegal verb tense errors.

Error Indicator:	**Past participle verb with *to be* as a helping verb (such as *was selected*, *will be driven*, etc.)**
Common Error(s):	Passive voice
Reviewed in:	Chapter Four

Error Indicator:	***They* and *their***
Common Error(s):	Faulty pronoun antecedent agreement
Reviewed in:	Chapter Five
Notes:	The plural personal pronouns *they* and *their* are often used incorrectly with singular antecedents.

Error Indicator:	**Quantifiers, such as *many*, *few*, and *some***
Common Error(s):	Incorrectly matched with count nouns or mass nouns
Reviewed in:	Chapter Six

Error Indicator:	**Introductory modifying clause**
Common Error(s):	Misplaced modifier
Reviewed in:	Chapter Six
Notes:	If a sentence begins with a modifying clause, the subject being modified should immediately follow the clause

Error Indicator: *Like* **or** *as*
Common Error(s):   Incorrect word choice
Reviewed in: Chapter Seven
Notes: The preposition *like* is used incorrectly for the conjunction *as*.

Error Indicator: *And* **and** *or*
Common Error(s):   Incorrect conjunction choice
    Faulty parallelism
Reviewed in: Chapter Seven and Chapter Eight
Notes: The coordinating conjunctions *and* and *or* are not interchangeable, so GMAC may use *and* when *or* is more appropriate, and vice versa. More commonly, though, *and* and *or* signify faulty parallelism between the verbs they are connecting.

Error Indicator: **Correlating conjunctions such as** *not only..but also* **and** *either..or*
Common Error(s):   Incorrect conjunction choice
    Faulty parallelism
Reviewed in: Chapter Seven
Notes: Correlative conjunctions must be properly matched with their partner. *Neither* must always be with *nor*, rather than *or*. The GMAT will match these conjunctions with a different ending. Also, the nouns or verbs that follow each part of a correlative conjunction must be parallel. In *not only X, but also Y*, the nouns or verbs that take the place of *X* and *Y* must have the same grammatical pattern.

Error Indicator: *Like, unlike, more, most, less, least, better,* **and** *worse*
Common Error(s):   Incomplete or illogical comparisons
    Faulty parallelism in a comparison
Reviewed in: Chapter Eight

Error Indicator: **A semicolon (;)**
Common Error(s):   A dependent clause on either side of the semicolon
Reviewed in: Chapter Eight
Notes: A semicolon must separate two independent clauses

You should study this list prior to the test. The more familiar you are with these error indicators, the more likely you are to spot them on the actual GMAT.

Even the most experienced test taker is bound to be faced with a sentence in which an error is not immediately present. The sentence might be grammatically correct, making answer choice (A) the best option. However, before choosing (A) and moving on, read each answer choice and compare it to the original sentence. What was changed? Was it changed for a legitimate reason? If not, you can eliminate the answer choice. But if the change does correct an error, you know that answer choice (A) is no longer correct.

You might also spot a major error immediately and select an answer choice that corrects your error. But do not move on yet! What if there is a minor error in the sentence which you have not noticed? You should always read all of the answer choices and compare them to the original sentence. If there is a minor error, it will be corrected in an answer choice which also corrects the major error. Failing to read all four answer choices can cause you to miss important questions on the test.

Let's look at an example to explore how to use the answer choices:

Several of the canvases that were singed and incinerated in yesterday's museum fire were painted by a famous Russian artist.

(A) Several of the canvases that were singed and incinerated in yesterday's museum fire were
(B) In yesterday's museum fire, several of the canvases that had been singed and incinerated were
(C) Yesterday several of the canvases that were singed or incinerated in the museum fire were
(D) Several of the canvases that were singed and incinerated in yesterday's museum fire had been
(E) Several of the canvases that were singed or incinerated in yesterday's museum fire had been

Reading the four new answer choices can help you find errors you might otherwise overlook.

Test takers might read this sentence and miss the two errors. The novice test taker would select Choice (A) and move on to the next question, but he would be wrong. The master test taker would start with Choice (B), and compare it to the original sentence:

Original:
Several of the canvases that were singed and incinerated in yesterday's museum fire were painted by a famous Russian artist.

Choice (B):
In yesterday's museum fire, several of the canvases that had been singed and incinerated were painted by a famous Russian artist.

First, Choice (B) moved the modifier *in yesterday's museum fire* to the front of the sentence. Did this modifier need to be moved? No. Is it incorrectly placed in this new location? No, but the sentence structure is changed. It's not an error, but was an unnecessary change. So look at the other difference between the original and (B). The first simple past tense *were* was changed to the past perfect *had been*. Remember, the past perfect is used to show the first event to take place in the past when there are two events from the past in the same sentence. Which happened first to the canvases? The singeing and incinerating or the painting? The painting occurred first, so *had been* should be attached to the second *were* in the sentence:

> Several of the canvases that were singed and incinerated in yesterday's museum fire *had been* painted by a famous Russian artist.

So we have found one error by looking at what was changed in Choice (B). Which answer choices use *had been* in place of the second *were*? Choices (D) and (E). We can eliminate Choices (A), (B), and (C).

Now compare the original sentence to Choice (D):

> *Original:*
> Several of the canvases that were singed and incinerated in yesterday's museum fire were painted by a famous Russian artist.

> *Choice (D):*
> Several of the canvases that were singed and incinerated in yesterday's museum fire had been painted by a famous Russian artist.

The only difference between these two sentences is the correction of the second *were* to *had been*. Some test takers might hastily choose (D) and move on, but the master test taker would check the final answer choice before making a decision:

> *Original:*
> Several of the canvases that were singed and incinerated in yesterday's museum fire were painted by a famous Russian artist.

> *Choice (E):*
> Several of the canvases that were singed or incinerated in yesterday's museum fire had been painted by a famous Russian artist.

Choice (E) also uses *had been*, but makes a second change that is so small it is often missed. *Singed* <u>*and*</u> *incinerated* became *singed* <u>*or*</u> *incinerated*. Can something be both *singed* and *incinerated* at the same time? No. It would be one *or* the other, making *or* the correct preposition. Choice (E) is the best answer.

We used the answer choices to find the errors in this sentence. This is an invaluable tool on the Sentence Correction portion of the GMAT. You do not have the time or the ability to record the original sentence and the answer choice on paper; you must make your comparisons by looking at the computer screen. Still, a quick study of each of the words in the original sentence compared to each of the words in the answer choices should alert you to possible errors in the sentence.

Eliminate Answer Choices

An important test-taking skill is the ability to eliminate answer choices. By disregarding certain answers, you save time and increase your chances of selecting correctly when forced to make an educated guess. As we saw in the previous example on analyzing answer choices, we were able to eliminate Choices (A), (B), and (C) after comparing Choice (B) to the original sentence. On a paper and pencil format test, we simply cross off these corresponding letters in the test booklet, but as discussed in Chapter One, the GMAT CAT format can present a challenge to students not used to finding test questions on a computer screen. Instead, we must use our scratch paper or personal whiteboard to create an answer chart, placing *X*s next to the rows for (A), (B), and (C).

While eliminating answer choices, do not mull over one choice too long. Because the test is timed, you cannot spend a lot of time on each answer choice. If you are not sure about the answer choice, leave it as a "contender" and move on. You might find an answer choice further down the list which will clearly eliminate the one you were pondering.

If you find that have eliminated all four of the possible corrections, choose Choice (A), representing no error in the sentence. On occasion you may eliminate all five answer choices. If this occurs, go back to the sentence and reevaluate each answer choice.

Substitute New Words and Phrases

Substitution is a key to the quantitative portion of the GMAT. We substitute numbers for variables and symbols for words. By turning the unfamiliar into the familiar, we are able to grasp concepts and problems which might have appeared unsolvable at first glance.

Substitution also works in the verbal sections of the GMAT. Taking unfamiliar words or language patterns and substituting more familiar forms can help you conquer the toughest test questions. We have highlighted several methods for substitution throughout this book, such as the use of *he* and *him* for *who* and *whom* when determining the correct pronoun choice. But you can also use substitution to test agreement, idiom, and other grammatical rules.

Take, for example, the following sentence with an idiom error:

The newly enacted term limits prohibited the popular city council chairperson to run for office during the next election.

The idiom occurs in *prohibited the popular city council chairperson to run.*

If the GMAT sentence is too lengthy or confusing, substitute words or variables into the entire phrase to shorten or clarify the expression:

> *prohibited the popular city council chairperson to run*
> prohibited X to Y
> prohibited me to work

Then substitute other words *for prohibited* and *to work*, to make sure that they are correct idiom:

> prohibited me to work
> kept me to work
> prevent me to work
> forbid me to work ✓

> prohibited me to work
> prohibited me of working
> prohibited me in working
> prohibited me from working ✓

At this point, you should realize that the infinitive *to work* belongs with *forbid*, but not *prohibited*. *Prohibited* needs a noun, followed by the preposition *from* and a gerund, such as *working*:

> prohibited X from Y
> prohibited me from working
> *prohibited the popular city council chairperson from running*

The correct sentence reads:

> The newly enacted term limits *prohibited the popular city council chairperson from running* for office during the next election.

This type of substitution can work in several grammatical areas on the GMAT. You can use it to check subject-verb agreement and pronoun-antecedent agreement, substituting a pronoun for a noun or a noun for pronoun:

> In South America and Southern Mexico, a colony of Driver ants, known for their fiercely defensive behavior, have been known to kill immobile livestock, such as tethered cows or corralled horses.   [*Incorrect*]

By removing the prepositional phrase with the subject and the modifying phrase in the center of the sentence, we can isolate the subject and verb:

> a colony have been known

Now, substitute a pronoun for the subject:

it have been known

This is obviously incorrect. The verb should be the singular *has*:

it *has* been known

Now you can correct the original sentence:

In South America and Southern Mexico, a colony of Driver ants, known for their fiercely defensive behavior, *has* been known to kill immobile livestock, such as tethered cows or corralled horses.   [*Correct*]

When presented with a pronoun, substitute the noun antecedent in its place to verify agreement:

During the charity auction, the organization collected over two hundred thousand dollars, nearly twice as much as they expected.

The pronoun in this sentence is *they*. Find its antecedent, and substitute it in the pronoun's place:

During the charity auction, the organization collected over two hundred thousand dollars, nearly twice as much as *the organization* expected.

they = the organization

Can the plural pronoun *they* refer to the singular subject *organization*? No. The correct pronoun must be singular:

During the charity auction, the organization collected over two hundred thousand dollars, nearly twice as much as *it* expected.

You may find other ways to use substitution as you practice for the GMAT. There are not any specific rules for its use; as long as you retain the same sentence structure, you are free to use other words or phrases to make the unfamiliar a little more familiar.

Rearrange the Phrase, Clause, or Sentence

Some sentences are easier to understand or analyze when they are rearranged. We have seen this while working with inverted subjects and verbs and sentences constructed in the passive voice. It is also an important skill in choosing between *who* or *whom*. Look at an example:

> NASA has agreed to send one American astronaut to the International Space Station for a six month experiment, although who it will send has yet to be determined.   [*Incorrect*]

The first step in determining the appropriate pronoun is to separate the clause containing *who* from the rest of the sentence:

> although *who* it will send has yet to be determined

You can even eliminate the excess modifiers and concentrate on the specific phrase with the pronoun:

> *who* it will send

We cannot clearly substitute *he* or *him* while the sentence is in the current arrangement:

> *he* it will send
> *him* it will send

Rearrange the phrase to find the clear pronoun:

> it will send *who*
> it will send *he*
> it will send *him* ✓

Because *him* works in the rearranged phrase, the correct pronoun is *whom*:

> it will send *whom*

Insert *whom* into the original sentence:

> NASA has agreed to send one American astronaut to the International Space Station for a six month experiment, although *whom* it will send has yet to be determined.   [*Correct*]

As in the example above, and covered extensively in Chapter Four, you can remove extraneous words, phrases, and clauses to isolate the offending error. Remember that subjects are never in prepositional phrases and that agreement errors can also occur in clauses.

Use Miscellaneous Strategies

We discussed Choice (A) in Chapter Two, but it bears mentioning again: Do not read answer choice (A). The first answer choice is an exact replica of the underlined portion of the original sentence. If you read Choice (A), you waste valuable time that can be spent on other answer choices or sentences.

If you know that the original sentence contains an error, but are unable to determine the proper correction, pick the shortest answer choice. This is particularly true for questions that have a wordy or awkward underlined portion. GMAC often tests for concise sentences—those that express the intended meaning in as few words as possible—thus the shortest answer is often correct.

Finally, after choosing an answer choice, read the entire sentence again, only this time with your correction in place of the underlined portion. Make sure that the sentence looks and sounds grammatically correct. If your answer choice meets these qualifications, choose it and move on to the next problem.

Practice

Here at PowerScore, we cannot adequately stress the importance of completing as many practice questions as possible. By working through real GMAT questions, you'll be able to implement strategies and concepts you've learned in this book, as well as discover patterns that tend to repeat throughout the test. It is extremely important to use real test questions during your study session; simulated questions do not always reflect the proper sentence structure or content that is used on the GMAT. Real sentence correction questions are available in two books produced by GMAC: *The Official Guide for GMAT Review* and *The Official Guide for the GMAT Verbal Review*. They also publish a guide for quantitative review. All three books are available on our website at www.powerscore.com, or by calling our offices at (800) 545-1750. We have provided you with twenty more practice questions in the following problem set, but we highly recommend that you complete all of the real questions in GMAC's two official guides.

Sentence Completion Strategies Problem Set

Please complete the problem set and review the answer key and explanations. Answers on page 239-245.

1. Although he had proposed funding cuts to the CIA <u>while being a senator</u>, John Kerry sought to bolster military spending after the American terrorist attacks.

   (A) while being a senator
   (B) while in Senate
   (C) at the time of him being a senator
   (D) as being a senator
   (E) as a senator

2. <u>An article about the "Seinfeld Curse," which was published just before *The New Adventure's of Old Christine* were cast</u>, predicted that Julia Louis-Dreyfus would be the only former Seinfeld cast member to succeed in another sitcom.

   (A) An article about the "Seinfeld Curse," which was published just before *The New Adventure's of Old Christine* were cast
   (B) An article about the "Seinfeld Curse," which was published just before *The New Adventure's of Old Christine* was cast
   (C) An article about the "Seinfeld Curse," published just before *The New Adventure's of Old Christine* were cast
   (D) *The New Adventure's of Old Christine* was cast just before an article about the "Seinfeld Curse" was published,
   (E) *The New Adventure's of Old Christine,* cast just before an article about the "Seinfeld Curse" was published

3. Due to the decrease in active lifestyles and the increase in high-fat diets, the adult obesity rate in the United Kingdom <u>increased by more than threefold</u> from 1980 to 2006.

   (A) increased by more than threefold
   (B) increased by more than triple
   (C) increased more than three times
   (D) more than tripled
   (E) had more than tripled

4. While some propose to improve bus transportation and timing for the school district's students by changing bus routes, others <u>by suggesting fining the bus company to increase the incentive for on-time pick-ups, and still others by demanding</u> the district use a different transportation company.

   (A) by suggesting fining the bus company to increase the incentive for on-time pick-ups, and still others by demanding
   (B) suggest fining the bus company to increase the incentive for on-time pick-ups, and still others demand
   (C) suggest the fine of the bus company to increase the incentive for on-time pick-ups, and still others by demanding
   (D) suggest the fining of the bus company to increase the incentive for on-time pick-ups, and still others are demanding
   (E) by suggesting the fining of the bus company and increasing the incentive for on-time pick-ups, and still others demand

5. According to the latest education report, <u>the number of teachers working without valid certificates has increased</u> by thirteen percent in the last ten years.

   (A) the number of teachers working without valid certificates has increased
   (B) teachers working without valid certificates have been increasing
   (C) the number of teachers working without valid certificates have increased
   (D) there have been increases in the number of teachers working without valid certificates
   (E) an increasing number of teachers have been working without valid certificates

Sentence Completion Strategies Problem Set

Please complete the problem set and review the answer key and explanations. Answers on page 239-245.

6. In addition to having more seats than the old theater, <u>the seats in the new theater are more customer-friendly than those in</u> the old theater, with reclining seat backs and cup holder armrests.

   (A) the seats in the new theater are more customer-friendly than those in
   (B) the seats in the new theater are more customer-friendly than that in
   (C) the new theater has seats that are more customer-friendly than those in
   (D) the new theater seats are more customer-friendly than
   (E) the customer-friendliness of the seats in the new theater is greater than those in

7. <u>Just as with</u> many of Bermuda's lakes and ponds, Trott's Pond is brackish because it is located near the Atlantic Ocean.

   (A) Just as with
   (B) As do
   (C) Just like
   (D) As
   (E) Like

8. A century of farming and development has changed the landscape of several of the battlefields; the memorial project <u>plans to reform and reconstruct them as they were during</u> the country's civil war.

   (A) plans to reform and reconstruct them as they were during
   (B) plans reforming and reconstructing them as they were during
   (C) plans to reform and reconstruct them as they had been during
   (D) plans to reform and reconstruct them as if during
   (E) plans the reformation and reconstruction of them as during

9. In James Cameron's 1984 classic *The Terminator*, the plot centers around the implications of time travel when a futuristic robot travels fifty-five years back in time and <u>it then attempts to change the outcome of events by assassinating the leader of a successful future uprising</u>.

   (A) it then attempts to change the outcome of events by assassinating the leader of a successful future uprising
   (B) then attempting to change the outcome of events by assassinating the leader of a successful future uprising
   (C) attempts to change the outcome of events by assassinating the leader of a successful future uprising
   (D) it attempts to change the outcome of events by assassinating the leader of a successful future uprising
   (E) it attempts to change the outcome of a successful future uprising by assassinating the leader

10. In states that allow a "Schools of Choice" program, academic success is a key component of a school district's enrollment: <u>not only is a report on students' standardized test scores published in the local newspapers, but on student dropout rates as well</u>.

   (A) not only is a report on students' standardized test scores published in the local newspapers, but on student dropout rates as well
   (B) not only is a report on students' standardized test scores published in the local newspapers, but also student dropout rates
   (C) published in the local newspapers are reports not only on students' standardized test scores, but also on student dropout rates
   (D) not only are students' standardized test scores published in a report in the local newspapers, but on student dropout rates as well
   (E) a report on students' standardized test scores is not only published in the local newspapers, but also on student dropout rates as well

Sentence Completion Strategies Problem Set

Please complete the problem set and review the answer key and explanations. Answers on page 239-245.

11. President Ronald Reagan met with Transportation Secretary Drew Lewis and the Federal Aviation Administration in July 1981 to discuss a possible air traffic controllers' strike and <u>how they would have to act legally and politically to handle them</u>.

   (A) how they would have to act legally and politically to handle them
   (B) how to handle them if legal and political action would be required
   (C) what would be necessary legally and politically for handling such an event
   (D) what legal and political action would be necessary in order to handle such an event.
   (E) the necessity of what kind of legal and political action in order to handle it

12. Although osteoporosis is most often associated with older adults, the disease can be prevented during childhood with sufficient intake of calcium and Vitamin D; <u>ensures that as a child grows, their</u> bone density will continue to increase.

   (A) ensures that as a child grows, their
   (B) ensuring that as a child grows, his or her
   (C) ensures that as children grow, their
   (D) these nutrients have ensured that when a child grows, his or her
   (E) these nutrients ensure that as children grow, their

13. With the addition of "shock jock" Howard Stern to its airwaves in 2006, Sirius made headway in <u>their competition with XM Radio in</u> satellite radio subscriptions, closing the margin to just under two million listeners.

   (A) their competition with XM Radio in
   (B) its competition with XM Radio for
   (C) its competition of XM Radio in
   (D) its competition with XM Radio in
   (E) their competition with XM Radio for

14. After hearing from dozens of local business owners and concerned community members, <u>it was decided by the town council to enact a smoking ban in all public and private buildings located within town limits</u>.

   (A) it was decided by the town council to enact a smoking ban in all public and private buildings located within town limits
   (B) the decision of the town council was to enact a smoking ban in all public and private buildings located within town limits
   (C) all public and private buildings located within town limits were banned from smoking by the town council
   (D) a smoking ban was enacted by the town council in all public and private buildings located within town limits
   (E) the town council decided to enact a smoking ban in all public and private buildings located within town limits

15. It is now believed that the the Mandiga people of Africa <u>visited the Americas nearly four hundred years before Christopher Columbus had made</u> his famous voyage.

   (A) visited the Americas nearly four hundred years before Christopher Columbus had made
   (B) had visited the Americas nearly four hundred years before Christopher Columbus had made
   (C) visited the Americas nearly four hundred years before Christopher Columbus was making
   (D) had visited the Americas nearly four hundred years before Christopher Columbus made
   (E) were visiting the Americas nearly four hundred years before Christopher Columbus had made

Sentence Completion Strategies Problem Set

Please complete the problem set and review the answer key and explanations. Answers on page 237-243.

16. A vault was so securely constructed and reinforced in the San Francisco bank that even a magnitude seven earthquake did not disturb the vault's contents.

    (A) A vault was so securely constructed and reinforced in the San Francisco bank that
    (B) So securely was a vault construction and reinforcement in the San Francisco bank
    (C) It was so secure that a vault was constructed and reinforced in the San Francisco bank
    (D) A vault that was so securely constructed and reinforced in the San Francisco bank
    (E) Constructed and reinforced so securely in the San Francisco bank was a vault that

17. Representatives from the college, one who is a member of the admissions board, will be available to talk to potential students about applications, personal statements, and standardized test scores.

    (A) one who
    (B) one of whom
    (C) one of which
    (D) one of them whom
    (E) with one of them who

18. The sex of baby alligators and many other reptiles—such as crocodiles and snapping turtles—are determined from the temperature of the nest; above ninety degrees yields males, while lower temperatures yield females.

    (A) are determined from the temperature of the nest; above
    (B) is determined from the temperature of the nest; temperatures above
    (C) is determined by the temperature of the nest; temperatures above
    (D) are determined by the temperature of the nest; those above
    (E) is determined from nest temperature; rising above

19. Unlike an interest-bearing checking account, which requires a minimum deposit and monthly balance, a customer who opens a free checking account is not required to maintain a specific balance.

    (A) a customer who opens a free checking account is not required to maintain
    (B) with a free checking account there is no requirement of
    (C) a free checking account does not require the customer to maintain
    (D) free checking account customers are not required to maintain
    (E) for the free checking account customer there is no requirement of

20. Each of the Pacific Northwest states—Washington, Oregon, Montana, and Idaho—were admitted in the Union in the nineteenth century, following the Lewis and Clark Expedition.

    (A) Each of the Pacific Northwest states— Washington, Oregon, Montana, and Idaho— were admitted in the Union
    (B) Washington, Oregon, Montana, and Idaho— each of the Pacific Northwest states—was admitted in the Union
    (C) Admitted to the Union, each of the Pacific Northwest states—Washington, Oregon, Montana, and Idaho—were
    (D) Washington, Oregon, Montana, and Idaho—the Pacific Northwest states—each one was admitted to the Union
    (E) Each of the Pacific Northwest states— Washington, Oregon, Montana, and Idaho— was admitted to the Union

Sentence Completion Strategies Problem Set Answer Key

Correct answers are in bold.

1. Although he had proposed funding cuts to the CIA <u>while being a senator</u>, John Kerry sought to bolster military spending after the American terrorist attacks.

   (A) while being a senator
   (B) while in Senate
   (C) at the time of him being a senator
   (D) as being a senator
   (E) as a senator

Being is rarely used correctly on the GMAT. In this sentence, it is wordy and unidiomatic. Choices (C) and (D) repeat this wordiness. Choice (B) causes some ambiguity in determining who or what was in the Senate. Choice (E) concisely corrects the error.

2. <u>An article about the "Seinfeld Curse," which was published just before *The New Adventures of Old Christine* were cast,</u> predicted that Julia Louis-Dreyfus would be the only former *Seinfeld* cast member to succeed in another sitcom.

   (A) An article about the "Seinfeld Curse," which was published just before *The New Adventures of Old Christine* were cast
   (B) An article about the "Seinfeld Curse," which was published just before *The New Adventures of Old Christine* **was cast**
   (C) An article about the "Seinfeld Curse," published just before *The New Adventures of Old Christine* were cast
   (D) *The New Adventures of Old Christine* was cast just before an article about the "Seinfeld Curse" was published
   (E) *The New Adventures of Old Christine,* cast just before an article about the "Seinfeld Curse" was published

The title of the television show, *The New Adventures of Old Christine*, might trick test takers into choosing a plural verb (*were*), but there is only one television show, thus requiring a singular verb (*was*). Choice (B) makes this correction.

3. Due to the decrease in active lifestyles and the increase in high-fat diets, the adult obesity rate in the United Kingdom <u>increased by more than threefold</u> from 1980 to 2006.

   (A) increased by more than threefold
   (B) increased by more than triple
   (C) increased more than three times
   (D) more than tripled
   (E) had more than tripled

Choice (A) uses the preposition *by*, but does not provide a noun object for the preposition, since *three-fold* is an adjective. Choice (B) makes the same error, but uses the adjective *triple*. Choice (C) changes the meaning of the sentence, indicating that adult obesity rates increased on three separate occasions. Choice (D) is correct because it is concise and it uses proper idiom. Choice (E) also uses correct idiom, but it incorrectly uses the past perfect tense (*had*), since there is only one past tense verb in the sentence.

4. While some propose to improve bus transportation and timing for the school district's students by changing bus routes, others <u>by suggesting fining the bus company to increase the incentive for on-time pick-ups, and still others by demanding</u> the district use a different transportation company.

(A) by suggesting fining the bus company to increase the incentive for on-time pick-ups, and still others by demanding

(B) suggest fining the bus company to increase the incentive for on-time pick-ups, and still others demand

(C) suggest the fine of the bus company to increase the incentive for on-time pick-ups, and still others by demanding

(D) suggest the fining of the bus company to increase the incentive for on-time pick-ups, and still others are demanding

(E) by suggesting the fining of the bus company and increasing the incentive for on-time pick-ups, and still others demand

The correct answer choice, Choice (B), creates a parallel construction with *some propose, others suggest, and still others demand*. Choices (A) and (E) lose parallelism with *by suggesting*. Choice (C) uses the wordy *the fine of the bus company* and loses parallelism with *by demanding*. Choice (D) also uses a wordy expression, *the fining of*. It also loses paralellism with *are demanding*.

5. According to the latest education report, <u>the number of teachers working without valid certificates has increased</u> by thirteen percent in the last ten years.

(A) the number of teachers working without valid certificates has increased

(B) teachers working without valid certificates have been increasing

(C) the number of teachers working without valid certificates have increased

(D) there have been increases in the number of teachers working without valid certificates

(E) an increasing number of teachers have been working without valid certificates

The sentence is correct. Because the subject is *number*, Choice (A) correctly uses the singular *has*. Choices (C), (D), and (E) violate subject and verb agreement by using *the number..have*. The verb in Choice (B) suggests that the thirteen point increase has occurred every year, rather than cumulatively over ten years.

6. In addition to having more seats than the old theater, <u>the seats in the new theater are more customer-friendly than those in</u> the old theater, with reclining seat backs and cup holder armrests.

(A) the seats in the new theater are more customer-friendly than those in

(B) the seats in the new theater are more customer-friendly than that in

(C) the new theater has seats that are more customer-friendly than those in

(D) the new theater seats are more customer-friendly than

(E) the customer-friendliness of the seats in the new theater is greater than those in

In the original sentence, the introductory clause (*In addition to having more seats than the old theater*) is modifying *seats*. But the correct referent is *the new theater*. Choices (A), (B), and (E) do not put *the new theater* next to the modifying clause, and are therefore incorrect. Choice (D) uses *the new theater* as an adjective to modify *seats*, so it is also incorrect. Choice (C) is correct.

7. <u>Just as with</u> many of Bermuda's lakes and ponds, Trott's Pond is brackish because it is located near the Atlantic Ocean.

    (A) Just as with
    (B) As do
    (C) Just like
    (D) As
    (E) Like

The correct answer is (E). Like is a preposition used to make comparisons, and the sentence is comparing Bermuda's lakes and ponds to Trott's pond. Choice (C) also uses the correct preposition, but becomes wordy when *just* is added. The use of as in Choices (B) and (D) create a modifying clause. Choice (B) uses a verb (*do*) that cannot be completed by any part of the sentence, and Choice (D) reads that Trott's Pond *is* many of Bermuda's lakes and ponds.

8. A century of farming and development has changed the landscape of several of the battlefields; the memorial project <u>plans to reform and reconstruct them as they were during</u> the country's civil war.

    (A) plans to reform and reconstruct them as they were during
    (B) plans reforming and reconstructing them as they were during
    (C) plans to reform and reconstruct them as they had been during
    (D) plans to reform and reconstruct them as if during
    (E) plans the reformation and reconstruction of them as during

This sentence does not contain an error. A simple past tense verb (*were*) is used in an independent clause which only has one past event occurring. Choice (C) violates this verb rule by using the past participle *had*. Choice (B) incorrectly uses the progressive form of *reform* and *reconstruct* with the verb *plans*, which needs the infinitives used in the original sentence. Choice (D) creates a dangling modifier, *as if during*. The use of *as during* in Choice (E) causes the reader to believe the reformation and reconstruction occurred during the civil war.

9. In James Cameron's 1984 classic *The Terminator*, the plot centers around the implications of time travel when a futuristic robot travels fifty-five years back in time and <u>it then attempts to change the outcome of events by assassinating the leader of a successful future uprising</u>.

    (A) it then attempts to change the outcome of events by assassinating the leader of a successful future uprising
    (B) then attempting to change the outcome of events by assassinating the leader of a successful future uprising
    (C) attempts to change the outcome of events by assassinating the leader of a successful future uprising
    (D) it attempts to change the outcome of events by assassinating the leader of a successful future uprising
    (E) it attempts to change the outcome of a successful future uprising by assassinating the leader

In the final clause, the subject is *robot*. There is no reason to name the subject again with the pronoun *it*. The nouns must be parallel, too: the robot *travels* and *attempts*. Only Choice (C) eliminates *it* and keeps the verbs parallel.

10. In states that allow a "Schools of Choice" program, academic success is a key component of a school district's enrollment: <u>not only is a report on students' standardized test scores published in the local newspapers, but on student dropout rates as well</u>.

   (A) not only is a report on students' standardized test scores published in the local newspapers, but on student dropout rates as well
   (B) not only is a report on students' standardized test scores published in the local newspapers, but also student dropout rates
   (C) published in the local newspapers are reports not only on students' standardized test scores, but also on student dropout rates
   (D) not only are students' standardized test scores published in a report in the local newspapers, but on student dropout rates as well
   (E) a report on students' standardized test scores is not only published in the local newspapers, but also on student dropout rates as well

The correlative conjunction *not only* always belongs with *but also*. This eliminates answer choices (A) and (D). There also must be parallelism between the X and Y components of *not only X, but also Y*. There are two reports: not only on test scores, but also on dropout rates. Choices (B) and (E) violate this parallelism rule. Only Choice (C) clearly connects the two reports while maintaining parallel structure and logical grammar.

11. President Ronald Reagan met with Transportation Secretary Drew Lewis and the Federal Aviation Administration in July 1981 to discuss a possible air traffic controllers' strike and <u>how they would have to act legally and politically to handle them</u>.

   (A) how they would have to act legally and politically to handle them
   (B) how to handle them if legal and political action would be required
   (C) what would be necessary legally and politically for handling such an event
   (D) what legal and political action would be necessary in order to handle such an event
   (E) the necessity of what kind of legal and political action in order to handle it

The original sentence has an implied pronoun: *them. Air traffic controllers* is used as an adjective, rather than a noun, so *them* does not have an antecedent. This eliminates Choices (A) and (B). Choices (C) and (E) are wordy and awkward. Choice (D) maintains parallel structure and is grammatically sound.

12. Although osteoporosis is most often associated with older adults, the disease can be prevented during childhood with sufficient intake of calcium and Vitamin D; <u>ensures that as a child grows, their</u> bone density will continue to increase.

   (A) ensures that as a child grows, their
   (B) ensuring that as a child grows, his or her
   (C) ensures that as children grow, their
   (D) these nutrients have ensured that when a child grows, his or her
   (E) these nutrients ensure that as children grow, their

The sentence has two errors. The first is the incorrect use of a semicolon. Two independent clauses must be joined by a semicolon, and Choices (B) and (C) place dependent clauses after the punctuation mark. The other error is the use of the plural *their* with the singular antecedent, *child*. Both (D) and (E) correct this error, but (D) is wordy and uses an unnecessary past participle with *ensure*. Choice (E) is best.

13. With the addition of "shock jock" Howard Stern to its airwaves in 2006, Sirius made headway in <u>their competition with XM Radio in</u> satellite radio subscriptions, closing the margin to just under two million listeners.

    (A) their competition with XM Radio in
    (B) its competition with XM Radio for
    (C) its competition of XM Radio in
    (D) its competition with XM Radio in
    (E) their competition with XM Radio for

The sentence has two errors. First, the plural pronoun *their* incorrectly refers to *Sirius*, a singular proper noun. Second, the correct idiom is *in competition with X for Y*. Only Choice (B) corrects both errors.

14. After hearing from dozens of local business owners and concerned community members, <u>it was decided by the town council to enact a smoking ban in all public and private buildings located within town limits.</u>

    (A) it was decided by the town council to enact a smoking ban in all public and private buildings located within town limits
    (B) the decision of the town council was to enact a smoking ban in all public and private buildings located within town limits
    (C) all public and private buildings located within town limits were banned from smoking by the town council
    (D) a smoking ban was enacted by the town council in all public and private buildings located within town limits
    (E) the town council decided to enact a smoking ban in all public and private buildings located within town limits

Who heard from the businesses and community members? The *town council*. Therefore, this noun must immediately follow the introductory clause. In Choice (A), *it* heard from the businesses and community members. In Choice (B), *the decision* heard from them. In Choice (C), it was *the buildings*, and in Choice (D), it was *the smoking ban*. Only Choice (E) makes this correction. Plus, (E) places the sentence in the active voice, rather than the passive voice used by the original sentence.

15. It is now believed that the the Mandiga people of Africa <u>visited the Americas nearly four hundred years before Christopher Columbus had made</u> his famous voyage.

    (A) visited the Americas nearly four hundred years before Christopher Columbus had made
    (B) had visited the Americas nearly four hundred years before Christopher Columbus had made
    (C) visited the Americas nearly four hundred years before Christopher Columbus was making
    (D) had visited the Americas nearly four hundred years before Christopher Columbus made
    (E) were visiting the Americas nearly four hundred years before Christopher Columbus had made

Remember to be on the lookout for the word *had*. It is used in a sentence with two events occurring in the past to indicate the event that occurred first. What happened first? The Mandiga voyage or the Columbus voyage? The sentence states that the Mandiga arrived first, so the use of the past participle *had* should be with *visited* rather than with *made*. Choice (D) makes this correction.

16. <u>A vault was so securely constructed and reinforced in the San Francisco bank that</u> even a magnitude seven earthquake did not disturb the vault's contents.

   (A) A vault was so securely constructed and reinforced in the San Francisco bank that
   (B) So securely was a vault construction and reinforcement in the San Francisco bank
   (C) It was so secure that a vault was constructed and reinforced in the San Francisco bank
   (D) A vault that was so securely constructed and reinforced in the San Francisco bank
   (E) Constructed and reinforced so securely in the San Francisco bank was a vault that

The correct idiom is *so X that Y*, which is used in the original sentence: *so securely contracted and reinforced that even an earthquake did not disturb its contents*. Choice (A) is correct.

17. Representatives from the college, <u>one who</u> is a member of the admissions board, will be available to talk to potential students about applications, personal statements, and standardized test scores.

   (A) one who
   (B) one of whom
   (C) one of which
   (D) one of them whom
   (E) with one of them who

The *one* is referring to one of the representatives, so we must use *who* or *whom* to refer to a person. This eliminates Choice (C). Just as we say *one of the representatives*, we must say *one of who* or *one of whom*. Since the pronoun is following the preposition *of*, it must be *whom*. *One of whom* in Choice (B) is the correct.

18. The sex of baby alligators and many other reptiles—such as crocodiles and snapping turtles—<u>are determined from the temperature of the nest; above</u> ninety degrees yields males, while lower temperatures yield females.

   (A) are determined from the temperature of the nest; above
   (B) is determined from the temperature of the nest; temperatures above
   (C) is determined by the temperature of the nest; temperatures above
   (D) are determined by the temperature of the nest; those above
   (E) is determined by nest temperature; rising above

This sentence has errors in several areas: subject and verb agreement, idiom, and semicolons. Begin with subject and verb agreement. The subject is *sex*, a singular noun, rather than *alligators*. The correct verb, then, is *is*, rather than *are*. This eliminates Choices (A) and (D). The next error is idiom. The correct idiom is *determined by* (not *determined from*), which eliminates choice (B). Finally, we must put an independent clause on each side of the semicolon. Choice (E) does not have a subject for *rising above* (what is rising above?), so it is a fragment. Only Choice (C) makes all three corrections.

19. Unlike an interest-bearing checking account, which requires a minimum deposit and monthly balance, <u>a customer who opens a free checking account is not required to maintain</u> a specific balance.

    (A) a customer who opens a free checking account is not required to maintain
    (B) with a free checking account there is no requirement of
    (C) a free checking account does not require the customer to maintain
    (D) free checking account customers are not required to maintain
    (E) for the free checking account customer there is no requirement of

This sentence contains an illogical comparison; *the interest-bearing checking account* is compared to *a customer*. It must compare the *an interest-bearing checking account* to *a free checking account*. Only Choice (C) makes this logical comparison (note that *free checking account* is an adjective in Choices (D) and (E)).

20. <u>Each of the Pacific Northwest states—Washington, Oregon, Montana, and Idaho—were admitted in the Union</u> in the nineteenth century, following the Lewis and Clark Expedition.

    (A) Each of the Pacific Northwest states—Washington, Oregon, Montana, and Idaho—were admitted in the Union
    (B) Washington, Oregon, Montana, and Idaho—each of the Pacific Northwest states—was admitted in the Union
    (C) Admitted to the Union, each of the Pacific Northwest states—Washington, Oregon, Montana, and Idaho—were
    (D) Washington, Oregon, Montana, and Idaho—the Pacific Northwest states—each one was admitted to the Union
    (E) Each of the Pacific Northwest states—Washington, Oregon, Montana, and Idaho—was admitted to the Union

Remember that *each* and *every* are always singular subjects. *States* is not the subject because it is in a prepositional phrase. Similarly, the names of the states are not a compound subject, because they are in a phrase separated by dashes. *Each* is the subject and should be paired with the singular *was*, rather than the plural *were*. Only Choice (E) makes this correction. Choice (B) incorrectly uses a compound subject with *was*. Choice (C) makes the same error as (A), and Choice (D) creates a fragment with the names of the states.

THE POWERSCORE GMAT SENTENCE CORRECTION BIBLE

CHAPTER TWELVE: TEST READINESS

The day before the test

On the day before your GMAT appointment, we recommend that you study very little, if at all. The best approach for most students is to simply relax as much as possible. Read a book, see a movie, or play a round of golf. If you feel you must study, we recommend that you only briefly review each of the concepts covered in this book.

If you are not familiar with the location of your test center, drive by the test center and survey the parking situation. This will alleviate anxiety or confusion on the day of the test.

Eat only bland or neutral foods the night before the test and try to get the best sleep possible.

The morning of the test

Attempt to follow your normal routine on the morning of the test. For example, if you read the paper every morning, do so on the day of the test. If you do not regularly drink coffee, do not start on test day. Constancy in your routine will allow you to focus on your primary objective: performing well on the test.

Dress in layers, so you will be warm if the test center is cold, but also able to shed clothes if the test center is hot.

You must arrive at the test center approximately 30 minutes before your scheduled appointment time.

We strongly believe that performing well requires confidence and a belief that you can perform well. As you prepare to leave for the test, run though the test in your head, visualizing an exceptional performance. Imagine how you will react to each math problem, essay question, and verbal problem. Many athletes use this same visualization technique to achieve optimal performance.

The following pages contain general notes on preparing for the day of the GMAT.

Do not study hard the day before the test. If you haven't learned the material by then, that final day won't make much difference.

At the test center

Upon check-in, test supervisors will ask you for acceptable personal identification (typically a driver's license or a passport). Supervisors are instructed to deny admission to anyone who does not present a photo ID containing a signature. They may also take a thumbprint, photograph you, or videotape you.

The test supervisors will assign each examinee a work station. You are not permitted to choose your own station.

Once you are seated, testing will begin promptly.

Food and drink are not allowed in the testing room.

You may not leave your work station during the timed portions of the test.

If you engage in any misconduct or irregularity during the test, you may be dismissed from the test center and may be subject to other penalties for misconduct or irregularity. Actions that could warrant such consequences include creating a disturbance, giving or receiving help, removing scratch paper or notes from the testing room, eating or drinking during the test, taking part in an act of impersonation or other forms of cheating, or using books, calculators, ear plugs, headsets, rulers, or other aids. The penalties for misconduct are high: you may be precluded from attending business school.

If you encounter a problem with the test or test center itself, report it to a test administrator. Reportable problems include power outages, computer malfunctions, and any unusual disturbances caused by an individual.

If you feel anxious or panicked for any reason before or during the test, close your eyes for a few seconds and relax. Think of other situations where you performed with confidence and skill.

After the test

At the end of the test you will be presented with the option of cancelling your score. This is the only opportunity you have to cancel your score, and you must make the decision without the benefit of knowing how you scored. Once a score is cancelled, it cannot be reinstated and you do not receive a refund of your test fee.

If you choose to accept your score, you will immediately see your unofficial scores from the multiple choice sections, and you can print out a copy of your results. Official test results will be mailed to you approximately two weeks after the test.

Yes, you read that correctly. You may be thumbprinted or photographed at the test center. This is done for test security purposes.

THE POWERSCORE GMAT SENTENCE CORRECTION BIBLE

Thank you for choosing to purchase the *PowerScore GMAT Sentence Correction Bible*. We hope you have found this book useful and enjoyable, but most importantly we hope this book helps raise your GMAT score.

In all of our publications we strive to present the material in the clearest and most informative manner. If you have any questions, comments, or suggestions, please do not hesitate to e-mail us at *scbible@powerscore.com*. We love to receive feedback, and we do read every e-mail that comes in!

Also, if you have not done so already, we strongly suggest you visit the website for this book at:

www.powerscore.com/scbible

This free online resource area contains supplements to the book material, provides updates as needed, and answers questions posed by students. There is also an official evaluation form that we encourage you to use.

If we can assist you in any way in your GMAT preparation or in the business school admissions process, please do not hesitate to contact us. We would be happy to help.

Thank you and best of luck on the GMAT!

THE POWERSCORE GMAT SENTENCE CORRECTION BIBLE

APPENDIX

List of Prepositions

Prepositions link nouns and pronouns to other words in a sentence:

> The pen is *on* the counter.
> The pen is *by* the counter.
> The pen is *near* the counter.
> The pen is *under* the counter.
> The pen is *past* the counter.
> The pen is *from* the counter.
> The pen is *across* the counter.
> The pen is *beneath* the counter.

There are over 100 prepositions in the English language. Here is a list of seventy-two of the most common prepositions:

aboard	between	inside	save
about	beyond	into	since
above	but	like	than
across	by	minus	through
after	concerning	near	throughout
against	considering	of	to
along	despite	off	toward
amid	down	on	towards
among	due to	onto	under
around	during	opposite	underneath
as	except	out	unlike
at	excepting	outside	until
before	excluding	over	up
behind	following	past	upon
below	for	per	versus
beneath	from	plus	with
beside	in	regarding	within
besides	including	round	without

Regular verbs follow a specific pattern when conjugated. Simply add an *-ed* to the past tense and past participle:

Verb	Present	Past	Past Participle
to open	open	open*ed*	had open*ed*
to treat	treat	treat*ed*	had treat*ed*
to wonder	wonder	wonder*ed*	wonder*ed*

Irregular verbs do not follow a pattern. Use this list to learn the irregular verb forms you may not know:

Verb	Present	Past	Past Participle
to arise	arise	arose	had arisen
to awake	awake	awoke/awakened	had awoken
to be	is/are	was/were	had been
to bear	bear	bore	had born/borne
to beat	beat	beat	had beaten/beat
to become	become	became	had become
to befall	befall	befell	had befallen
to begin	begin	began	had begun
to behold	behold	beheld	had beheld
to bend	bend	bent	had bent
to bet	bet	bet/betted	had bet/betted
to bid	bid	bid	had bid
to bind	bind	bound	had bound
to bite	bite	bit	had bitten
to bleed	bleed	bled	had bled
to blow	blow	blew	had blown
to break	break	broke	had broken
to breed	breed	bred	had bred
to bring	bring	brought	had brought
to broadcast	broadcast	broadcast	had broadcast
to build	build	built	had built
to burn	burn	burnt/burned	had burnt/burned
to burst	burst	burst	had burst
to buy	buy	bought	had bought
to cast	cast	cast	had cast
to catch	catch	caught	had caught

Verb	Present	Past	Past Participle
to choose	choose	chose	had chosen
to cling	cling	clung	had clung
to come	come	came	had come
to cost	cost	cost	had cost
to creep	creep	crept	had crept
to cut	cut	cut	had cut
to deal	deal	dealt	had dealt
to dig	dig	dug	had dug
to dive	dive	dove	had dived
to do	do	did	had done
to draw	draw	drew	had drawn
to dream	dream	dreamed/dreamt	had dreamed/dreamt
to drink	drink	drank	had drunk
to drive	drive	drove	had driven
to eat	eat	ate	had eaten
to fall	fall	fell	had fallen
to feed	feed	fed	had fed
to feel	feel	felt	had felt
to fight	fight	fought	had fought
to find	find	found	had found
to flee	flee	fled	had fled
to fling	fling	flung	had flung
to fly	fly	flew	had flown
to forbid	forbid	forbade	had forbidden
to forget	forget	forgot	had forgotten
to forgive	forgive	forgave	had forgiven
to forsake	forsake	forsook	had forsaken
to freeze	freeze	froze	had frozen
to get	get	got	had got/gotten
to give	give	gave	had given
to go	go	went	had gone
to grind	grind	ground	had ground
to grow	grow	grew	had grown
to hang	hang	hung	had hung
to have	have	had	had had
to hear	hear	heard	had heard
to hide	hide	hid	had hidden
to hit	hit	hit	had hit

Verb	Present	Past	Past Participle
to hold	hold	held	had held
to hurt	hurt	hurt	had hurt
to input	input	input	had input
to keep	keep	kept	had kept
to know	know	knew	had known
to lay	lay	laid	had laid
to lead	lead	led	had led
to leave	leave	left	had left
to lend	lend	lent	had lent
to let	let	let	had let
to lie	lie	lay	had lain
to light	light	lighted/lit	had lighted/lit
to lose	lose	lost	had lost
to make	make	made	had made
to mean	mean	meant	had meant
to meet	meet	met	had met
to pay	pay	paid	had paid
to plead	plead	pled/pleaded	had pled/pleaded
to prove	prove	proved	had proved/proven
to put	put	put	had put
to quit	quit	quit/quitted	had quit/quitted
to read	read	read	had read
to rid	rid	rid	had rid
to ride	ride	rode	had ridden
to ring	ring	rang	had rung
to rise	rise	rose	had risen
to run	run	ran	had run
to say	say	said	had said
to see	see	saw	had seen
to seek	seek	sought	had sought
to sell	sell	sold	had sold
to send	send	sent	had sent
to set	set	set	had set
to sew	sew	sewn/sewed	had sewn/sewed
to shake	shake	shook	had shaken
to shear	shear	sheared	had shorn/sheared
to shed	shed	shed	had shed
to shine	shine	shined/shone	had shined/shone

Verb	Present	Past	Past Participle
to shoot	shoot	shot	had shot
to show	show	showed	had shown/showed
to shrink	shrink	shrank/shrunk	had shrunk
to shut	shut	shut	had shut
to sing	sing	sang	had sung
to sit	sit	sat	had sat
to slay	slay	slew	had slain
to sleep	sleep	slept	had slept
to slide	slide	slid	had slid
to sling	sling	slung	had slung
to slit	slit	slit	had slit
to smell	smell	smelled/smelt	had smelled/smelt
to speak	speak	spoke	had spoken
to speed	speed	sped/speeded	had sped/speeded
to spell	spell	spelled/spelt	had spelled/spelt
to spend	spend	spent	had spent
to spin	spin	spun	had spun
to spit	spit	spit/spat	had spit/spat
to split	split	split	had split
to spoil	spoil	spoiled/spoilt	had spoiled/spoilt
to spread	spread	spread	had spread
to spring	spring	sprang/sprung	had sprung
to stand	stand	stood	had stood
to steal	steal	stole	had stolen
to stick	stick	stuck	had stuck
to sting	sting	stung	had stung
to stink	stink	stank/stunk	had stunk
to strew	strew	strewed	had strewed/strewn
to stride	stride	strode	had stridden
to strike	strike	struck	had struck/stricken
to string	string	strung	had strung
to strive	strive	strived/strove	had strived/striven
to swear	swear	swore	had sworn
to sweep	sweep	swept	had swept
to swell	swell	swelled	had swelled/swollen
to swim	swim	swam	had swum
to swing	swing	swung	had swung
to take	take	took	had taken

Verb	Present	Past	Past Participle
to teach	teach	taught	had taught
to tear	tear	tore	had torn
to tell	tell	told	had told
to think	think	thought	had thought
to throw	throw	threw	had thrown
to thrust	thrust	thrust	had thrust
to tread	tread	trod	had trod/trodden
to upset	upset	upset	had upset
to wake	wake	woke/waked	had woken/waked
to wear	wear	wore	had worn
to weave	weave	wove	had woven
to wed	wed	wedded/wed	had wedded/wed
to weep	weep	wept	had wept
to wet	wet	wet/wetted	had wet/wetted
to win	win	won	had won
to wind	wind	wound	had wound
to withdraw	withdraw	withdrew	had withdrawn

Note: Words formed with a prefix, such as *mishear*, *override*, and *rethink*, are conjugated in the same manner as the root word:

Verb	Present	Past	Past Participle
to hear	hear	heard	had heard
to mishear	mis*hear*	mis*heard*	had mis*heard*

Verb	Present	Past	Past Participle
to ride	ride	rode	had ridden
to override	over*ride*	over*rode*	had over*ridden*

Verb	Present	Past	Past Participle
to think	think	thought	had thought
to rethink	re*think*	re*thought*	had re*thought*

The following chart presents common idioms that can appear on the GMAT. Most of the Xs and Ys represent nouns, pronouns, or noun phrases. To create an idiomatic expression, substitute words or phrases for the X and Y as in the following example:

> *consult with* <u>X</u> *about* <u>Y</u>
> *consult with* <u>my doctor</u> *about* <u>treatment</u>   [*Correct*]

Any other prepositions used with *consult* in this format are unidiomatic.

> *consult* my doctor *for* treatment   [*Incorrect*]
> *consult on* my doctor *about* treatment   [*Incorrect*]
> *consult with* my doctor *for* treatment   [*Incorrect*]
> *consult in* my doctor *about* treatment   [*Incorrect*]

The following list of idioms is not inclusive, and the most common idiom errors are discussed in Chapter Eight. However, this list is an excellent supplement for possible errors on the GMAT

Common Idiomatic Expressions

a lot of X	appropriate to X
account to X for Y	approve of X
accuse X of Y	argue about X
acquaintance with X	argue with X for Y
adapt to X	ashamed of X
affection for X	ask X for Y
afraid of X	ask X of Y
agree to X	assure X of Y
agree with X about Y	at the top of X
alarmed at X	attraction to X
a lot of X	aware of X
amazed at X	bargain with X for Y
amused at X	because of X
amused by X	believe in X
angry at X	blame X for Y
angry with X	blind to X
apologize to X for Y	by means of X
apparent to X	call to X from Y
appeal to X	capable of X
apply to X for Y	certain of X

Common Idiomatic Expressions

challenge X to Y

characteristic of X

cheat X of Y

close to X

comment on X

communicate with X

communicate X to Y

comparable to X

compare to X

compare with X

competition with X for Y

complain to X about Y

composed of X

concerned about X

concerned with X

confess to X

confidence in X

confident of X

congratulate X on Y

conscious of X

consideration for X

consult with X about Y

consult with X on Y

contempt for X

contented with X

contrast with X

contribute to X

control over X

converse with X about Y

convict X of Y

convince X of Y

copy from X

correspond with X

count on X for Y

cure for X

deal with X

decide on X

dedicate X to Y

defend X against Y

defend X from Y

delight in X

delighted with X

demand X of Y

depend on X for Y

deprive X of Y

designed for X

desire for X

different from X

disagree with X about Y

disappointed in X

disappointed with X

disgusted with X

displeased with X

distrust of X

do X about Y

doubt about X

dream about X

dream of X

due to X

duty to X

engaged to X

escape from X

excel in X

exception to X

excuse for X

excuse X from Y

explain X to Y

failure of X in Y

faithful to X

fascinated with X

fearful of X

for the sake of X

full of X

grateful to X for Y

Common Idiomatic Expressions

guard against X

guess at X

hear about X

hear of X

hint at X

horrified at X

in case of X

in common with X

in favor of X

in place of X

in search of X

independent of X

influence over X

inform X of Y

inquire into X

insist on X

intent on X

interested in X

interfere with X

introduce X to Y

invite X to Y

irrelevant to X

laugh at X

lecture on X

listen to X

look at X

look for X

made of X

make X for Y

mistaken for X

need for X

obligation to X

on account of X

opportunity for X

opposition to X

pay X for Y

pay X to Y

pity for X

point at X

prefer X to Y

prejudice against X

protect X from Y

provide X for Y

punish X for Y

qualified to do X

quarrel with X over Y

quote X from Y

reason for X

reason with X about Y

recover from X

related to X

rely on X

remind X of Y

reply to X about Y

require X of Y

research in X

responsible to X

result from X

result in X

result of X

rob X of Y

satisfactory to X

search for X

send for X

shocked at X

shocking to X

similar to X

smile at X

stare at X

start with X

supply X with Y

sure of X

take advantage of X

take care of X

Common Idiomatic Expression

talk over X with Y	threaten X with Y
talk to X about Y	tired of X
tell X about Y	trust in X
thankful for X	trust X with Y
think about X	wait for X
think of X	weary of X
think over X	

List of Wordy Expressions ▮▮▮▮▮▮▮▮▮

The following list reveals possible GMAT errors and their concise corrections. You should watch for wordiness errors in Sentence Correction questions, as well as avoid using wordy expressions in your writing samples.

Wordy Expression	*Concise Correction*
adequate number of	enough
adjacent to	next to, near, by, beside, close to
afford an opportunity	allow, let, give
after the conclusion of	after
ahead of schedule	early
a large proportion of	many, most, much (or be specific)
almost all	most
along the lines of	like, similar, similar to
already exist	exist
an estimated	about, nearly, almost, more than
are in possession of	have, has, owns
arrange to return	return
as a result of	because, because of, since
as long as	if, since
as of now; as of [date]	about; on, from
assuming that	if
as to	about, on, to, of (or leave out)
as well as	and, also
at all times	always (or leave out)
at an early date	soon
at the end of	after
at the present time	now
at this point in time	now
at this time	now
at the time	when, then
bring to a conclusion	conclude or end, finish
by means of	by, with

Wordy Expression	Concise Correction
come to the realization	realize
come to an agreement	agree
concerning the matter of	about
conduct experiments	experiment
consensus of opinion	consensus
course of	during, while, in, at
despite the fact that	although, even though, despite
draw to your attention	show, point out, show you, remind you
due to the fact that	because, because of, since, for, as
during such time, during the time	during, while, when
effect many changes	change
except when	unless
excessive number of	too many
extend an invitation	invite
for the purpose of	for, to, of
for the reason that	because, since, for
for the sum of	for
give an indication of	show, signal, hint, suggest
give consideration to	consider
has been proved to be	is
has the capability	can
have an effect on	affect
hold a conference, hold a meeting	confer, meet
in addition	also
in addition to	besides, beyond, and, as well as, also
in a timely manner	on time, at once, quickly, promptly
in an effort to	to
in close proximity to	near
in conjunction with	with, and
in connection with	about, of, in, on, over, with
in most cases, in most instances	often, mostly, usually
in order to	to
in place of	for
in possession of	has, have
in reference to	about, on, for
in regard to; in relation to	about, for, on; about, in, with, toward, to,
in respect of	for, about, of
in spite of (the fact that)	despite, although
in terms of	in, with, for, at, by, about
in the amount of	for, of, the
in the context of	in, about, for
in the course of	during, while, in, at
in the event that	if
in the neighborhood of	near, about, nearly
in the very near future	soon
in the vicinity of	in, near, close to, about, around, round

Wordy Expression	_Concise Correction_
in view of the fact that	because, since
in this day and age	today, nowadays
in view of the fact	because, since
is found to be	is
is in a position to	can
is of the opinion	thinks
it would appear that	apparently
it is probable that	probably
limited number	few
located in, located on	in, on, found
made a statement	said
make a decision	decide, determine
make an application	apply
make reference to	refer to
none at all	none
not in a position to	unable to, cannot
notwithstanding the fact that	although, even if, however, despite
of major importance	is important
on a daily basis, on a regular basis	daily, regularly
on behalf of	for
one of the	a, an, one
on most occasions	usually
on the part of	by, among, for, of
over the duration of	during
realize a savings of	save
refer to as	call, name
regardless of the fact that	although, despite
regards to, with regard to	about, as for, for, in, of, on
relating to	about, on
serves the function of being	is
some of the	some
subsequent, subsequent to	after, later, next, then, following
sufficient number of	enough, plenty
take action	act
take exception to	challenge, disagree (with), object
take into consideration	consider
to a certain degree	in part, less often, less so, partially, some
to a large degree	largely
to whatever extent	however
under the provisions of	under, by
until such time	until, when
was of the opinion that	believed, thought, said, think
with a view to	to
with reference to	about
with regard to	about, for, on

CHAPTER ANSWER KEY

Notes

Detailed answers to every question in this book are found in the text of the chapter or in the chapter answer key. The consolidated answer key in this section is intended for quick reference.

Chapter Four: Errors Involving Verbs

Subject and Verb Agreement Problem Set

1. D
2. B
3. E
4. C
5. A
6. E
7. E
8. B

Verb Tense Problem Set

1. E
2. C
3. B
4. B
5. D
6. D
7. A
8. E

Irregular Verbs Problem Set

1. E
2. A

Verb Voice Problem Set

1. C
2. B

Noun Agreement Problem Set

    1.   E
    2.   A
    3.   D
    4.   E

Pronoun and Antecedent Agreement Problem Set

    1.   D
    2.   D
    3.   B
    4.   B

Relative Pronouns Problem Set

    1.   D
    2.   A
    3.   B
    4.   B

Ambiguous and Implied Pronouns Problem Set

    1.   C
    2.   A
    3.   E
    4.   E
    5.   B
    6.   A
    7.   D
    8.   C

Chapter Six: Errors Involving Modifiers

Adjective Versus Adverb Problem Set

    1.   D
    2.   B

Quantifier Problem Set

    1.   C
    2.   E

Modifier Placement Problem Set

    1.   A
    2.   E
    3.   B
    4.   E
    5.   C
    6.   D

Verb Forms as Modifiers Problem Set

    1.   A
    2.   C
    3.   E

Chapter Seven: Errors Involving Conjunctions

Conjunctions Problem Set

    1.   B
    2.   B
    3.   C
    4.   E

Comparisons Problem Set

1. D
2. C
3. B
4. E
5. A

Parallel Structure Problem Set

1. D
2. C
3. A
4. E
5. E
6. C
7. D
8. B
9. C
10. B
11. D
12. C

Semicolons Problem Set

1. B
2. B

Idiom Problem Set

1. A
2. E
3. B
4. D
5. B
6. C
7. C
8. E
9. B
10. D
11. D
12. C
13. B
14. C
15. E
16. A

Chapter Nine: Errors Involving Style

Wordy Language and Redundancy Problem Set

1. C
2. E
3. A
4. D
5. E
6. B

Chapter Ten: Multiple Errors

Double and Triple Errors Problem Set

1. D
2. B
3. C
4. A
5. C
6. C
7. B
8. E
9. E
10. D
11. A
12. D
13. C
14. E
15. B
16. A
17. C
18. D
19. D
20. B

Sentence Correction Strategies Problem Set

1. E
2. B
3. D
4. B
5. A
6. C
7. E
8. A
9. C
10. C
11. D
12. E
13. B
14. E
15. D
16. A
17. B
18. C
19. C
20. E

GLOSSARY

Examples, if provided, are indicated in italics.

active voice: A preferred form of a verb in writing that allows the subject to perform the action in a sentence (*Vincent picked a flower*).

adjective: A word which describes or modifies a noun or a pronoun. Examples include *happy*, *clever*, and *quick*. Adjectives are one of the eight parts of speech.

adjective phrase: A phrase that modifies a noun or a pronoun.

adverb: A word which describes or modifies a verb, adjective, or adverb. Examples include *happily*, *cleverly*, and *quickly*. Adverbs are one of the eight parts of speech.

adverb phrase: A phrase that modifies a verb, adjective, or adverb.

ambiguous pronoun: A pronoun without a clear antecedent. Two or more nouns or pronouns may be possible antecedents.

antecedent: The word or phrase replaced by a pronoun.

clause: A group of related words that contain both a subject and a verb.

collective noun: A singular count noun that identifies a group, such as *committee*, *choir*, and *faculty*.

common noun: A noun that names common things, such as *woman*, *highway*, and *marina*, unlike a proper noun, which names specific things, such as *Beth*, *Interstate 95*, and *Broad Creek Marina*.

comparative degree: The level of intensity conveyed by adjectives and adverbs (*cold, colder, coldest*).

compound predicate: A predicate with two or more verbs performed by the same subject (The boy *finished first and won the prize*).

compound subject: A subject with two nouns or pronouns that perform the same action in the sentence (*The boy and girl* won prizes).

conditional statement: A statement that uses the word *if* in a dependent clause to state an outcome in an independent clause (*If I finish first, I will win a prize*).

conjunction: A word which links words or phrases. Examples include *and*, *although*, and *yet*. Conjunctions are one of the eight parts of speech.

coordinating conjunction: A conjunction used to connect two words, phrases, or clauses which share grammatical structure. The seven coordinating conjunctions are *and*, *but*, *or*, *yet*, *for*, *nor*, and *so*.

coordination: The linking of two independent clauses by a coordinating conjunction (*I do not like the actress <u>but</u> I enjoyed the movie*). Coordination puts equal emphasis on both clauses.

correlative conjunction: A conjunction that always occurs in a matched pair (*not only...but also, neither...nor*).

count noun: A noun that can be counted (one *poster*, three *friends*, hundreds of *acres*), unlike a non-count noun that cannot be counted (some *air*, little *juice*, a good deal of *laughter*).

dangling modifier: A modifier that does not have a referent in the sentence. Dangling modifiers often occur in introductory phrases or clauses (*Having returned the shirt,* a gift certificate was issued).

demonstrative pronoun: A pronoun that points to nouns that are nearby in time or in space. There are four demonstrative pronouns: *this*, *that*, *these*, and *those*.

dependent clause: A clause that depends on an independent clause to make sense. Dependent clauses could not stand alone as a sentence, even if a period were added. Dependent clauses carry less weight and importance than an independent clause (*After Logan completed the police academy,* she was hired as a full-time deputy).

direct object: The noun or pronoun in the predicate that receives the action of the verb (I <u>drank</u> *the soda*).

expletive construction: An inverted sentence that begins with *there* or *it* (*It is common to see alligators on the banks of the lagoon*).

gerund: A verbal that ends in -*ing* but functions as a noun (*Dancing* is one of my favorite hobbies).

helping verb: A verb such as *be*, *shall*, *can*, *must*, or *would* that is added to an action verb to help express time and mood.

idiom: An expression that is natural to native speakers of the language. Idioms often do not make literal sense (*back in the day*, *kick the bucket*).

illogical comparison: A faulty comparison of two unlike things (Unlike her co-worker's *monitor*, *Cheryl* has a much larger screen).

implied pronoun: A pronoun without any antecedent (During the Monday night game, *they* said that the quarterback had a disagreement with his wide receiver).

indefinite pronoun: A pronoun that refers to a person or thing that is identified, but isn't specific, such as *everybody*, *few*, *each*, and *somebody*.

independent clause: A clause that could act as a sentence if a period were added to the end. Independent clauses carry more weight or importance than a dependent clause (After Logan completed the police academy, *she was hired as a full-time deputy*).

indirect object: The noun or pronoun in the predicate that is indirectly affected by the verb (Uncle Fred bought *Blake* a car).

infinitive: A verbal that uses the root of the verb combined with *to*, such as *to be*, *to sleep*, and *to dream*. Infinitives can function as adjectives or adverbs, but most often serve as nouns.

intensive pronoun: A pronoun that intensifies or emphasizes the antecedent. Intensive pronouns take the same form as reflexive pronouns, but they follow the noun more closely (As for me *myself*, I prefer the orange Jeep).

interjection: A word used to convey emotion. Examples include *Ouch*, *Wow*, and *Hey!* Interjections are one of the eight parts of speech.

interrogative pronoun: A pronoun used to ask questions. The four main interrogative pronouns are *who*, *whom*, *which*, and *what*.

intransitive verb: A verb that does not take a direct object.

inverted sentence: A sentence in which the subject comes after the verb (There <u>are</u> only *two houses* on my street).

irregular verb: A verb whose past tense and past participle are not formed by adding *-ed*. *Operate* is a regular verb: he operat*ed*, he had operat*ed*. *Drive* is an irregular verb: he *drove*, he had *driven*.

linking verb: A verb that links a noun or pronoun to additional information about that noun or pronoun. It does not show action (The story *seems* suspicious. The storm *is* approaching. The entrée *tastes* like chicken).

mass noun: Often referred to as a non-count noun. A noun that cannot be counted (some *air*, little *juice*, a good deal of *laughter*) unlike a count noun that can be counted (one *poster*, three *friends*, hundreds of *acres*).

misplaced modifier: A modifier that is placed too far away from its intended referent and therefore appears to be modifying the wrong referent. Misplaced modifiers often occur in introductory phrases or clauses (*Having returned the shirt,* a gift certificate was issued to Erin).

modifier: A word, phrase, or clause that provides information about another word phrase or clause in the sentence (The *largest* planet *in that solar system* turns *slowly* on its *tilted* axis).

non-count noun: Often referred to as a mass noun. A noun that cannot be counted (some *air*, little *juice*, a good deal of *laughter*) unlike a count noun that can be counted (one *poster*, three *friends*, hundreds of *acres*).

noun: A word that names a person, place, or thing. Examples include *chairman*, *kitchen*, and *symbol*. Nouns are one of the eight parts of speech.

noun phrase: A phrase that contains a noun and any words that modify the noun.

object of the preposition: The object in the prepositional phrase controlled by the preposition (<u>to</u> the *store*, <u>by</u> the *desk*, <u>from</u> my favorite *aunt*).

participle: A verbal that functions as an adjective and most often ends in *–ing* (present participles) or *–ed* (past participles).

passive voice: A less preferable form of a verb in writing in which the subject does not perform the action in a sentence (*A flower was picked by Vincent*).

personal pronoun: A pronoun that refers to a specific person or thing, such as *I*, *he*, *hers*, and *us*.

phrase: A group of related words that do not contain a subject and a verb. A phrase can have a subject or a verb, but not both.

plural noun: A noun that names more than one person, place, or thing (*cats, houses, ideas*).

plural verb: A form of a verb that agrees with a plural noun (the girls *vote*, they *dance*). Compare to a singular verb, which agrees with singular nouns (the girl *votes*, he *dances*).

predicate: The part of the sentence that contains the verb as well as the objects and phrases controlled by the verb. (The talented musician *learned to play the piano as a young boy*).

preposition: A word used to link a noun or pronoun to other words. Examples include *about, to, by, from,* and *near.* Prepositions are one of the eight parts of speech.

prepositional phrase: A phrase containing a preposition, the object of the preposition, and any modifiers. All prepositions appear in prepositional phrases.

pronoun: A person, place, or thing which replaces a noun. Examples include *she, their, everyone, all,* and *who.* Pronouns are one of the eight parts of speech.

proper noun: A noun that names specific things, such as *Beth, Interstate 95,* and *Broad Creek Marina,* unlike a common noun, which names common things, such as *woman, highway,* and *marina.*

quantifier: A modifier that indicates the quantity of something (*two, several, a lot, hundreds*).

redundancy: A state of wordiness in which ideas are repeated (*recent newlyweds*).

reflexive pronoun: A pronoun that reflects back onto the noun. The reflexive pronouns are *myself, yourself, herself, himself, itself, ourselves, yourselves,* and *themselves.*

relative pronoun: A pronoun that connects a phrase to the antecedent. There are four specific relative pronouns: *who, whom, that,* and *which.*

simple predicate: The main verb, verb phrase, or compound verb with all modifiers removed (The elderly woman politely *asked* for assistance crossing the street).

simple subject: The main noun or pronoun with all modifiers removed (The elderly *woman* politely asked for assistance crossing the street).

singular noun: A noun that names one person, place, or thing (*cat, house, idea*).

singular verb: A form of a verb that agrees with a singular noun (the girl *votes,* he *dances*). Compare to a plural verb, which agrees with plural nouns (the girls *vote,* they *dance*).

split predicate: A divided predicate in which part occurs after the subject and part occurs before the subject (*Although he attended the conference,* Roberto *did not believe in the underlying principles of the theory*).

subject: The part of the sentence that contains the word or phrase that performs the action of the verb in the sentence. The subject is a noun, pronoun, or noun phrase and names whom or what the sentence is about.

subordinating conjunction: A conjunction used to introduce a dependent clause. Examples include *although, once, rather than,* and *until.*

subordination: The linking of a dependent clause and an independent clause by a subordinating conjunction (*Although I do not like the actress, I enjoyed the movie*). Subordination puts more emphasis on the independent clause.

tense: The form of a verb used to express the point in time that the action, or lack of action, takes place.

transitive verb: A verb that takes a direct object.

verb: A word showing action or state of being. Examples include *walks, thinks,* and *will be driving.* Verbs are one of the eight parts of speech.

verbal: A word that is based on a verb, but functions as another part of speech in the sentence. Verbals include infinitives, gerunds, and participles.

CONTACTING POWERSCORE

Contact Information

PowerScore GMAT Sentence Correction Bible Information:

Student Web Section: www.powerscore.com/scbible
E-mail: scbible@powerscore.com

PowerScore GMAT Course Information:

Effective GMAT Preparation
Full and Weekend Courses
99th Percentile Instructors
Real GMAT Questions

Web: www.powerscore.com/gmat

PowerScore GMAT Tutoring Information:

One-on-one meetings with a PowerScore GMAT expert.

Web: www.powerscore.com/gmat/gmatutoring.htm

PowerScore Business School Admissions Consulting Information:

Personalized application and admission assistance.

Web: www.powerscore.com/gmat/mbadmissions.htm

PowerScore International Headquarters:

PowerScore
37V New Orleans Road
Hilton Head Island, SC 29928

Toll-free information number: (800) 545-1750
Facsimile: (843) 785-8205
Website: www.powerscore.com
E-mail: gmat@powerscore.com